THE ERA
WAS LOST

JUSTICE, POWER, AND POLITICS

Heather Ann Thompson and Rhonda Y. Williams, editors

Editorial Advisory Board
Dan Berger
Peniel E. Joseph
Daryl Maeda
Barbara Ransby
Vicki L. Ruiz
Marc Stein

The Justice, Power, and Politics series publishes new works in history that explore the myriad struggles for justice, battles for power, and shifts in politics that have shaped the United States over time. Through the lenses of justice, power, and politics, the series seeks to broaden scholarly debates about America's past as well as to inform public discussions about its future.

A complete list of books published in Justice, Power, and Politics is available at https://uncpress.org/series/justice-power-politics.

THE ERA WAS LOST

The Rise and Fall of New York City's Rank-and-File Rebels

GLENN DYER

THE UNIVERSITY OF NORTH CAROLINA PRESS

Chapel Hill

© 2024 The University of North Carolina Press

All rights reserved

Designed by Jamison Cockerham
Set in Scala, Officina Serif, and Irby
by codeMantra

Cover art © Hum Images / Alamy Stock Photo.

Manufactured in the United States of America

LIBRARY OF CONGRESS CATALOGING-IN-PUBLICATION DATA
Names: Dyer, Glenn (Historian), author.
Title: The era was lost : the rise and fall of New York City's rank-and-file rebels / Glenn Dyer.
Other titles: Justice, power, and politics.
Description: Chapel Hill : University of North Carolina Press, [2024] | Series: Justice, power, and politics | Includes bibliographical references and index.
Identifiers: LCCN 2024021621 | ISBN 9781469682051 (cloth) | ISBN 9781469682068 (paperback) | ISBN 9781469682075 (epub) | ISBN 9781469682082 (pdf)
Subjects: LCSH: Strikes and lockouts—New York (State)—New York—History—20th century. | Labor unions—New York (State)—New York—History—20th century. | BISAC: POLITICAL SCIENCE / Labor & Industrial Relations | SOCIAL SCIENCE / Sociology / Urban
Classification: LCC HD5326.N7 D94 2024 | DDC 331.892/9747109046—dc23/eng/20240612
LC record available at https://lccn.loc.gov/2024021621

CONTENTS

Acknowledgments vii

List of Abbreviations ix

INTRODUCTION 1

1 Rank-and-File Strikes in Transit and Plumbing 11

2 Militancy, Alienation, and the Wallace Effect 39

3 Strike Fever 65

4 Fading Fires 97

5 Taxi Drivers' Rage 111

6 Rank-and-File Resistance to Fiscal Austerity 129

CONCLUSION 155

Notes 163

Bibliography 205

Index 217

ACKNOWLEDGMENTS

There are many people who supported this project over the years and without whom this book would have never seen the light of day. At the CUNY Graduate Center, K. C. Johnson was an incredible adviser and mentor who provided invaluable feedback, commentary, and assistance when this book was simply a proposal. Thomas Kessner and Joshua Freeman read multiple drafts more times than they would have liked and both helped me greatly.

I also owe a debt of gratitude to the research staff at the Tamiment Library and Robert F. Wagner Labor Archives, where the bulk of my research was performed; they are certainly happy that I have not been back. The archivists at the International Brotherhood of Electrical Workers Local 3 Archives also helped me greatly as did those of the New York City Municipal Archives. I would also like to thank the editorial staff at the University of North Carolina Press, particularly Dawn Durante, who helped turn a stalled review process into an actual book. Finally, I would particularly like to thank the many former union members that I interviewed for this project as well as those who saw fit to document their battles through the years. Without those interviews or documents, this book would not exist.

To my mother and father, I thank you not only for the support and love you have shown me but also for embodying the most trenchant of working-class norms. While you often wondered where I came from, it was always from you. Finally, to my wife and sons, thank you for everything that you are and will become.

ABBREVIATIONS

AFL-CIO American Federation of Labor—Congress of Industrial Organizations

BCTC Building and Construction Trades Council

BWAC Bell Workers Action Committee

CCC Citywide Coordinating Committee to Save New York Schools

CLC Central Labor Council

CWA Communications Workers of America

DC 37 District Council 37

EFCB Emergency Financial Control Board

HUC Harlem Unemployment Center

IBT International Brotherhood of Teamsters

LEG Law Enforcement Group of New York

MAC Municipal Assistance Corporation

MBPU Manhattan-Bronx Postal Union

MLC Municipal Labor Committee

NALC National Association of Letter Carriers

NALC	Negro American Labor Council
NYT	New York Telephone
OCB	Office of Collective Bargaining
PBA	Patrolmen's Benevolent Association
PERB	Public Employees Relations Board
SSEU	Social Service Employees Union
TA	Transit Authority
TAC	Teachers Action Caucus
TDU	Taxi Drivers Union
TTU	Telephone Traffic Union
TWU	Transport Workers Union
UA	United Action
UA	United Association of Plumbers and Pipefitters
UFT	United Federation of Teachers
USA	Uniformed Sanitationmen's Association

THE ERA WAS LOST

Introduction

On a chilly day in early January 1969, New York City's most powerful labor leaders gathered for a special meeting to discuss the "strike fever" that gripped the city. For the previous three years union members had gone on strike against the wishes of employers, government officials, and union representatives. Transit workers had pushed their storied leader Mike Quill into a strike in 1966, shutting down the city's subway system for over a week. In 1967, workers as varied as waiters, cargo handlers, lifeguards, and parking enforcement officers wildcatted over grievances, and in 1968 alone, sanitation workers forced their leaders to strike, burying the city under thousands of tons of trash; utility workers who manned and maintained the city's power grid rejected a union-endorsed contract and threatened to plunge the city into darkness; and fuel oil drivers rejected a contract put to them by their union, defending picket lines with golf clubs and Molotov cocktails and cutting off home heating to tens of thousands during the Hong Kong flu pandemic.

Harry Van Arsdale Jr., head of the city's AFL-CIO Central Labor Council and former business manager of the International Brotherhood of Electrical Workers Local 3, decried the upheaval, believing that it undermined labor's political power. At the same meeting, his counterpart in the International Brotherhood of Teamsters, Joint Council 16 president Joseph Trerotola, agreed, describing himself as "disturbed" by the growing upheaval. Special guest Governor Nelson Rockefeller blamed rising inflation for the disorder but also the mood of the late 1960s, arguing that young people just wanted "action."[1] A discussion ensued among various union heads including Albert Shanker of the United Federation of Teachers, Victor Gotbaum of District Council 37, and James Beamish of Local 1-2 Utility Workers. Union leaders suggested numerous methods to bring their members to heel, including mandatory arbitration, cooling-off periods, and even the use of computers to centralize data, keep dues in order, and check membership statuses.[2] While New York City's labor leaders could be a parochial and fractious lot, in early 1969, they were unified at least temporarily in favor of reasserting order and authority over their members.

Between 1965 and 1975, New York City's union members fomented a powerful yet inchoate wave of strikes, electoral drivers, and organizing efforts that challenged the entrenched power of employers, labor leaders, and politicians. By the early 1960s, many American unions had become relatively stable bureaucracies that were increasingly insulated from their members, and in spite of New York labor leaders' uniquely devout commitment to a kind of municipal-level New Deal liberalism, their organizations were often equally bureaucratized or nondemocratic.[3] With rising anger about work conditions, sellout contracts, ineffective union leadership, racism, and political disempowerment, union members as different as postal workers, plumbers, lifeguards, and teachers all rebelled against their leaders in a "rank-and-file rebellion" that swept through New York City.[4]

Recent works by Jefferson Cowie and Lane Windham are divided on the nature of this period and what it meant for the American working class. For Cowie, who borrows Bruce Schulman's measure of a "long 1970s," it is the "last days of the working class," replete with failed insurgencies, a rightward political turn, and rising cynicism.[5] For Windham, the 1970s marked the "first days of a reshaped and newly energized working class," led by new political subjects—young people, women, and people of color—and involved unionization drives, successful or not, as the proper measure of "working class motivation and mobilization."[6] Though she emphasizes workers' optimism, Windham ultimately concurs with Cowie that workers eventually lost, bringing to the forefront the opposition of powerful and well-organized elites.

While both are excellent histories, they adopt a broad-strokes approach that erases the intricacies of important local environments of struggle, of which New York's rank-and-file upheaval is a particularly potent example. In the middle of the twentieth century, labor's power was ascendant in the city, and as a result of the postwar struggles to build a "working-class New York," workers in the city possessed a powerful class consciousness, with distinct norms and behaviors that challenged employers' control.[7] Strikes were common but had declined by the first half of the 1960s. By 1966, however, they began to rise in number but, more important, transform in character: they became much larger, with nearly 500,000 workers taking part in strikes between 1968 and 1970 alone; they were increasingly disruptive, shutting down deliveries of heating oil, threatening electrical generation, and paralyzing the city's transportation networks; and a growing number were the result of rank-and-file anger, involving contract rejections, attacks on union officials, and wildcat activity. In other cases, insurgent electoral campaigns were interwoven with the broader restiveness, sometimes unseating entrenched leaders.[8] Though they worked for different employers and toiled in very different conditions, workers in New York City radicalized and emboldened one another, and in 1970 when the city's postal workers led an illegal strike that grew into a nationwide walkout, one of the strikers argued, "Everybody else strikes and gets a big pay increase. . . . The teachers, sanitationmen and transit workers all struck in violation of the law and got big increases. Why shouldn't we?"[9] The powerful resonance of rank-and-file challenges within the city crossed the boundaries of gender, race, skill, and workplace, challenging Windham's dyad of pessimistic, backlashing white workers and optimistic, young, female, and Black workers.

While the rebellion in postwar New York City—America's largest industrial center—merits more study, it must be understood as an urban phenomenon. Studies of municipal unions in the city, including Gerald Podair's, Marjorie Murphy's, and Daniel Walkowitz's work, contextualize rank-and-file teacher and caseworker militancy within the city's political and racial dynamics, but they do not highlight the interconnection across sectors and the lasting political impact generated by this broader movement.[10] Kieran Taylor's chapter on the Detroit-based League of Revolutionary Black Workers grounds the organization in urban changes, but his focus is on a single organization and rebellion among largely Black workers. Further, this research suggests only a small back-and-forth between militancy in different sectors and racial groups and does not document deep lasting impact on the polity.[11] While it is outside of the purview of this study to comment on the dynamics of every American city, New York City's rank-and-file rebellion was distinct from Detroit's—and certainly many others'—in its size, degree of its interracial and cross-sector resonance, and level of political entanglement and impact on the urban polity.

My work builds on histories of class in New York City and the 1960s and 1970s more generally but fills several important gaps in the literature. I uncover influential and largely unexamined rank-and-file movements, such as the Black-led Rank and File Committee for a Democratic Union in the Transport Workers Union (TWU), which helped spark the 1966 transit strike, and that of Communications Workers of America (CWA) Local 1101. I also focus on electoral campaigns and strikes in building trades unions and the Teamsters, organizations whose reputation for conservatism has overshadowed their postwar-era militancy. Across various chapters I draw together diffuse and fleeting strikes and protests by highlighting ways that workers mimicked and referenced one another, and I also show how New York's rebel rank and file significantly influenced unions nationwide, while outside influence on New York was relatively minimal. I also pay particular attention to the interplay between workers' rebelliousness and politics, discussing George Wallace's 1968 presidential campaign in New York and the myriad ways that rank-and-filers of all kinds butted heads with mayor John Lindsay and supported his opponents. Furthermore, I uncover the expansive rank-and-file movement against union leaders and the business elite during the city's 1975 fiscal crisis, which has still received little research in spite of excellent recent works like Kim Phillips-Fein's. Ultimately, my research provides a novel interpretation by foregrounding rank-and-file struggles—not simply labor writ large—playing a central role in increasing political polarization in New York City and hastening the decline of the city's social democracy.[12]

My work deepens our understanding of the political shifts of the 1960s and 1970s. Workers in New York City at that time were not reducible to a simple left-right polarity.[13] Rather, they took part in varied and sometimes contradictory activities: seeing a fleeting hope or protest vote possibility in George Wallace's racist populism, explicitly and implicitly demanding greater control of their working lives, and challenging their subordinate status within America's socioeconomic hierarchy. While some workers certainly turned rightward, when they did it was not always the case that workers "vot[ed] against their material interests." Many workers, especially, but not only, city employees, found themselves directly facing off with liberal Republican mayor John Lindsay, who would often deride workers' demands as racist power brokering, counterposing them to the interests of the city's growing Black and Hispanic populations. For some, like the predominantly white sanitation union, strikes and mobilizations became a way to challenge the mayor and his rejection of their interest in favor of both Black and Puerto Rican residents of the city. At the same time, taxi drivers saw their livelihoods declining alongside the rise of the primarily Black and Hispanic livery car industry, and once again Mayor Lindsay largely took the side of livery drivers and companies. In response to such battles, some white workers moved rightward, though not because of confusion about their material interests, while others saw their labor struggles fail, no longer engaging in the collective action that had undergirded liberalism in the city.[14]

While the rank-and-file upheaval of the 1960s and 1970s was potent, it ultimately failed, collapsing under the pressure of government and corporate recalcitrance as well as confusion and disarray. Nationally, rank-and-file rebellion continued with several important wildcat and reform movements taking hold, but New York's strike wave mostly collapsed in the first years of the 1970s, minus a short-lived revival during the 1975 fiscal crisis.[15] Early on, workers were able to win some of their wage and benefit demands and unseat some corrupt leaders, but in many cases strikers were outflanked by their bosses or were only able to obtain catch-up contracts due to rising inflation. Amid increasing political polarization and a worsening economy, workers lost many big public battles. Rather than being a tale of working-class heroics and long-term victories, New York's era of rank-and-file upheaval is largely characterized by defeat. While this conforms in some ways to Cowie's and Windham's arguments, unlike the rest of the nation, New York City retained a high unionization rate and unions wield significant political power in the city to this day. Thus, my work is not about the decline of labor overall but rather a story of the defeat of the union rank and file and the changing attitudes, beliefs, and politics that resulted from those defeats. For many, the aftermath of the labor activism and strikes was largely about keeping one's head above water, embracing individual survival, and developing an incredible wariness, if not outright rejection, of workplace militancy. This social and political legacy cannot be understated, and to date New York City has had no further strike waves.[16]

Sourcing the study of New York's rank-and-file rebellion requires the use of a wide range of primary materials. The records of New York City unions and labor organizations provided the richest documentation of the era's struggles. Important collections include those of the Building and Construction Trades Council, AFL-CIO Central Labor Council, CWA, District Council

37, International Brotherhood of Electrical Workers Local 3, New York Metro Area Postal Union, Social Service Employees Union, TWU Local 100, and United Federation of Teachers (UFT). Each of these collections contains important meeting minutes that discuss internal upheaval, correspondence from angry members, voting records of insurgent campaigns, and flyers and leaflets from opposition groups. The bulk of the above union collections are held at the Tamiment Library and Robert F. Wagner Labor Archives, which also has important serials and rank-and-file collections including those of the Bell Workers Action Committee, Harlem Fight Back, United Action, Taxi Rank and File Coalition, and the transit workers' *Rank and File News* as well as the Anne Filardo Papers on Rank and File Activism in the UFT. The James Haughton Papers at the New York Public Library's Schomburg Center for Research in Black Culture give insight into the significant impact of the Harlem riots on Black labor militants and their attempts to build the activity of rank-and-file organization within the TWU and in the country as a whole. The New York Municipal Archives have myriad holdings from the John Lindsay and Abraham Beame eras that document labor unrest during the 1960s and 1970s, whether in the form of notes on mediation proceedings, strike case files, or reports on work stoppages in key economic sectors. Complementing municipal records are the John Lindsay Papers at the Yale University Archives, which contain daily crisis calendars, negotiation notes, internal communications, strike response plans, and copies of workers' publications produced by municipal employees. Finally, I consulted several other collections, including the Jack Bigel Collection at Baruch College, which contains material relevant to the New York City fiscal crisis; the archives of the Joint Industry Board of the Electrical Union, which contain important documents from not only the electricians union but also the Taxi Drivers Union; the Nelson A. Rockefeller gubernatorial papers at the Rockefeller Archive Center; and the Theodore Kheel Arbitration Awards and E. Wight Bakke Papers at the Kheel Center for Labor-Management Documentation and Archives at Cornell University, both of which give some insight into workers' informal resistance practices.

While some rank-and-file organizations are well represented in archival collections, recovering some workers' voices required greater creativity. Oral history has been invaluable to reconstructing internal upheaval within several unions, and especially so with unions whose archives are either not made accessible to researchers or have not survived. During my research, I conducted interviews with former members of the Local 2 plumbers union, CWA Local 100, Taxi Drivers Union, TWU, and Teamsters Local 553 fuel oil drivers, each of whom gave firsthand accounts of working conditions, internal union politics, and rank-and-file attitudes and concerns during the period. Contemporary print media including the *New York Times*, *Daily News*, *New York Post*, and *El Diario La Prensa* provide extensive accounts of strikes, but more important, they contain interviews with workers and photographs of picket lines, which help recover workers' sentiments in the period. Important holdings at the Tamiment Library include the extensive New Yorkers at Work Oral History Collection and the copious Taxi Rank and File Coalition Oral History Collection, which also extend our understanding of the predominant attitudes, concerns, and desires of the city's rank and file and prominent labor activists. Without oral history, an investigation into the era's upheaval would be woefully incomplete, because in many cases, archival sources from unions and rank-and-file organizations are incomplete, edited, or completely unavailable to researchers. For example, fuel oil rank-and-file publications are not available and the union's records are not open to the public. I was also unable to access the Uniformed Sanitationmen's Association archives, nor was I able to find any rank-and-file-produced leaflets or publications. In some cases, the lack of sources has made the story more difficult to reconstruct, but I have done my best to use oral history and nonunion archives to make up for the occasional dearth of union sources.

My study is organized chronologically. Chapter 1 investigates rank-and-file upheaval within the TWU and the United Association of Journeymen and Apprentices of the Plumbing and Pipefitting Industry Local 2 between 1964 and 1967. Black workers influenced by the civil rights movement and the 1964 Harlem riots were a growing minority in the TWU, and the Black-led Rank and File Committee for a Democratic Union emerged in 1965, pushing for greater contract demands and running an opposition bid to take the reins of the union. While other works have argued for a diffuse sentiment that led TWU president Mike Quill to strike, I argue that Black workers and the Rank and File Committee were critical in pushing Quill to the 1966 subway strike and in turn sparked a broader wave of militancy in the city. Though historians have given more attention to the transit strike, the plumbers of Local 2 also struggled with their leaders in the mid-1960s, and their corrupt leader, Jack Cohen, led a strike to attenuate growing anger in the union. Cohen miscalculated, however, and his inability to deliver on the much-coveted hiring hall—that would allow the union to allocate work—led to his and his cronies' ejection from office. The strike continued for several months and was only ended when the international of the United Association of Journeymen and Apprentices of the Plumbing and Pipefitting

Industry threatened to put the local union into trusteeship and force the plumbers back to work. While popular imagery primarily portrays building trades workers as bigoted, some of them took part in important challenges to their labor leaders and some of the city's biggest businesses. This tale of internal upheaval helps reexamine the militancy of such workers as well as their role in the city's wider labor movement.[17]

The second and third chapters try to capture the breadth of the rebellion, delving into its myriad manifestations between 1967 and 1972. The first half of chapter 2 explores rank-and-filers' use of wildcat strikes, absenteeism, and contract rejections to exercise greater control over their working lives, and it also explains the growing alienation and anger that beset many workers. Unexpected sources of militancy, including rising crime and job safety, sparked rebellion in the ranks of some unions, as did a broader discontent with the workers' place in America's socioeconomic hierarchy. The second half of the chapter explains how such anger fed into the rank-and-file 1968 sanitation strike and how it developed into fleeting support for George Wallace's 1968 presidential run, in which the southern segregationist openly appealed to New York's rank-and-filers with populist rhetoric and public events prominently featuring union leaders. Chapter 3 investigates distinct moments of rebellion, including the contract rejections of Teamsters Local 553, the continued and ultimately failing efforts of the TWU Rank and File Committee, and a gathering of radical rank-and-filers in New York City, none of which have received much mention in labor histories of postwar New York. The chapter concludes with an examination of the more prominent 1970 postal wildcat strike and the 1970 Hard Hat Riot. These five vignettes help elucidate the limitations workers confronted during the rebellion, including union leaders, recalcitrant employers, internal divisions, and their own attitudes toward the workplace and workplace struggle. Within these limitations and early defeats, the legacy of defeat, frustration, and withdrawal begins to take shape.[18]

The final three chapters explore the decline of the rank-and-file rebellion amid large-scale public defeats, growing political polarization, and elite resistance. Chapter 4 focuses on the militant CWA Local 1101 telephone workers. In the telephone industry, the principled unionism of older workers combined with the restiveness of the young, generating one of the city's most militant rank and files, which took part in myriad wildcat strikes and acts of sabotage. In 1971, however, Local 1101 rejected a contract put to them by not only their local but their international leadership, leading their own strike against the powerful New York Telephone. After seven months, New York

Telephone defeated the union, firing militant workers, and the CWA International split up the insurgent local. In the words of one rank-and-filer, "The era was lost"; defeat and demoralization set in just as the local and national economic picture began to seriously deteriorate.[19] Chapter 5 focuses on the newly unionized yellow cab drivers. The taxi drivers took part in an inchoate fight against their union leaders. Internal divisions made workers fight with one another, but they also fought against the growing livery cab industry, which both the union leadership and some rank-and-filers associated with growing crime and permissiveness in the city. A left-wing rank-and-file organization emerged from this maelstrom, putting forward a significant, albeit short-lived challenge. Amid the division and polarization, taxi rank-and-filers were unable to make serious progress and saw their efforts defeated by union leaders or their anger channeled into a racist battle against the livery industry. The sixth, and final, chapter explores the brief revival of rank-and-file rebellion amid the business elite's attempts to impose fiscal austerity on New York City. While Kim Phillips-Fein's recent work only touches on it, there is a rich history of militant social workers, sanitationmen, police officers, and teachers leading mobilizations and strikes and challenging the causes and meaning of the city's budgetary shortfalls. Worker activism against fiscal austerity lends support to the left historiography on the 1975 fiscal crisis, as workers rejected elite narratives that put the blame on municipal workers, racial minorities, and social democratic provisions like the welfare and city university systems. Resistance to the business elite's agenda ultimately failed, however, and New York's workers, both as union members and community members, bore the brunt of budget cuts, declining services, and a broken social fabric.[20]

While the defeat of New York's rank-and-file rebellion occurred in the early 1970s, its legacy retains relevance to national politics and the lives of working-class people today. My conclusion discusses this persistent importance, in particular how defeat led to new working-class norms that focused on individual survival and self-preservation in the face of a deteriorating local economic reality. Many authors have discussed the turn away from liberalism in the 1960s as a turn rightward, but I contend that the turn away from such expansive social values was also a result of working-class defeat and withdrawal. Furthermore, the short-lived support for Wallace in 1968 presaged the swing constituencies that dominate many elections today. Nowhere has this been more relevant than in the rise of Donald Trump, who, like Wallace before him, employed populist, antiliberal rhetoric to tap into white working- and middle-class Americans' growing anger. Trump's

Democratic opponents, including Joe Biden and Hillary Clinton, powerfully echoed Mayor Lindsay when they denounced many of Trump's supporters as racist and sexist cretins. While such political dynamics remain incredibly relevant, so do the impasses of the rank-and-file rebellion. Notably the upheaval of the 1960s and 1970s was the last strike wave in American history, and in an age of increasing wealth inequality and virulent polarization, working-class people's lives and aspirations remain stunted, much like those of their forebears.[21]

ONE

Rank-and-File Strikes in Transit and Plumbing

On New Year's Day 1966, tens of thousands of Transport Workers Union (TWU) Local 100 members walked off the job for pay raises and better health and welfare benefits, shutting down the city's subway and bus services for twelve days. While newly elected mayor John Lindsay declared that he still thought it was a "fun city," several union leaders found themselves jailed for violating a state law that barred municipal unions from striking.[1] Later that same year, the normally cacophonous construction sites that exemplified the city's postwar building boom would fall silent. The 4,000 plumbers of the United Association of Journeymen and Apprentices of the Plumbing and Pipefitting Industry (UA) Local 2 struck their employers in hopes of gaining greater control over work allocation.

In 1965 and 1966, unrest within the ranks threatened Michael Quill and the rest of the TWU leadership. Older workers called Quill a fraud, arguing that in spite of his militant posturing, contracts he negotiated were always inadequate. Some of them were skilled tradesmen who saw themselves falling behind skilled workers in the private sector, while others were long-term employees who felt they were barely keeping up with inflation. Meanwhile, the union's growing number of Black members became increasingly emboldened due to the era's civil rights struggles and experiences with racial discrimination on the job. While historians have pointed out some of the rank-and-file influence in the 1966 strike, they have primarily attributed it to amorphous sentiment. I argue, however, that the Rank and File Committee for a Democratic Union, a growing Black-led opposition group, played a key role in challenging the TWU leadership in the run-up to the strike. In the aftermath of the Harlem riot of 1964, motorman and activist Joseph Carnegie began to agitate within the ranks of the TWU, and in concert with older, white, left-wing activists, he established the Rank and File Committee, running an electoral slate to challenge Quill during the TWU's 1965 contract negotiations. Though unsuccessful at gaining electoral power, the committee's pickets, interventions, and electoral bid helped push Quill to a strike. With both widespread anger and an internal opposition group, Quill needed a large settlement to appease his members, and he reluctantly led them off the job when negotiators for the incoming Lindsay administration failed to meet his demands.[2]

Though historians have given it little attention, the 1966–67 UA Local 2 strike provides another important window into rank-and-file challenges. The ruling faction of the union, the Yellow Ticket, colluded with management and failed in some ways to keep up with more powerful building trades unions. Unlike the more powerful Local 3 electricians union, plumbers lacked a hiring hall, and contractors controlled work assignments. Cronyism and corruption within the union worsened the distribution of the work. Plumbers increasingly supported an opposition faction, the Blue Ticket. More pragmatic than politically minded, the Blue Ticket gained some power prior to the 1966 strike, when its leader Michael Pappalardo was elected business agent. With a new round of elections set for December 1966, UA president Jack Cohen gambled on a strike to win the long sought-after hiring hall, hoping to shore up support against the Blue Ticket. For five months, plumbers in Manhattan and the Bronx stayed off the job, paralyzing billions of dollars of construction in the world's most lucrative real estate market. Buoyed by the region's economic strength, many plumbers found intermittent work out of state and with the help of this backup work rejected contract after contract. In the December elections, they would fully repudiate the Yellow Ticket's control, voting in the Blue Ticket and a new union head, Pappalardo. With many plumbers working out of state and in it for the long haul, the UA International leadership negotiated a new deal with the plumbing contractors in early 1967, ultimately forcing the plumbers of Local 2 to accept it under threat of trusteeship.³

"Quill Deserves an Emmy": Transit Rank and File and the 1966 TWU Strike

TWU Local 100, which still represents New York City's bus and subway workers, emerged from the massive Congress of Industrial Organizations unionization drive of the 1930s. As in many other fights to build industrial democracy, the TWU brought together workers of a variety of different skills—maintenance men, guards, station agents, motormen, and conductors—but in this case they also brought together workers across the hundreds of miles of rails and roadways of North America's largest transit system. In its early days, the TWU was majority Irish American, and its leaders up until the 1960s reflected this ethnic composition.⁴ During the union's first two decades, leader Michael Quill advocated a style of unionism that helped foster the rise of "social democratic New York," advocating increased wages and benefits for workers as well as the maintenance of a low fare for the working people of the city.⁵ Furthermore, Quill and others in the TWU openly advocated against racially discriminatory hiring practices while also pushing for both the city and the state to assume a greater role in subsidizing the operations of mass transit. The union weathered employer attacks when the industry was private and survived government attacks when transit infrastructure was municipalized in the 1940s, and by the 1950s the TWU's position had stabilized to the point that its representation of transit workers was no longer seriously contested from without.⁶

In 1948, TWU International president Quill, with the help of Mayor William O'Dwyer, purged Local 100 leader and avowed communist Austin Hogan and several of his allies. Hogan and his supporters had become a threat to Quill, and Hogan's political ties were becoming a liability in an increasingly anti-communist political environment. In addition to these purges, Quill and city administrations came to a broader ideological agreement, with Quill advocating exclusive bargaining rights for the TWU on the basis that it would foster greater industrial peace.⁷ Though Quill maintained an emphasis on some social goals, he reneged on others, trading fare increases for wage gains that same year. Historian Mark H. Maier argues that this decline in social commitment was also reflected in the TWU's accession to declining service quality. In his words, after the late 1940s, "the union never seriously linked the interests of subway workers to those of subway riders."⁸ With service decline came thousands of layoffs, which would become a sore point for some workers in subsequent years.⁹ In 1954, Quill acceded to Transit Authority (TA) demands for the first day of sick leave to be unpaid, rolling back an earlier win. Later that same year, members displayed their displeasure with his leadership when nearly a third of the more than 40,000 transit workers stopped paying union dues.¹⁰

With the union facing diffuse opposition such as the refusal to pay dues, skilled workers began to organize against the TWU leadership in the second half of the 1950s. The TWU's negotiation of across-the-board wage increases resulted in skilled workers' wages not keeping pace with those of the rest of the city's craft workers. Dissatisfaction set in, and some skilled workers hoped to use strikes to get better representation in the TWU while others hoped to completely secede from the union.¹¹ The motormen who drove the city's subway trains became some of Quill's strongest opponents.

Between 1955 and 1958, motormen and mechanics organized several wildcat strikes that tied up trains and buses across the city. In 1955, 150 motormen carried out a short walkout that disrupted train traffic for several hours. In June 1956, 400 walked off the job when instructed to train potential scabs.¹² In December 1957, motormen led a walkout of many craft associations in another failed attempt to push for recognition of their unions. In spite of their strikes, the Motormen's Benevolent Association and other independent craft organizations rapidly faded away when they failed to win union recognition elections in the late 1950s.¹³ Their efforts, however, demonstrated the ability of a small number of well-placed rank-and-filers to disrupt the subway system.

Alongside the efforts of skilled TWU members to establish their own craft representation was the left-wing Rank and File Committee of the TWU. The committee originally emerged as an opposition group during the anti-communist purges of the late 1940s, running slates and pushing for a more broadly militant position in contract negotiations. Its membership initially grew because many leaders were older, respected union members, but under the constant attacks of Quill and anti-communist city organizations, the committee was bleeding members by the mid-1950s.¹⁴ Though many of its leaders were skilled workers, the Rank and File Committee was vehemently against the craft union drivers of the late 1950s, calling such attempts "a weapon of the raiders and splinter groups who would smash our union."¹⁵ Instead, it advocated for its own broadly social view of transit that was not too far off from Quill's and the TWU's original positions, including maintaining an industrial union, keeping the fare low, and upgrading and adequately servicing the subway system. They opposed some of the TWU leadership's 1950s trade-offs, such as the end of first-day sick leave and layoffs. Another source of their discontent was the TWU's unwillingness to adequately defend its members from TA-issued workplace violations, some of which were incurred in the process of maintaining the timely operation of route schedules.[16] Additionally, the rank-and-file group, like most members of the TWU, was very concerned by the rates of compensation. At the same time that the TWU's skilled workers were losing pace with the rising wages of other crafts, so, too, were its less skilled members not keeping pace with newly unionized civil servants.[17] While it would publicly criticize contracts, the Rank and File Committee always supported the union and told other rank-and-filers to "stick with the TWU," eventually folding as an organized opposition group in the late 1950s after members retired or found their efforts ineffectual.[18]

New discontent and worker self-organization began to emerge in the 1960s on account of demographic shifts within the union. The TWU's leadership and rank and file had been strongly Irish American from the founding of the union, but the union was already 10 percent Black during the late 1930s.[19] After 1945, however, with a growing influx of Blacks and Latinos to the city, the TWU's membership became increasingly integrated. This was not a natural or inevitable process, however, and several unions, especially those in the building trades, were racially exclusionary. By contrast, the TWU leadership, and Quill in particular, supported efforts to prevent racial discrimination in hiring and promotions. At the TWU's 1961 national convention, Martin Luther King Jr. went so far as to praise the TWU's "crusading spirit which broke through the open shop stronghold, [and] also broke through the double walled citadels of race prejudice," continuing, "It is pathetic that our nation did not begin decades ago, as did you, to deal with the evil of discrimination."[20] While Quill supported antidiscrimination efforts, Black rank-and-file advocates in fact provided much of the impetus for improvements, as TWU leaders were sometimes reluctant to make racial equality a key public issue for fear of fueling opposition factions or management attacks that could divide the union.[21]

By the early 1960s, more than one-third of the TWU's membership was Black, and in the summer of 1962, the city's *Amsterdam News* gave public attention to Black transit workers when it published a four-part series, "The Transit Authority and Its 12,000 Negroes." Reporter James Booker found a high degree of racial segmentation in the workforce, with Blacks more often found in menial jobs and only a few in supervisory positions.[22] Interviewees expressed a wide array of complaints including abuse by white supervisors and preferential treatment of whites in promotions.²³ They also described mistreatment by the TA court, the employer's main disciplinary mechanism, arguing that Blacks were punished much more severely than whites.²⁴ Black rank-and-file organizers agreed with the *Amsterdam News*'s assessment, though they were more interested in fighting on behalf of workers through the labor movement than promoting Blacks to management.²⁵

Early 1960s organizers included Frank Robinson, motorman Joseph Carnegie, James Gordon of the 207 Street shop, private lines bus driver Kermit Saltus, and Abram Allick of the track department.²⁶ As these organizers described it, the failure of the early 1950s left-wing rank-and-file group and the craft strikes and organizing of the later 1950s led to widespread disillusionment among white and Black transit workers. They hoped, however, to initiate a new round of organizing in the early 1960s based on the growing numerical importance of Blacks in the TWU.²⁷ In 1961 Black rank-and-filers began organizing for greater Black representation, with fifteen signing a letter calling on TWU leaders to appoint a Black leader to the Local 100 executive board. Though their group was small, their fellow Black workers supported their efforts even though they remained reluctant to join in rank-and-file efforts.²⁸ That same year, these organizers also helped elect a handful of Black delegates from Local 100 to attend the TWU's national convention, where they pushed for Black representation in the International's hierarchy. Shortly thereafter, Quill appointed Roosevelt Watts to the International's executive board, and by the end of the year Watts was also appointed vice president of Local 100. Though organizers like Carnegie, Gordon, and Robinson believed that Watts would be primarily loyal to Quill, the speed at which the TWU leadership had acceded to their demands emboldened them.²⁹

In 1962, Carnegie, Gordon, and Allick began participating in the Negro American Labor Council (NALC), led by storied labor and civil rights leader A. Philip Randolph, meeting other Black organizers interested in mobilizing Black workers to win the struggle for civil rights and the advancement of working-class people as a whole.³⁰ Some New York NALC members were already involved in an ongoing battle with the International Ladies Garment Workers Union over its organizing practices and lack of Black and Puerto Rican leadership, a campaign that resonated with TWU rank-and-file organizers.³¹ While many NALC members focused primarily on organizing Black workers, Carnegie was more concerned about the direction of the labor movement, including its decline in militancy, sellout contracts, internal corruption, and the acceptance of automation's job elimination. The Greater New York chapter's willingness to speak out on such issues swiftly created a backlash, and AFL-CIO leaders pressured Randolph to denounce them. Through a combination of red-baiting and deft maneuvering, Black union officials loyal to Randolph ousted many of the militants.[32]

Internal divisions also began to develop among Black transit organizers. Carnegie and Gordon wanted to avoid the creation of a formal organization. They feared mimicking the ossification of the labor movement and had "no intention of becoming a stagnant docile, black base for a few people to bargain with the TA and the union for jobs for themselves."[33] In spite of such reservations, they helped found the Transit Fraternal Association (TFA) in the spring of 1963. In Carnegie's estimation, organizers like Allick and Saltus began to move away from engaging with their fellow rank-and-filers, rejecting mass agitation for dialogue with the leaderships of the TWU and TA.[34] Carnegie, who was the TFA's coordinator, maintained a strong emphasis on mass mobilization and rank-and-file engagement, hoping to spur greater Black involvement with the labor movement.[35]

The growing split among the earlier organizers was best exemplified later that spring when Carnegie and allies in the NAACP Labor and Industry Committee pushed for a public protest against the arrest of thousands of young people during the southern civil rights movement's Birmingham campaign. May 2–3, thousands of children as young as six marched in Birmingham as part of ongoing attempts to defeat segregation in the city, resulting in more than 1,000 arrests and influential media coverage that included attacks with water cannons and police dogs.[36] That weekend, Carnegie contacted his allies in the NAACP including James Haughton, head of the Labor and Industry Committee, and New York City NAACP president Rev. Richard Hildebrand. Together they began organizing for an emergency demonstration, with Hildebrand contacting Randolph to obtain the support of Harry Van Arsdale Jr., head of the city's AFL-CIO Central Labor Council, and Carnegie working with the TFA and transit rank-and-filers. Van Arsdale argued there was too little time to convene the Central Labor Council and provided little help, and Allick of the TFA wavered on the use of the organization's name to endorse the rally. Disgusted with the vacillation, Carnegie organized leafleting independently, and in response the TWU released its own leaflet supporting the Birmingham movement. Hundreds of Blacks maintained a vigil at New York's city hall for three nights, and on May 8 a rally took place of some 1,500 white and Black New Yorkers with speakers like mayor Robert Wagner, NAACP president Roy Wilkins, and Hildebrand.[37]

Divisions between Carnegie, Gordon, and the TFA became stronger during the summer of 1963. The NAACP's Labor and Industry Committee held a one-day conference on organizing in the city with caucuses from transit, textile, and building trades taking part. There, Gordon, Carnegie, and Allick drafted resolutions that their caucus would not only attack racism in the TA but also call for the end of the semiautonomous agency. The TFA initially printed 5,000 copies to distribute to transit rank-and-filers, but Allick withheld the leaflets for several weeks for fear of damaging the association's standing with the TA. Signaling the TFA's increasing emphasis on negotiations over mobilization, Allick instead organized a private meeting with the TA and the TWU's Watts to discuss job discrimination.[38] By the end of 1963, this early wave of mobilization had resulted in some concessions, but rank-and-file organizers like Carnegie and Gordon found the changes to be inadequate and not in keeping with the broader goals of empowering rank-and-file transit workers.

Roughly one year later, riots in Harlem and Bedford-Stuyvesant reinvigorated Black rank-and-file organizing in the TWU. In mid-July 1964, white police lieutenant Thomas Gilligan shot and killed fifteen-year-old James Powell after Powell and several other youths were involved in an altercation with a building superintendent on the city's wealthy Upper East Side. Several days of protests and rioting ensued, spreading to Bedford-Stuyvesant in Brooklyn and sparking a wave of unrest that would hit several cities in the Northeast over the course of the summer.[39] Carnegie was convinced that the Harlem riots were a turning point in Black struggle. In his mind, the so-called leadership of the Black community, which claimed to speak on behalf of Black people, was actually very far behind the common person who had rioted in defense of Black rights. In fact, those leaders were now playing a game of catch-up.[40]

While he was inspired by the riots, Carnegie believed that Black communities needed some kind of organized force to focus the militant activity and that the time had come to establish independent, Black-led organizations in both neighborhoods and workplaces.[41] In an initial organizational effort, Carnegie leafleted three transit depots with flyers denouncing police brutality and the lack of criminal charges for the officer involved. His efforts put him in touch with many sympathetic Black workers, but both TWU and TA officials warned him to stop distributing the leaflets.[42] Carnegie's evolving perspective, and perhaps renewed faith in the struggling masses, operated as a self-criticism of his past activities: he had agitated within the union in recent years and only reluctantly organized a fraternal association. In mid-September 1964, Carnegie announced to the Labor and Industry Committee that he was laying the groundwork for a transit rank-and-file organization that would build upon increasing Black militancy, long-term disappointment with the transit union, and impending contract negotiations in 1965.[43]

The Labor and Industry Committee's chairman, James Haughton, bolstered Carnegie's new organizing activities. Born to working-class West Indian parents, Haughton attended City College and then both Princeton and New York University for graduate school, working briefly for Mobilization for Youth in the city's Lower East Side. Significantly, Haughton was A. Philip Randolph's protégé and under his aegis formed the NALC.[44] Haughton left the NALC when rank-and-file organizers in New York were ejected, and in 1962 he took the reins of the NAACP's Labor and Industry Committee upon NAACP head Reverend Hilderbrand's invitation.[45] In 1964, while Carnegie was beginning to strategize for rank-and-file renewal among transit workers, Haughton founded the Harlem Unemployment Center, an organizing space that would seek to assail discriminatory hiring in the building trades and serve as a meeting hall for rank-and-file groups attempting to undermine racism within unions.[46] Carnegie's Rank and File Committee would meet at the Harlem Unemployment Center throughout its life, and this organizational tie would persist for years, shaping rank-and-file efforts to come.[47]

While the early months of the Rank and File Committee are not well documented, its record becomes clearer in the second half of 1965 as it began to publicly challenge TWU Local 100's leadership over contract negotiations. In mid-June 1965, at the enlarged joint executive board meeting that brought together both TWU leaders and representatives from various divisions, committee members aired a long list of rank-and-file grievances, demanding higher wages, a greater social commitment to service upgrades, and democratic unionism. Their intervention led to a confrontation with TWU stewards, and after some pushing and shoving, stewards ejected the Rank and File Committee members from the meeting.[48] A few weeks after this open confrontation with union leadership, the committee organized a picket of TA offices in downtown Brooklyn against subway entrance closures and an increased fare. Committee members argued that better services and a low fare were in the interest of working New Yorkers like themselves and that any subsequent fare increases would be blamed on transit workers who were only trying to better their piteous lot.[49] Inspired by the growing militancy of Black communities, the committee resisted every effort to depoliticize negotiations, appealing to both their fellow TWU members and the community at large.[50]

The committee's emphasis on the politics of TA funding reflected the complicated nature of transit negotiations. After municipalization, negotiations involved a web of actors and institutions, including transit boards, the mayor, and his various representatives; even state officials were dragged into the mess from time to time. One of the TA's counterarguments to aggressive TWU demands was that transit should be a self-sustaining institution.[51] To the committee, the notion that the TA would ever be self-sustaining was absurd. Their leaflets pointed out that money always came from the city and that most contract demands were met through deals hammered out between the TA, the mayor, and the TWU leadership. Furthermore, the city had originally taken over the industry because it wasn't profitable, and the committee believed it was absurd to insist on this standard now that it was under municipal control. In August 1965, when the committee organized another demonstration against declining services and the possibility of an increased fare, they called upon mayoral candidates to take a position on upcoming contract negotiations of the TWU. To reinforce the point, their August flyer concluded with a powerful declaration: "Transit is not self-sustaining now and it never will be."[52] By insisting on this fact, they advocated an inherently political understanding of transit functions and financing, linking their demands to a much broader environment of struggle across the city.

Amid the committee's weeks of agitation, the TWU first made its contract demands public. In late July, much earlier than anticipated, the union called for a thirty-cent wage increase, increased holidays, and greater TA contributions to workers' retirement packages. All told, this deal would cost the TA nearly $100 million, whereas the final settlement from the down-to-the-wire 1964 negotiations had totaled only $40 million.[53] While the package was larger than the previous contract agreement, which some workers had picketed, the committee was unsatisfied, continuing its efforts to push for an even more substantial contract. In August, the committee organized a picket of city hall, claiming responsibility for the TWU's early issuance of demands and arguing, "The only reason our union has submitted demand to the Transit Authority so soon, without the approval of the membership of the TWU, is because of their embarrassment by rank-and-file members of the TWU."[54]

The committee continued its agitation at the TWU's October constitutional convention. Transit workers elected Pat DeVito as a delegate, and he used the opportunity to speak out in support of more aggressive demands for the upcoming contract. While he spoke out for higher wages and a shorter workweek, Quill loyalists quickly roughed him up and shouted him down. A week later, DeVito sent a letter of protest directly to Quill wherein he denounced his silencing but still expressed hope that Quill would be supportive of his positions.⁵⁵ He had some cause to believe in Quill: after months of the committee's agitation, Quill used the convention as a platform for dramatically increasing TWU Local 100's contract demands. Before delegates and elected officials of the entire union, Quill announced that in addition to the previous $100 million package, he would now seek a thirty-two-hour, four-day workweek, a 30 percent pay increase, retirement after twenty-five years, and a no-layoff clause.⁵⁶

In October, the committee looked to intensify the pressure with an electoral drive. Named for its presidential candidate and financial secretary-treasurer, respectively, the Carnegie-DeVito slate was the only serious competitor for the TWU leadership in 1965.⁵⁷ Carnegie was a natural choice for president as he was the chair of the committee, a long-standing rank-and-file activist, and a vocal advocate for Black rights. DeVito as the second-in-command was also a clear choice; he was a staunch militant during the 1950s—one of the organizers of the original rank-and-file committee—and he had maintained agitational activity into the early 1960s.⁵⁸ Significantly, the slate featured another Black candidate, George Hayes, for the position of third vice president.⁵⁹

Electoral materials did not foreground racial matters as much as picketing leaflets did. The committee's electoral platform called for wage parity with other city workers, a shorter workweek, improved working conditions, a twenty-five-year pension, elimination of the TA court, and an end to contract ratification by mail.⁶⁰ While Carnegie's earliest efforts involved consolidating Black support, the committee was now vying for power in a general election in a majority-white union. It is unsurprising then that its electoral materials appealed to the broadest cross section of workers in the union.⁶¹ That being said, the slate's promotion of two Black candidates, one for president and one for third vice president, was a visible reminder of the committee's stance on racial equality, and if the committee won the election, it would be in a better position to push for such antidiscrimination demands.⁶²

Later that month, Local 100 president Daniel Gilmartin advocated a transformation of the TWU's electoral process: the mail ballot. While contract votes had often been conducted by mail, elections were conducted via polling places spread throughout the city.⁶³ Gilmartin publicly advocated the mail ballot as a way to increase participation in elections, which in recent years had seen a roughly two-thirds participation rate on the part of transit workers.⁶⁴ While he did not mention the committee in the meeting minutes, the mail ballot was also a method whereby the union could privately conduct vote counts and more easily control electoral outcomes. The union already used it for contract ratification, and the committee advocated for its abolition.[65] Though the local's top official proposed the change, several executive board members were wary of the mail ballot, with one voting against it and five abstaining from the vote altogether. In spite of the opposition, Gilmartin's proposal won the day with the remaining twenty-two delegates voting in favor.[66]

In November the TWU directly attacked the committee's electoral efforts. Less than a month before the election, the TWU disqualified Hayes on the grounds that he did not attend sufficient union meetings. He disputed his disqualification as dubious, arguing that he tried to attend the meetings, but because they lacked a quorum his attendance was not counted. Unsympathetic to Hayes's pleas, the TWU leadership removed his name from the December 1965 ballot.[67]

The transformation of the voting structure, the shouting down of opponents, the dubious disqualification of candidates, and the upward revision of contract demands all demonstrate that the TWU bureaucracy was very concerned with the committee's opposition. While it was doubtful that the new organization would sweep elections, Quill and Gilmartin took no chances with their restive membership base, and their countermeasures are broadly indicative of the lengths union leaders would go to in order to maintain their grip on power, damaging the democratic nature of their organizations and reinforcing their membership's claims that entrenched leaders were self-perpetuating cliques.

When the 1965 TWU elections finally took place in mid-December, the Carnegie-DeVito rank-and-file slate lost, but the electoral showing indicated sizable discontent within the union ranks. After the TWU tallied the new mail ballot votes, incumbent president Gilmartin received 12,183 votes to Carnegie's 3,678.[68] While nowhere close to unseating the leadership, it was the best showing of any opposition candidate since the beginning of the decade. In 1961 an opposition candidate garnered only 1,000 votes to Gilmartin's more than 10,000, and in 1963 the Gilmartin slate had run unopposed.[69] In 1965, of the roughly 60 percent of the TWU workers who voted via mail-in ballots, roughly one-quarter voted for the Rank and File Committee's opposition slate for every position, and the committee managed to win in the Surface Maintenance Division.[70] All told, nearly 4,000 workers across a dozen divisions were willing to vote for untested rank-and-file candidates amid one of the union's most contentious negotiations. Though Carnegie believed they had no chance of winning, the election did give the committee some basis to claim that it spoke on behalf of angry TWU members.[71]

While most workers voted for the incumbent leadership, Quill and Gilmartin now had to deliver the demands promised at the October constitutional convention. Many TWU members were long dissatisfied with contracts, and as some saw it, the contracts that Quill called victories were actually delivering weak wage gains and undermining the union. To these workers, Quill's negotiating style was only playacting, and his self-proclamations as champion of the workingman rang hollow.[72] While anger at the disjunction between a fiery negotiating style and actual delivery could perhaps be attributed to a few disillusioned men, Alan Lawrence of the TWU's public relations team confirmed that Quill's "orchestration process" was meant to convince rank-and-filers that each contract was the best that could be obtained.[73] In the run-up to the 1966 strike, skilled workers complained that Quill's tough talk far outweighed the actual delivery of tangible gains at TWU meetings and publicly aired their grievances with the city's three major newspapers.[74]

The 1965–66 negotiations began to break down in the late fall as the state, city, and TA all sought to avoid taking direct responsibility for meeting transit worker demands. Mayor Wagner appealed to Governor Rockefeller for state assistance in meeting demands, but Rockefeller also wanted no part. After failing to get outside support, the outgoing mayor foisted negotiations on the incoming Lindsay.[75] Lindsay, meanwhile, wanted little to do with the TWU, which he believed to be an antireform power broker. During early negotiations, the mayor-elect publicly refused to even send a representative.[76] Lindsay began secret negotiations in December, but talks ultimately went nowhere. Though technically an autonomous entity, the TA hoped that either the city or state would intervene on its behalf with new subsidies to meet TWU demands.[77] Quill advocated that everyone from Robert Moses, Rockefeller, and Port Authority director Austin Tobin take part in negotiating a settlement. Lacking a significant counterproposal from either Lindsay or the TA, Quill had little to offer his rank and file, and when the clock struck midnight on December 31, the TWU ordered its members to strike.[78]

When the strike began, the TWU directed motormen across the city to park the system's thousands of trains in their proper rail yards or in designated tunnels and stations to avoid the possibility of a winter storm. As workers left the job, the TWU leadership quickly organized picketing through forty-two headquarters that registered thousands of members for four-hour stints. Because of the transportation hardships caused by the strike itself, the TWU allowed workers to choose their own sites.[79] Most signed up to picket close to home, where they walked orderly lines carrying union-printed "No Contract No Work" signs.[80]

During the strike, transit workers openly discussed rank-and-file anger with news outlets, with many of them pointing to the fact that Quill had lost a large amount of support in the union due to the brokering of weak deals. One worker argued that for his militant posturing, "Quill deserves an emmy [sic]." Another clearly laid out the leadership's conundrum: "Quill couldn't dare come back with what was offered. . . . He wouldn't have a union if he did."[81] Even though the rank and file did not organize the strike, some believed that Quill had struck in spite of himself to obtain a good contract.[82]

The strike resonated with many rank-and-file union members in the city. A week into the transit shutdown, Local 3 electrician Charles Henricks took the opportunity not only to express his support for Van Arsdale's stance on the transit strike but also to express his displeasure with Van Arsdale's leadership of the Local 3 electricians union. Complaining of high dues, discontinued union meetings, and intermittent work—an issue central to the plumbers strike of 1966—Henricks concluded that "it is conditions like this that strain our loyalty to the union."[83] Others in the building trades would remember the strike for its militancy, arguing like Henricks that in spite of it making it difficult for them to get to work, they supported the transit strikers.[84] But the building trades were not unique: young militants in the Communications Workers of America visited pickets and attended support rallies during their lunch breaks, showing their support for the striking workers and bringing back leaflets and signs to share with their coworkers. Some workers connected to the strike through blood relations, with family members who were transit workers, while others simply understood the strike to be part of the broader terrain of working-class New York.[85]

The 1966 transit strike and settlement emboldened many workers across the city to strike in the years that followed. With its twelve-day strike, the union won a 15 percent pay increase for its 30,000 members, a $500 yearly contribution to each worker's retirement fund, an additional paid holiday, three-day leave for deaths in the family, and increased health and welfare benefits. While some workers were angry that the pay increase was not front-loaded—they would only reach the full increase by July 1, 1967—it was a significant pay increase by any standard.[86] An illegal, citywide strike had generated a positive outcome for TWU workers, and this lesson particularly affected teachers, sanitationmen, social workers, and other municipal employees.[87]

In the immediate aftermath of the strike, the Lindsay administration feared the settlement's impact. Lindsay publicly proclaimed the strike's resolution a success, but in a working paper on municipal labor relations, the city's chief labor negotiator, Herbert L. Haber, argued that the transit strike "makes it hard to conceive of municipal employee organizations of any strength or sophistication, agreeing to settlements that are not in the neighborhood of these terms." He predicted that if the city stood firm against such efforts, "conflict, mass demonstrations, slow-downs and strikes [would occur] as unions are driven to obtain percentage settlements close to the transit agreement."[88]

Haber's prediction would prove largely correct, but the transit strike's impact was not purely municipal. In March 1970 militant postal workers in New York City sparked a nationwide wildcat strike, and in an interview on the picket lines, a letter carrier acknowledged the influence of the transit strike, stating: "Everybody else strikes and gets a big pay increase . . . The teachers, sanitationmen and transit workers all struck in violation of the law and got big increases. Why shouldn't we? We've been nice guys too long."[89] In another *New York Times* piece covering the strike, an anonymous but prominent union official (as identified by the paper) argued: "Postal workers in New York City watched city workers against the city. They were illegal strikes. . . . And what happened? Those strikers got fat raises."[90]

The 1966 transit strike also heightened political polarization in the city, painting Lindsay's mayoralty as anti–working class. The media seized upon the diametrically opposed personalities and politics of Mike Quill and John Lindsay, and Quill fed this dynamic, deliberately mispronouncing the mayor's name as "Lindsley," calling him a pipsqueak and lightweight, and heaping more and more invective upon him as the contract deadline approached.[91] Significantly, the clash with the transit workers led Lindsay to make a career-defining speech in which he railed against the "power brokers" such as organized labor that he believed held the city hostage.[92] Lindsay's position garnered him some support among people hostile to labor and with some civil rights organizations distressed by the impact of the strike on New York's poor minority populations. Two days after Lindsay's power broker speech, Van Arsdale told his fellow union leaders that a "lynch labor" atmosphere permeated the city and the state.[93] This legacy of division was compounded by events shortly following the strike: on January 28, 1966, roughly two weeks after the strike's conclusion, the TWU's storied leader died of heart failure. For some of the city's workers, Quill's death was easily explained. In the words of a Local 2 plumber who would go on strike later that year, "Lindsay killed Quill."[94]

"He's on the Dime and He Can't Even Run the Meeting Right:" The Local 2 Plumbers Strike

UA Local 2 was a craft union of some 4,000 members that covered plumbing in the Bronx and Manhattan, the epicenter of New York City's construction boom.[95] Since being disbanded amid racketeering and corruption charges in the early 1990s, the union traced its history to the labor struggles of nineteenth-century New York, when many plumbers were affiliated with the Knights of Labor.[96] For some time, it was the largest plumber local in the country, and in the early part of the twentieth century, it was among the militant skilled trades whose members took part in a variety of cross-trade solidarity strikes.[97] The Great Depression hit the union hard and rolled back some of its gains, but in the aftermath of the war, a building boom and transformed labor relations led to the flourishing of Local 2 and the UA International.[98] Notably, Local 2 was the home union of George Meany, the first president of the AFL-CIO in the aftermath of its merger. Meany started in Local 436 plumbers, winning election as a business agent and then making a quick lateral move out of the union and into the New York State Federation of Labor's office of the president and eventually to the top of American labor's hierarchy. While authors have called the building trades unions corrupt, nepotistic, and sometimes reactionary—all three being true of the Local 2 leadership—such depictions do not fully encapsulate the plumber rank and file.[99]

In the mid-1960s, a construction boom was in full swing in New York City, with massive new skyscrapers reshaping the city's skyline as well as important investments in municipal infrastructures such as hospitals and schools. Nearly $1 billion of new construction was slated for 1966 alone, an increase from the already-massive $800 million construction investment in the previous year.[100] For workers in the building trades, plentiful investment meant more available work, and such high demand for skilled laborers created the material basis for a strengthening of their bargaining position. During the 1960s, the unionization rate for the city's some 200,000 building trades workers was as high as 80 percent, and these jobs brought with them rapidly rising wages and growing fringe benefits that outpaced many other workers'. Some have even gone so far as to label this period a "golden age" in which "construction workers especially prospered."[101] Unlike municipal employees or transit workers, who saw weak gains or fell behind comparable trades, workers in the building trades obtained growing wages and benefit packages. But not every union did equally well; some had shorter workweeks, some had higher wages, others had hiring halls, and others had dental plans and paid vacations.[102] While the plumbers of Local 2 kept up in the wage battle, many of them experienced periodic bouts of unemployment that cut into their earnings and savings.[103] Thus, while it may have been a golden age when compared to the travails of the Depression and the anti-union assault that would come in the 1980s and '90s, construction workers still found themselves contesting the length of working days, labor processes, and employers' rights to allocate work.[104]

The growing confidence that accompanied the city's postwar building boom also manifested in on-the-job behavior. Plumber pride was built on a combination of respect for both physical prowess and mental ability. Strength was essential on the job, whether it involved lugging heavy construction materials up many flights of stairs or being able to thread pipe by hand. Men used the job to show off such skills, with some individuals hoisting bathtubs over their heads—normally a two-man job—and mounting more than ten flights of stairs. Others did fingertip push-ups at lunchtime, much to the awe and enjoyment of their coworkers, while some, like Jack Basilico, a former boxer born in East Harlem, garnered fame for their violent defense of the union: when civil rights protesters tried to block entrance to the union's headquarters in Manhattan, Basilico beat up several of them.[105] The pride, however, was not simply in the physical side of the work. Plumbers also looked fondly upon the ability to navigate a wide variety of materials, plan and properly organize work with other trades, and negotiate the minutiae of contracts and regulations. Physical toughness was still paramount, however, as injuries, life threatening and not, abounded on work sites that were both harsh and crude.[106]

In the postwar era, pride and self-confidence grew among plumbers both on the job and outside of it. With increased work opportunities, many Depression-era work-site behaviors, including skill hoarding and public deference to contractors, waned as both younger apprentices and some older workers rejected them.[107] Outside of work, plumbers and other skilled tradesmen took enjoyment in disrupting the sheltered spaces of higher-class New Yorkers by "wearing rough work clothes as a badge of honor, riddling their speech with curses, and harassing women who passed by construction sites."[108] This low-intensity counterculturalism was incredibly gendered, often taking on a sexist bent, but alongside other behaviors on the job it reflected a growing confidence among blue-collar workers.[109]

In the mid-1960s, business manager Jack Cohen and his political faction, the Yellow Ticket, ran UA Local 2. Essentially, the Yellow Ticket was a patronage system held together by its ability to provide material incentives for both union members and bosses. Without a hiring hall, plumbing contractors ultimately decided who worked and who did not. In situations where contractors could not fill jobs with their own preferred plumbers, contractors would call the union to send men of its choosing. Until 1964, the Yellow Ticket controlled all of the union's highest-ranking offices, and through these offices, they doled out jobs to supporters and denied them to challengers.[110] While guaranteeing work to loyalists was important, Cohen had to convince a majority of rank-and-file plumbers to support him, and this task included delivering contract improvements as well as solving disputes at work sites with contractors and between trades. In 1962, for example, Cohen and the plumbers feuded with the carpenters over who had the right to install sinks in the International Ladies Garment Workers Union's new co-op housing. The battle halted construction for two weeks and was essentially a dispute between unions about guaranteeing work for their respective memberships. To maintain the respect of the members, the Yellow Ticket had to stand fast against encroachment from other trades.[111] Events such as these shed some light on the limitations of both union and worker aspirations in the building trades, as they both exhibited and reinforced parochialism among the trades.

Another way that the Yellow Ticket maintained its power was through collusion with contractors, a relationship that was smoothed over by bribes.[112] A sliver of corruption came to light in 1963 when Cohen was indicted on bribery charges for allowing a contractor to do off-site work in exchange for $4,000. In other words, when contractors used nonunion labor, Cohen and his cronies were willing to look the other way—for a price. Ironically, Cohen's indictment gained him a modicum of respect outside of his loyalists, as many plumbers admired his taking the full rap for corruption and not fingering any of his fellow leaders.[113]

The Yellow Ticket's attempts to maintain its power produced loyalty among some plumbers and garnered wealth for the leaders, but the ticket began to lose ground to a competing organization within the union, the Blue Ticket. Like the Yellow Ticket, the Blue Ticket opposition lined up behind a single leader, Michael Pappalardo, an Italian American from East Harlem who joined the union during the Depression. Pappalardo was a skilled organizer and street politician who was able to build a competing organization within the union by being a "good labor man who stood behind the men," straightening out problems on job sites and standing up against employer abuses.[114]

Pappalardo's efforts gained him respect from other plumbers, but his refusal to join the Yellow Ticket made him a target of the leadership, which prevented him from working for extended periods of time. He built up his organization by using the familial and personal connection at the heart of the hiring process and relying on blood relatives to back him as well as an extended network of work assistance that created loyalty to his group. When the Yellow Ticket kept him off the job for several weeks, loyal supporters beat a Yellow Ticket business agent who had blacklisted Pappalardo.[115]

Through steady organizing, Pappalardo became the first non–Yellow Ticket business agent when he was elected in the early 1960s. In a sense, the Blue Ticket was a competing patronage machine, albeit more militant.[116] While some men became supporters of the Blue Ticket by virtue of their personal connections, others had ethnic motivations for joining, as many Italian and Jewish members joined up with the Blue Ticket. Opposition grew within the union when Cohen was indicted for taking bribes from contractors, but long-standing grievances concerning the precarity and availability of work predominated.[117]

A letter from Local 2 plumber Dennis Kelly to mayoral candidate John Lindsay in the summer of 1965 exemplifies these problems. Kelly called on the would-be mayor's help in transforming the plumbers local from a corrupt, undemocratic institution into an organization that actually had its members' best interests in mind. Kelly outlined financial irregularities such as the nondisbursement of vacation benefits and the withholding of medical benefit disbursements, for which the union offered no explanation. In addition to these financial issues, Kelly also complained of a variety of other problems in relation to the conduct of union business. He argued that though unemployment in the union was high, work was not being properly distributed among members. Kelly closed his cry for help by emphasizing that the "officials of Local 2 and the Plumbing Industry Board are pursuing a policy that is not only detrimental to Local 2 members, but it is also undemocratic and completely un-American."[118] Kelly would not have a hard time finding common ground with workers in other trades.[119]

Interunion competition and a desire for greater control over the normally precarious allocation of work drove the demand for a hiring hall. Plumbers in Local 2 looked on in envy at the electricians of Local 3, who had won a hiring hall from contractors.[120] In spite of years of anger, plumbers—like many other trades—made little headway because both employers and the union hierarchy preferred it that way. If plumbing contractors controlled hiring, they could choose loyal employees and manipulate plumbers into cutting corners and overlooking work rules. The Yellow Ticket benefited from the lack of a hiring hall, handing out jobs to its supporters.[121]

As one former plumber described it, the process of obtaining work could be agonizing. In some cases, men would shape up at jobs much like longshoremen did on the docks, with some men picked by a foreman and others sent off to find work elsewhere. Aside from attending morning shape-ups, men would also chase down work, calling contractors to inquire about openings or driving from job site to job site in the Bronx and Manhattan in hopes of talking a foreman into giving them a chance. Plumbers used personal connections to get vetted, or in some cases plumbers even underbid one another, taking pay cuts in exchange for work.[122] Though the building boom had made work more readily available in the 1960s—a young plumber related that he was out of work twice in the 1960s for an extended period of time—plumbers feared bouts of unemployment.[123] While a hiring hall would not solve the problem of intermittent work, plumbers hoped that available work would be more fairly distributed.[124]

The precarious and uneven distribution of work within the building trades speaks to the importance of kinship and friendship therein. Many plumbers active in the 1966 strike entered the trade through fathers and uncles and other times through marriage into a family of plumbers. At the time, Local 2's constitution stipulated that two current members vouch for any individual's induction as a plumber.[125] By requiring new members to be sponsored, new plumber hires were practically required to come through networks of family, friends, and, as many of the workers were Catholic, institutions such as parochial schools, churches, and fraternal organizations that were central to the social lives of many white ethnics in New York City.[126]

In many ways, the vetting process for union entry acted as a mutual aid mechanism for working-class New Yorkers, but familial arrangements sometimes favored employers.[127] Plumbing contractors could tap family connections to fill short-term employment gaps, saving themselves the trouble of having to find new workers or taking on the cost of training them. Plumbers were more likely to share important knowledge and skills with family members—not rejecting them as potential future competition—and the contractors could know that they spent little money training a man who would eventually leave their company and work for one of their competitors.[128] While plumbers and other building trades workers used their personal connections and vetting processes to help one another, this helped maintain a racially exclusionary union.[129]

In spite of massive demographic shifts in New York City, in 1964 Local 2 had fewer than twenty-five Black members out of 4,000. Local 2 was in no way exceptional, and in spite of public protest the building trades as a whole were racially exclusionary.[130] Black workers reported that they were denied entry to unions. Some would apply for apprenticeships but never hear back. In other cases, unions gave Black plumbers the runaround, repeatedly telling them they had incorrectly filled out their paperwork or lacked proper documentation; after several trips to the union offices, most would get the message and give up.[131] Blacks that had worked in the building trades in the South were caught in a catch-22: contractors would tell them to obtain a union card, but the union would tell them to be hired by a contractor first. Both the employers and the union could blame the other and deny culpability.[132]

If Blacks or Latinos managed to somehow make it into the union, they would often be relegated to B-card status, which only allowed them to do small jobs and repairs, making an inconsistent income even more unpredictable. Local 2 in particular was known for the refusal to issue licenses to Blacks or Latinos who were trained or had experience from out of state, which, given the massive migration patterns of Black and Latino New Yorkers, would have been the majority.[133] Excluding Blacks and Latinos from the building trades kept them out of a line of work that had few educational barriers to entry and carried better wages than most others.[134] In the mid-1960s, construction work could have been a boon for nonwhite, working-class New Yorkers; instead it became a divisive political battleground that damaged the standing of organized labor.[135]

The hiring practices of the building trades and the plumbers in particular became increasingly politicized in the 1960s. In 1963, activists with the Congress of Racial Equality and the NAACP led protests and nonviolent direct actions for the hiring of Black workers in the city's construction industry. Protests shut down city and state construction sites in Harlem, Brooklyn, and the Bronx, as Black activists pushed for expanded opportunities for minority workers in the industry.[136] To avoid further protests, Harry Van Arsdale Jr. announced a plan for Local 3, the city's most powerful craft union, to induct Black and Latino apprentice electricians. In doing so, Van Arsdale hoped to appease Black civil rights leaders and also maintain the union's control over its membership process. All told, Van Arsdale brought in 240 Black apprentices and sixty Puerto Ricans out of a new class of some 1,000 apprentices.

The city's plumbers unions, however, made no efforts to integrate whatsoever, and in 1964, the New York City Commission on Human Rights decided to target Local 2.[137]

That April, the commission attempted to force the hiring of four nonunion Latino and Black plumbers at the Bronx Terminal Market. After initial resistance, Astrove, the company that held the contract, agreed to hire the four men, and the commission hoped they could then obtain union membership.[138] When the commission contacted Local 2, however, the union immediately protested that this was in violation of their contract. Using the guise of an earlier dispute around sanitation, Local 2 leaders pulled men off the job, with one rank-and-filer later telling the National Labor Relations Board that the dispute occurred because "we don't work with non-union people."[139]

Other accounts from activists at the time allege that the Local 2 plumbers and the four nonunion plumbers were changing into their work clothes and an unidentified union business agent told Local 2 men that they were going on strike due to sanitary conditions. One plumber argued that the sanitary conditions were nothing new. A short argument ensued, and the plumbers walked off the job. While most left work without conflict, an activist's account also mentions that during the initial walkout one plumber shouted obscenities and racial slurs at the nonwhite plumbers.[140]

For two weeks, Local 2 refused to work while the four city hires showed up each day only to be turned away. Eventually the plumbers went back to work, and three of the hires took a union-administered exam, which they subsequently failed.[141] The union refused to submit the tests for outside review. The twenty-day walkout made national headlines, drawing in the UA International, AFL-CIO president George Meany, and even President Lyndon Johnson. While some of the men were initially reluctant to walk out, all ultimately agreed that they would not work with nonunion workers, and in the aftermath of the dispute plumbers thought that the Black and Latino workers were not following the proper procedures, specifically entering through the union's apprenticeship program.[142] For years, civil rights organizations had documented hiring problems and discrimination, and few unions were addressing the problem, forcing activist organizations and the city government into action.[143] Meanwhile, Local 2 members had effectively enforced a closed shop on most job sites through a refusal to work with nonunion workers for decades, and their militant defense of a closed shop at Astrove became a militant attempt to prevent integration of the union, pitting the union in a public conflict with the city government and the city's racial minorities. While the 1964 walkout was not a rank-and-file hate strike, it still heightened the political divide between organized labor and the city's growing Black and Latino communities, reinforcing organized labor's reputation as a racially discriminatory institution that lacked interest in the plight of working-class Blacks.[144]

In spring 1966, union negotiators met with plumbing contractors to discuss a new contract, and hiring remained a key issue.[145] Local 2 leaders called for pay raises, a shorter workweek, a dental plan, elevators on job sites, and most important, a hiring hall. Several of these were demands to catch up with the gains of the more powerful Local 3 electricians, including the hall.[146] Plumbing contractors rejected the hiring hall demand, and negotiations reached an impasse.[147]

At a boisterous union meeting in the summer of 1966, Cohen gave an impassioned speech against the plumbing contractors who had for so long dictated the terms of plumbers' hiring and firing. Trying to rouse his members, he called for a strike to achieve the long-desired goal of rank-and-file plumbers: a hiring hall.[148] Both Yellow Ticket and Blue Ticket loyalists as well as many other plumbers were excited by the list of the demands and the possibility of a strike, especially as several other trades looked to walk off the job as well.[149]

At the meeting, Pappalardo enthusiastically endorsed the strike call, and Cohen called for a voice vote of all plumbers present. The men in the hall stood and roared their approval of the strike move, opening up a months-long labor dispute that would rock the city.[150] While Cohen could appear to be a militant leader rallying his troops, for years his Yellow Ticket had benefited from allocating work assignments to loyalists and Cohen had done little to remedy this issue. Some workers suspected Cohen was leading a strike not because he was a bold advocate of the working class but rather because he was a corrupt leader who was losing his grip on power.[151]

During the first two months of the strike, negotiations improved little, but the plumbers remained firm in their resolve.[152] The union had originally argued for a full hiring hall, but it then reduced its demand to 40 percent control and then 25 percent by October. Contractors offered Cohen a compromise, agreeing to some wage increases and an all-but-worthless hiring hall that would allow the union to select two out of every nineteen jobs, or slightly less than 10 percent. Denouncing the contract at a meeting of plumber rank and file, Cohen asked for a vote of no confidence, with nearly all members standing against the contract.[153] The Blue Ticket's Pappalardo agreed with this contract rejection, arguing that the terms were insufficient; he even went so far as to praise his competitor's stance, lauding the rejection of the builders' terms, which he considered a deceitful reneging on earlier talks.[154]

While it may seem that Pappalardo and Cohen were undergoing a rapprochement, this was not the case at all. Records from the Lindsay administration confirm just how important the power struggle within the union was to the continuation of the strike. Henry Shemin, Lindsay's commissioner of labor, who was in daily contact with union representatives and contractors, claimed that the Yellow Ticket leaders hoped to use the issue of the hiring hall to consolidate their support within the union and that upcoming elections were hindering a settlement.[155]

During the strike, Cohen eschewed picket lines and relied instead on the favorable economic climate, ordering his men to find work in other UA jurisdictions. In response to his call, Local 2 members used their personal and familial connections to organize alternative work, working short jobs in states across the northeast including New Jersey, Pennsylvania, Connecticut, and Delaware. Seeking out-of-state work was an alternative to plumbers exhausting their own savings or having to go through the nearly two-month wait for welfare benefits. Tight-knit groups of men shared job opportunities among themselves, sometimes commuting together in the early morning hours or renting hotels to be closer to distant work sites.[156]

While more plumbers began working out of state, striking construction workers in other trades began returning to work. By the end of August, operating engineers went back, and by mid-September, Local 1 plumbers were also back on the job in Brooklyn and Queens.[157] With men working out of state and without ongoing pickets, other trades even began to violate the plumbers strike, turning on water at job sites in Manhattan and the Bronx. To enforce the strike, a group of Local 2 business agents from both the Blue Ticket and the Yellow Ticket went to scabbing work sites with chains to prevent water from being turned on, threatening members of other trades.[158] Out-of-state work quickly became an important part of the strike, with both contractors and city officials arguing that the men were not really on strike if they were simply doing the same work elsewhere.[159]

With out-of-state work holding the strike steady into November, employers began seeking help to end the strike from public officials and the union international. After the plumbers rejected their contract in late October, the Building Trades Employers Association (BTEA) called on government intervention by Governor Rockefeller and Mayor Lindsay. The BTEA also began negotiations directly with the UA International.[160] With the combined pleas of contractors and the city, the labor organization sent a special representative, John Regan, to help foster an accord. Regan met with employers, assuring them he would do his best to end the strike.[161] They drew up a contract, but Local 2 leaders opposed it, and on November 2, with deputy mayor Timothy Costello presiding, builders and plumbers met for two hours to no avail, prompting a builder's representative to state, "To me, it looks hopeless."[162]

In spite of both Cohen's and Pappalardo's opposition, Regan forced Local 2 leadership to present his contract to the union's membership on November 5. Regan hoped that with significant forewarning, a greater number of plumbers would attend the meeting and pass the contract.[163] Regan's plan completely backfired when the rank-and-file of Local 2 voted down the contract by a massive margin: 1,369 to 382.[164] Dismayed by the contract rejection, the BTEA telegrammed President Johnson, governor Nelson Rockefeller, and US senators Jacob Javits and Robert Kennedy, warning that the strike had the possibility of lasting well into the next year and that action was necessary to "restore industrial order."[165]

Negotiations remained at an impasse throughout November, but in early December state intervention alongside pressure from the UA International forced another contract vote on the plumbers. Mayor Lindsay and employers had asked the state industrial commissioner to appoint a board to make recommendations to settle the strike, and on December 7, after weeks of consideration, the board, headed by Theodore W. Kheel, recommended improved wages, a study of employment conditions, and an alternative to the union hiring hall: a jobless registry that would allegedly help employers more easily sort out who should be assigned work.[166] Though they originally called for this state intervention, employers rejected these recommendations and insisted on yet another weak contract.[167]

When president Jack Cohen brought these recommendations before Local 2 members—only a few days before the union elections—he recommended their rejection, perhaps suspecting that the plumbers would reject them anyway. The meeting went on for hours, with rank-and-file members attacking the leadership for failing to deliver and the contractors for refusing to give plumbers their due.[168] Finally, after the anger and frustration built, Cohen called for a voice vote on the contract, and in a roar, members roundly voted it down. Kheel commented the following day that negotiations were deadlocked and that he doubted that further negotiations on his part were even worthwhile. He still recommended that the union take a proper machine vote, but there are conflicting accounts as to whether such a vote actually happened.[169]

On the night of the Local 2 elections in early December, the tide turned against Cohen and the Yellow Ticket. Despite half of Local 2's plumbers working out of state, thousands of plumbers filled the Manhattan Center. As the meeting got underway, various officials spoke on the merits of their respective factions and the deficiencies of their opponents, but when business agent John Barnett, a Yellow Ticket leader, began to denounce Pappalardo and the Blue Ticket, a brawl broke out that brought pandemonium to the hall. Men piled on top of one another, trading punches and bloodying one another's faces. As one participant remembered it, even men who were normally friendly on the job found themselves exchanging blows in the name of their chosen faction.[170] The fight only ended when shouts rang out that the police were on their way. To avoid police scrutiny, plumbers and officials got right back to the meeting as if the brawl had never happened![171]

When the police arrived, the fight was already over, but they arrested several men who were visibly bloodied. While the police led some plumbers away in handcuffs, the mood of the meeting had changed significantly. Factionalism had started a brawl during the meeting, but the men were united in its aftermath.[172] Voting got underway, and in a few hours all of the ballots were counted to a stunning surprise: Blue Ticket men won nearly every position. Cohen lost the presidential election to Pappalardo, and Local 2 seated four new business agents with three Yellow Ticket incumbent business agents voted out.[173] As Pappalardo's nephew Rocky Maio remembered the event, the consensus among the men came down to a simple phrase that encapsulated the Yellow Ticket's and Jack Cohen's loss of control: "He's on the dime, and he can't even run the meeting right."[174]

A combination of factors changed the plumbers' minds, including Cohen's ineptitude, corruption, and inability to produce a decent contract after more than four months on strike. Even Cohen's own loyalists rejected him, arguing that he had proven himself an ineffective leader. Cohen had called a strike with rank-and-file support in order to maintain his power, but when he could neither deliver nor control his union, the men ousted him and nearly every single one of his supporters.[175]

While plumbers had made their discontent felt at the polls yet again, the UA International made its final move to put an end to the strike. In the last days of December 1966, Local 2 representatives and contractors met in Washington, DC, to hammer out an agreement, settling on a contract that looked remarkably similar to earlier rejected offers. Having failed to obtain victory in previous votes, the international completely sidestepped internal democratic mechanisms and threatened the union with trusteeship if the strike continued.[176] In spite of much autonomy, UA locals, like many other union locals, were dependent on their charter from the international, and the governing body had the right to put any local into trusteeship should it deem fit, a severe sanction that submitted the local to direct international control.[177] President Peter T. Schoenmann of the UA International justified this move by arguing that plumbers working out of state were prolonging the strike unnecessarily and primarily to the detriment of their nonworking brothers. While a little less than half of the union was working, it was actually much easier for unemployed plumbers to attend union meetings and vote for a contract because of their proximity to the meeting.[178]

The international's threats forced the newly elected Pappalardo to be the bearer of bad news. In his first meeting before the rank and file, he recommended approval of a contract he had previously argued against, announcing to more than 2,000 plumbers that should they reject this contract, Local 2 would be placed in trusteeship and have the contract imposed anyway. The meeting lasted for three hours, and the *Daily News* described it as an "emotion-charged meeting that threatened several times to erupt into violence."[179] Much of the meeting involved the newly elected Blue Ticket pleading with the rank and file to accept the contract and save the union from the threat of the international. After hours of talking, shouting, and jeering, a desperate plea from former Local 2 president Cohen to allow the membership to vote resulted in a hastily taken yea vote in favor of the contract.[180] Ironically, the international's final account of the Local 2 negotiations for 1966–67, which it published in its general membership journal, portrayed the affair as a rising vote of confidence in the contract.[181]

While they did not obtain a hiring hall, plumbers won a wage increase and dental plan but ultimately gained no control over the allocation of work within the industry. Many Pappalardo loyalists would have continued striking if he had ordered it, but they also understood the precarious situation of the local.[182] After a six-month strike, employer resistance, and threats from the UA International, other plumbers saw the impossibility of achieving the hiring hall and were content to simply get back to work.[183]

Rank-and-file opposition to the Yellow Ticket helped provoke a lengthy strike whose results were ultimately mixed. On the one hand, it showed that building trades unions could oppose their entrenched leaderships as well as the power of contractors to dictate the terms of life and labor. The incumbent leadership, under the helm of Cohen, refused to negotiate an inferior contract that would result in his being labeled a "sellout" by the membership, and when they could not deliver, they were ejected from office. On the other hand, their strike showed to what lengths political actors locally and nationally would go in order to ensure labor peace. The international showed its hand quickly, working very hard to end rather than win the strike. With help from the international, employers were able to maintain control of hiring. A favorable national boom in construction as well as a viable oppositional faction undergirded the plumbers' resistance, but those two factors were not enough to deliver everything the men wanted. Though plumbers won a wage increase and dental plan and also voted out incumbent leaders, the inability to win the hiring hall was a defeat that would not be overturned until roughly twenty-five years later.[184]

A Rising Rebellion

The dramatic rank-and-file-driven strikes, which paralyzed the city's critical public transportation system and its multibillion-dollar construction industry, announced the beginning of a wave of upheaval. Transit workers inspired others in the public sector, but that electricians, postal employees, and communications workers also saw the strike as something to emulate signaled that many workers across the city were frustrated by weak contracts and leaders who could not deliver. In the building trades, the plumbers' struggle helped set a tactical precedent, and in the years that followed, steam fitters, sheet metal workers, and elevator constructors followed Local 2's lead, voting down leadership-endorsed contracts and fighting for increased wages and trade-specific improvements.[185] In spite of strong divisions—racial, craft, and sector—segments of working-class New Yorkers influenced and emboldened one another, and a tactical and experiential transmission would unfold in the years to come.

These strikes also exposed some initial limitations within the city's rank-and-file struggles. Though the Rank and File Committee had pushed the TWU leadership toward better demands and more militant action, it was ultimately unsuccessful in taking the reins of leadership. After the 1966 strike, the question remained: Workers could rebel, but could they seize power? The plumbers meanwhile were able to throw out their old leaders, but they were ultimately unable to achieve the long-sought-after hiring hall. Employer resistance and, just as significant, resistance from their own international crushed their efforts; in the face of such stiff opposition there was very little recourse but to let some demands fall by the wayside. In the years to come, workers in a variety of other industries would confront similar obstacles, experimenting with different methods to overcome these roadblocks and in other cases accommodating themselves to a situation that seemed impossible to change. Though dramatic, many of these rank-and-file moments would be ultimately fleeting.

TWO

Militancy, Alienation, and the Wallace Effect

Rank-and-file militancy intensified in the aftermath of the transit and plumbers strikes. It was not simply that strikes were growing: more of them were wildcats (walkouts not authorized by union officials) or began with workers rejecting contracts put to them by their union leaders. Informal practices of resistance such as absenteeism and shirking of duties proliferated alongside these public displays of rank-and-file anger. In the late 1960s, workers across the country seemed to be suffering the "blue-collar blues" and the "white-collar woes."[1] While the workplace was often the site of rebellion, New York City's working people were not just angry about work. A growing number detested mayor John Lindsay and hated the inferiority they felt as working people. In his 1968 presidential run, the racist, populist George Wallace sought to tap into this growing anger, connecting with the city's rank-and-file rebels in both sentiment and, to a lesser degree, votes.

This chapter delves into the alienation and discontent that drove New York City's rank-and-file upheaval by examining its myriad sources and manifestations. The first third examines its diverse expressions between 1967 and 1968—wildcat strikes, contract rejections, and absenteeism—while also uncovering its many sources. Far from a coherent, singly motivated, or linear movement—such as a classical story of workers versus bosses—varied and often very contradictory experiences and contexts led rank-and-file workers to rebel in similar ways. The second part examines the rank-and-file-driven 1968 sanitation strike and how it embodied a broader social discontent in New York City. In February 1968, Uniformed Sanitationmen's Association (USA) president John DeLury completely lost control of a contract rally, and his men forced him into a strike he did not want. While economic issues drove USA members, an increasing discontent and anger with their social position in the city's socioeconomic hierarchy also fueled their unrest. Tired of being looked down upon as garbagemen, they unleashed their anger on New York and singled out Mayor Lindsay for particular scorn. Their strike, like that of the Transport Workers Union (TWU) before them, heightened political tensions in the city and cemented Lindsay's legacy as broadly anti–working class. The third part of this chapter explores how George Wallace's 1968 presidential run sought to tap into this growing worker alienation in New York City. While New York was foreign territory for the southern segregationist, Wallace won some support from militant workers in the city when deploying populist language and making direct overtures directly to union members. Labor leaders chalked up the support to a combination of confusion and racism, and the latter has been shown to play a role in some workers' support for Wallace. Discontent with liberal institutions, many of which were doing very little to meet the demands of white working people, has been underemphasized in the literature. In New York City, Mayor Lindsay, who often pitted the interests of the working-class whites against that of poor Blacks, exacerbated these tensions, as did entrenched union leaderships who offered up weak contract gains in often worsening work environments. New York's rank-and-file rebellion overlapped with shifting the electoral alliances and constituencies that eventually came to define decades of American politics.[2]

Wildcats, Contract Rejections, and Workplace Rebellion

Labor upheaval, catalyzed by the TWU and the plumbers of Local 2, continued in 1967 and 1968. In New York City there were 201 and 191 strikes in those years, respectively, and though this total represented a smaller number of strikes than had occurred in the early 1960s, the strikes involved more workers than in previous years and resulted in many more days idle. Worker participation in strikes had hit a nadir in 1963, with only 54,000, but steadily climbed upward, hitting a peak for the decade with just over 200,000 in 1968. Days lost climbed significantly from mid-decade, with employers losing nearly 3.3 million workdays in 1968, a more than 50 percent increase from the previous year.[3] While strikes grew in number and size, workers' actions were transforming qualitatively; in fact, some of the largest strikes in 1967 were rank-and-file-led wildcats.[4]

During World War II and in its immediate aftermath, unions in the United States overwhelmingly agreed to "no strike" clauses that legally barred workers from engaging in any type of work stoppages for the duration of the contract.[5] Wildcats had reached a high point during that period, with many taking place in arms production plants, but by the mid-1960s, they began to increase across the entire country and across different sectors.[6] For many unions, enforcing no-strike clauses was no easy task, and some workers used short-term walk-offs in lieu of much slower grievance mechanisms.[7]

In January 1967, just as the plumbers of Local 2 were being forced back to work, over 1,000 drivers of the Railway Express Agency wildcatted.[8] In May, restaurant workers in the Pan Am building began a wildcat when one of their coworkers was fired for being rude to customers who did not tip. For three days, the wildcat shut down four restaurants of Waldorf Associates.[9] In June, when Greyhound management tried to change shift schedules on the Providence–New York route from two days on/two days off to two days on/one day off, drivers walked out, picketing buses, feigning being hit, and blocking traffic at the Port Authority bus terminal. The wildcat spread along the line to Albany and Montreal and brought pleas from union heads to end the strike.[10] In October, a three-day wildcat strike of some 2,500 longshoremen shut down the Port of Newark-Elizabeth, one of America's largest shipping terminals.[11] While in some unions wildcats were one-off affairs, Long Island Rail Road engineers used wildcats and slowdowns in 1967 and 1968 to resist scheduling changes that would reduce their overtime pay. In fact, the union had not struck since 1960.[12]

A statewide wildcat strike by Communications Workers of America (CWA) Local 1101 in the summer of 1967 revealed not only the growing aggressiveness of New York's workers but also the growing concern with safety in a changing city. The wildcat began on the last day of July, four days after the robbery and nonfatal shooting of a twenty-two-year-old telephone repairman and change collector in Brooklyn's Bedford-Stuyvesant neighborhood.[13] In the city's growing Black ghettoes, thieves targeted the mostly white collectors who serviced pay phones, and in May, a worker had refused to work unaccompanied in Harlem, prompting ponderous negotiations between union and management. After New York Telephone refused workers' demands to be paired up for assignments in dangerous areas after the July attack, twenty-eight people walked off the job in north Brooklyn without union authorization, and within a week nearly 25,000 workers were on strike.[14]

Increased labor demand had made many telephone workers confident enough to engage in such a strike, and this event was important for the development of solidarity within the CWA.[15] The severity of the attack on the repairman exposed the growing dangers that many of the CWA's outdoor workers faced, bridging the gap between those who worked in neighborhoods and those who worked inside New York Telephone plants. In Brooklyn, where the strike was initiated, the wildcat brought older and younger workers together in collective action, bridging some of the generational divide. As one CWA rank-and-filer remembered it, this massive wildcat for job safety prompted a new era of militancy, which will be examined in a later chapter.[16]

With the strike spreading, the union intervened in support of the wildcat's aims while calling for its end. Previous negotiations had yielded little, but with this near-total walkout, management nominally agreed to the strike demands but, in exchange, wanted to punish the wildcat leaders. In response, the union called for statewide solidarity and assumed full control of the strike.[17] After nine days and intense negotiations, the CWA ultimately agreed to the firing of three workers involved in the walkout but obtained a forty-five-day pairing experiment in the neighborhoods of the South Bronx, Bedford-Stuyvesant, Brownsville, East New York, Williamsburg, and Harlem.[18]

The entanglement of crime, race, and geography in New York City was complex, and the attacks on the CWA's predominantly white workforce in the city's Black ghettoes had important ramifications. Michael W. Flamm's work has shown that law and order was an increasingly powerful conservative talking point after 1963, with large numbers of white working-class voters supporting law-and-order measures in New York City. Michael Javen Fortner has shown, however, that the Black working class embraced law and order in the face of increasing violence as well, which in turn fostered acceptance for harsher punishment of drug addicts and criminals and the eventual establishment of the Rockefeller Drug Laws.[19] Such sentiment could be found on the wildcat picket lines in 1967, with one Black CWA member declaring, "There's more crime in poor neighborhoods, and it has nothing to do with your race. A junkie or hood will hit anyone." As another put it, "Decent people of any race don't throw things at telephone men."[20] While historians have discussed the rise of "law and order" discourse in national and local politics, the Local 1101 strike suggest its salience as a workplace issue.[21] In fact, such demands for pairing in the face of crime and violence were not confined to telephone workers.

In late May 1967, a police officer attacked a "meter maid" who he believed had unfairly issued a summons to a motorist. A scuffle ensued, and when the news spread, some twenty parking enforcement officers walked off the job.[22] The women complained not only of this incident but of widespread harassment by both the police and civilians. In New York, the white-collar, all-female force was established in 1960, and strict weight requirements were in place, which caused public conflict with the union in 1965 and resulted in one of their newer members attending a weight-loss camp in Florida.[23] Meanwhile, the police department engaged in a multiyear jurisdictional battle with the parking enforcement officers over what violations and citations were allowed to be issued.[24] It was not unusual for conflict to take place between police officers and parking enforcement, but after their two-day wildcat, the striking parking enforcement officers won a pairing agreement, which Local 1101 members would obtain several weeks later.[25]

After many abortive attempts to establish a union, taxi drivers, with the help of Harry Van Arsdale Jr., established the New York City Taxi Drivers Union in 1965 with a combination of well-organized garage elections and a two-week strike. Medical benefits, vacation days, and pensions quickly followed for cab drivers.[26] While these gains were significant, many taxi drivers felt that they were long overdue and that Van Arsdale was not delivering quickly enough. In spite of its fledgling status, the union quickly became the site of diffuse rank-and-file challenges only a year after its founding.[27]

Opponents of the leadership fell into two camps in the late 1960s. One side wanted greater taxi driver representation but respected Van Arsdale's leadership in the unionization drive.[28] The other oppositionists despised Van Arsdale, believing him to be a paternalist that lacked direct knowledge of drivers' daily concerns as well as confidence in drivers' ability to run their own affairs.[29] Several opposition slates ran in 1966, and though the incumbents defeated them, the collective votes of the oppositionist were substantial.[30]

The next year, as negotiations stalled between the newly established union and fleet owners, rank-and-file dissidents organized pickets and walk-offs in Manhattan when union leaders postponed a strike deadline. Drivers went on strike at four garages in Queens, Manhattan, and the Bronx, paralyzing roughly 250 cabs.[31] At a union meeting in Queens, Van Arsdale asked the 3,000 assembled taxi drivers to stand in support of extended negotiations;

very few did, and as a result, he fled the meeting as drivers called him a sellout and dictator.32 The following day, angry taxi drivers wildcatted against their union's decision to continue negotiations rather than strike. Picketing dozens of fleet garages, they prevented thousands of taxis from going out and scared many on-duty drivers from working anywhere near the pickets.33

A mere two days after the driver-led wildcats, the union and fleet owners reached an accord that would see an increase in pay for taxi drivers as well as a concerted effort on the part of union leadership and owners to push the city to increase fares.34 Mayor Lindsay's support of fare increases, however, was contingent on greater city oversight of the taxi industry as well as plans to issue new medallions, regularize livery cabs, and address some drivers' refusal to pick up Black passengers.35 Drivers who owned their own cabs and who stood to benefit from fare increases more than their fleet driver counterparts were particularly angry at the mayor, threatening the city with more wildcats.36 But at the end of January 1968, the mayor acceded and the city council approved fare hikes, avoiding further walkouts.37

While wildcat strikes grew in number, so, too, did contract rejections. In late January 1967, tugboat operators, who helped larger ships dock and delivered sand, gravel, fuel oil, and jet fuel, rejected a union-leadership-endorsed contract.38 In April, firemen rejected a contract endorsed by their association's heads for a third time and in the very same meeting also rejected a proposal that the next contract only be approved by top leadership.39

In June 1967, welfare caseworkers of the Social Service Employees Union went out on strike and rejected their leadership's recommendation to return to work while negotiations continued. Instead, they organized a picket of city hall, and Lindsay denounced them for "their callous exploitation of innocent welfare clients."40 Ironically, the predominantly female Social Service Employees Union had advocated for not only their own economic well-being but also for that of their clients. Many young women entering the profession in the 1960s faced huge caseloads and lacked the resources to service their abysmally poor clients. As a result, in 1966 the Social Service Employees Union rank and file and union leadership struck the city's welfare centers to assert their right to bargain for greater benefits for welfare clients. The entry of many young leftists and the creation of leftist groups within the union helped push the union leadership and rank and file toward confrontation by 1967, but the strike actions ultimately failed to crush Lindsay's resolve.41

Not to be outdone, on the first day of September 1967, New York City teachers walked off the job, testing the limits of the newly established Taylor Law and pushing Mayor Lindsay into a contentious political situation.

School was delayed for weeks, and the city's newspapers assailed the teachers, calling them greedy public servants who had forgotten their professional commitments. When United Federation of Teachers (UFT) president Albert Shanker finally negotiated a contract, a sizable minority of the rank and file voted against it, calling him a power-hungry sellout.[42]

Worker dissatisfaction also found an outlet through absenteeism.[43] Though many workers considered white-collar labor an escape from blue-collar drudgery, professionals experienced what some called the "white-collar woes."[44] New York City teachers, for example, exhibited a higher absentee rate than those in other major cities such as Chicago, Pittsburgh, and San Francisco. In fact, most teachers in New York took all ten of their paid sick days each year, shortening by a day almost a quarter of their workweeks. The UFT's Shanker was quick to defend them as a necessary measure for people who were "on the stage six hours a day."[45]

Arbitration papers for transit workers in the city, in particular among bus drivers, give us insight into the practice among workers with much less sick leave. Theodore Kheel, the Amalgamated Transit Union and TWU mediator, dealt with these issues repeatedly in the late 1960s and early 1970s. Workers would routinely fake sicknesses, either calling in the day prior or even only an hour before their shift. The problem became so pronounced that the Transit Authority would call workers on the phone to verify that they were at home and on occasion send a Transit Authority doctor to assess them.[46] While absenteeism was often stretched to its feasible limits, sometimes it went much further, with one worker fired for missing thirty days of work in 1968![47]

In addition to absenteeism, many white- and blue-collar workers engaged in activity that decreased the intensity of their workday. In some cases, these were long-standing practices; in the early 1960s, the chairman of Walworth, a valve and tool manufacturer, complained that his office workers "used to have trouble with the trains. . . . Then they had to have a coffee break of about thirty minutes, and then by 11:30 they were making plans for lunch, and most of them were back by 2 P.M. Then they had to leave to catch the train by 4:30."[48]

In the late 1960s, such practices were relatively common in many blue-collar jobs. A young radical worker in the fuel oil industry found that many of his coworkers would park their trucks and take naps. Since they worked independently and were paid hourly and radio monitoring equipment was not installed in trucks, drivers could make money while sleeping off part of their workday.[49] In the same years, younger telephone workers would sometimes sabotage equipment to spark short walk-offs, purposely interrupting the workday in a way their older counterparts did not.[50] In other industries, workplace norms dictated a slower pace of work, and fuel deliverers at airports maintained a large number of breaks, shirking their duties or deliberately working slowly and sometimes facing harsh disciplinary responses from management.[51] Meanwhile construction workers routinely took tools and construction materials home, and some engaged in sabotage to shut down job sites.[52]

For some workers, the workplace itself, not simply rules and wages, was a source of discontent. In his "Confessions of a Working Stiff," Patrick Fenton described the daily experience of unionized baggage handlers in the late 1960s at John F. Kennedy Airport in Queens, who—as he succinctly put it—had two things in common: "They hate the work they are doing and drink a little too much."[53] Baggage handlers worked outdoors and in cargo holds of airplanes, unloading and transporting anything from mail to luggage within the airport grounds. Fenton described the work as terribly monotonous, and its monotony was to blame for its destructive effects on the lives of baggage handlers. Indignities spanned the range from deafening noise and roll calls to horrible weather and clock-watching managers. Older workers were the least content, and they complained often that their economic obligations—families, mortgages, and car notes—kept them on the job. At the end of the day, Fenton described how his fellow workers would "head down to the locker room, heads bowed, like a football team that never wins."[54] While "Confessions of a Working Stiff" was certainly stylized for effect, the conditions Fenton described were also found in other workplaces. In addition to being poorly paid, postal workers worked in increasingly automated workplaces and complained of fatigue and boredom.[55] Autoworkers bemoaned the repetitive and monotonous nature of their work and were diagnosed with the "blue-collar blues."[56]

Though Fenton describes a disheartening situation, some of this discontent manifested in collective action. In August 1967, nearly 500 Pan American airline employees walked off the job over unresolved grievances and deadlocked contract talks, ending their walkout after two days when the leaders of the Brotherhood of Railway, Airline, and Steamship Clerks Local 3055 ordered them back to work.[57] In May the following year, more than 100 cargo handlers working for Pan American walked off the job in response to the dismissal of one of their workmates. The strike spread from the cargo holds to the mail rooms, with another fifty Pan Am employees walking out. Union representatives for Local 3055 intervened, brokering a deal to bring the issue to mediation and putting an end to the walkout.[58]

Some younger people in the 1960s expressed a generational discontent with workplace discipline. Refusing to fall in line was reflected in high turnover rates and absenteeism, and some young people articulated the desire to have the mental and physical space to explore things outside of work.[59] Young people's more vocal opposition was in some ways a result of better times: they had more job opportunities available to them in an era of low unemployment and lacked the experience of severe economic downturns.[60] Cultural practices of the young also brought conflicts with management: United Parcel Service workers briefly went on strike against being disciplined for having long hair and wearing turtlenecks in 1969.[61] Young people's attitudes sometimes reflected a broader youth movement that questioned hegemonic institutions including the workplace, family, and government.[62] In the summer of 1968, when nearly 700 young lifeguards and lifeguard supervisors organized a one-day wildcat against poor work conditions and ongoing grievances, their union leaders in District Council 37 denounced them as "a bunch of wild kids."[63]

Increasing neighborhood-based Black militancy helped spur increased Black organizing in the workplace. Wilbur Haddock was a member of Congress of Racial Equality's Bronx chapter, working at a racially stratified Ford production plant in Mahwah, New Jersey. Influenced by mobilizations in the city, in the mid-1960s he pushed the United Auto Workers to take a stronger stand against job discrimination and racial segregation in the workplace. Efforts foundered, however, and in the late 1960s Haddock helped form the United Black Brothers, which would organize outside of the union's framework, building its base of support primarily among urban Blacks, who had more experience and proximity to ongoing civil rights struggles. In June 1969, the United Black Brothers led a wildcat strike that shut down the Ford plant for two nights after a supervisor allegedly called a Black worker a racial slur.[64]

Black Nationalism and growing racial pride influenced Haddock's group and many other newer Black labor groups. While the Harlem riots contributed to the acceleration of Black activism in the TWU, in July 1967 Detroit, Newark, and New Haven exploded as ghettoized Black people looted stores, burned buildings, and fought back against the National Guard's attempt to impose order.[65] While many whites looked on the events as outbreaks of lawlessness and crime, many Blacks saw the riots as politically motivated rebellion, and even those who were not direct participants sympathized with the riots or were proud that they had occurred.[66] The 1968 Ocean Hill–Brownsville strike, which saw the primarily white and Jewish UFT facing off with Black community control advocates, added to racial nationalism in the city.⁶⁷ As Detroit-based organizer Simon P. Owens recalled, many new Black caucuses around the country were much more radical in orientation, focusing less on traditional rank-and-file activism and more on revolutionary aspirations and style. In some cases, the radical aesthetics and revolutionary stance of younger Blacks alienated older coworkers and, in Owens's estimation, allowed union leadership to more easily undermine them.⁶⁸

Worker dissatisfaction and practices such as absenteeism—as well as sabotage and wildcat strikes—caused concern among government officials and major corporations. By the last quarter of the 1960s, profits began to decline across most sectors and productivity growth began to slow. Aggressive workers were not solely to blame, of course, and as economist Robert Brenner argues, international competition played a driving role in the declining rate of profit.⁶⁹ That being said, worker discipline is always a concern for businesses, and amid a declining rate of profit, absenteeism, shirking work duties, and pilferage cost owners more money.⁷⁰ While there was some dispute at the time concerning the degree to which workers' actions were responsible for declining profits, by the second half of the 1960s, profits had fallen 33 percent in manufacturing and 22 percent in white-collar work, generating managerial anxiety and catalyzing attempts to reorganize the workplace in order to turn the trend around.⁷¹

Alienation and New York's Garbagemen

While many remember 1968 as a year of student protest and rioting in the aftermath of Martin Luther King Jr.'s assassination, in New York, the growing alienation of working-class people was also front and center. In February, the rank and file of the USA forced their longtime leader into a nine-day strike, leaving hundreds of thousands of tons of garbage to accumulate along the city's tight streets. Organized as Local 831 of the International Brotherhood of Teamsters, the 10,000 sanitation workers rejected a contract put to them by their founding president, John DeLury, pelting him with eggs and chasing him off a speaker's platform in front of city hall. There was more at stake than mere bread-and-butter concerns; as Charles R. Morris put it, New York's sanitationmen "were angry at the city, angry at the changes in working conditions, angry at the apparent preferences shown minorities; they felt like second-class citizens ('garbagemen') and wanted to strike almost for catharsis."⁷² Combining grievances both on and off the job, the sanitation strike gives us an important window into the myriad factors that spurred the city's rank-and-file-led strikes. It also reveals important fault lines in labor's body politic, with the overwhelmingly white sanitation workers embodying white working-class anger at Lindsay.

Relations between the Lindsay administration and the USA leadership between 1966 and 1968 led to increasing anger on the part of rank-and-file sanitation workers. As city officials predicted, the 1966 transit strike made unions more confident that major gains could be achieved by challenging the mayor.[73] When the USA's contract expired on July 1, 1966, DeLury chose not to call a strike, expecting a big settlement and assured by Lindsay that all wage and benefit gains would be retroactive. Lindsay appeared to be changing course with unions, avoiding direct confrontations and employing an appeasement strategy that previous mayors had used.[74]

Relations quickly took a turn for the worse when Lindsay appointed Samuel J. Kearing Jr. to the position of sanitation commissioner. Amid ongoing negotiations, Kearing began an investigation into USA members, which resulted in the suspension of nearly two dozen sanitation workers for taking bribes. DeLury responded with a work slowdown, urging his men to operate only trucks that met safety standards, leaving nearly a quarter of the city's sanitation fleet idle.[75] Within a week, the union won a $450 raise, increased city payments toward a dental plan, and diverted an increased margin of city payments into pension funds. DeLury thought the deal kept up with the pattern set by the TWU, and upon agreeing to it, he put in a good word for the mayor, saying, "Mayor Lindsay's labor policy is beginning to take shape. So long as we have his cooperation, we pledge him ours."[76]

In spite of conciliatory words and contracts, Commissioner Kearing continued investigations, and in 1967, he reassigned some 450 sanitationmen from twenty-five sites in response to allegations of large-scale corruption.[77] Kearing also attacked the union with a series of cost-cutting measures, including eliminating a paid workday for participation in any one of the city's large parades (such as Saint Patrick's Day and Columbus Day).[78] While Kearing attacked the union, he advocated solving the city's sanitation problems with increased hiring, pleasing union officials and USA members. When he hired some 200 new sanitationmen without Lindsay's approval, Lindsay fired him for ignoring the chain of command.[79]

The biggest point of contention between the administration and the USA leadership was the newly created Office of Collective Bargaining (OCB). Lindsay hoped that the tripartite commission—made up of one city representative, one union representative, and one impartial mediator—would streamline labor relations in the aftermath of the transit strike. DeLury resented the institution, preferring direct negotiations with the mayor, which he felt were a sign of respect for the powerful organization he had built.[80] When the USA's 1967 contract expired, DeLury refused to negotiate with the OCB, not only out of anger at the institution but also in hopes that several ongoing disputes with public sector employees would help raise the bar for his own contract negotiations.[81] DeLury's plan backfired, however. After seven months without a contract, he issued a hard deadline to the city in January but ultimately balked when the city did not budge.[82]

On the icy morning of February 2, DeLury and the USA leadership called a mass rally of sanitationmen at city hall, pulling men off the job across the five boroughs in what was an unofficial strike. By 7:00 a.m., some 7,000 USA members had gathered, and DeLury hoped that the rally would bring about the necessary pressure to produce a sellable contract.[83] But as he walked through the crowd, DeLury faced intense hostility, with sanitationmen jeering and jostling him and some trying to hit him with eggs.[84] Like the transit workers had done with Mike Quill, the sanitationmen called DeLury's bluff. The men believed that others looked down on their occupation, taking for granted a public service that was both backbreaking and dangerous. Similar to a growing number of workers, sanitationmen felt very strongly that they occupied a low rung in the social hierarchy, but unlike other workers, they felt that their line of work singled them out; many were enraged daily at being called garbagemen.[85] Their resentment made its way up the city's social hierarchy, and as one sanitation worker concluded in the aftermath of the strike, "We're hard-working men, and the Mayor just doesn't understand us."[86]

While widespread anger at both the mayor's and DeLury's lack of delivery existed, it was not without forewarning: several days earlier, when DeLury had failed to lead his men out on strike, the union's 700 shop stewards rejected his contract recommendations.[87] Such rejections were becoming more common in the city, and in the days before, 3,500 Local 272 Teamster garage workers rejected a contract and went on strike, and a bus strike on Long Island paralyzed the commutes of more than 20,000 riders after drivers there rejected a contract.[88] Less than two months earlier, an angry meeting of taxi drivers had forced the city's most powerful labor leader to flee through a side door. When calling his men out for a threatening rally that bordered on a strike, DeLury not only miscalculated his own control over his members but also underestimated the degree to which rank-and-file upheaval had emboldened workers in New York.

What began for DeLury as a piece of political theater, a mass rally with him at the helm, evolved quickly into a worker-driven meeting where grievances were aired against both the city and the union president. DeLury presented an OCB-written contract, which was voted down, and when he motioned for a mail-in strike vote, the angry ranks shouted him down again, forcing DeLury—who had overseen only one, single-day strike in his thirty years as USA president—to declare, "I accept a motion for go, go, go."[89]

While internal issues helped spur the strike, the growing political dissensus in New York City also played a part. Many white rank-and-file union members had come to associate Lindsay's mayoralty with one that actively promoted the welfare of racial minorities at the expense of whites. Lindsay tended to agree, telling one reporter after his first year in office: "I understand how they feel . . . and I don't resent it. But this had to be the year of the poor in New York."[90] In Lindsay's mind the poor were Black and Puerto Rican New Yorkers, and standing opposite the progress of racial minorities was New York's more well-off, white working class, many of whom were organized in or affiliated by family relations with labor unions, whom Lindsay had portrayed as entrenched power brokers that upheld unfair advantages for whites.[91] Lindsay played this card during the transit strike and would do so again during the sanitation strike, attacking their efforts with crisis rhetoric, or using what DeLury called a "rash of clamors" to whip up antilabor sentiment.[92]

Lindsay's denunciation of union power and his broader disregard for many whites led to a widespread feeling among white working-class people that the mayor favored poor Blacks and Puerto Ricans over poor and working-class whites.[93] As one union cab driver put it in 1967, "You tell me what he's ever done for white people."[94] For sanitation workers, the growing resentment against the mayor compounded their on-the-job grievances. As such, going on strike in 1968 developed as a way to not only make militant demands but also avenge themselves of the denigration of their occupational and class status.

Determined not to lose the battle against yet another municipal labor union, the Lindsay administration hoped to use emergency powers to put down the strike, a move that inadvertently united the labor movement behind the striking sanitation workers.[95] Lindsay's first major countermeasure came on the fourth day of the strike when he called 3,000 municipal workers to emergency trash duty. The move enraged District Council 37's Victor Gotbaum and John Cassesse of the Patrolmen's Benevolent Association, and both threatened a massive strike if their members were brought in as scabs.[96] Days later, Lindsay ordered the Emergency Control Board to declare a public health emergency on the grounds of possible typhoid and cholera outbreaks and the growing number of trash fires.⁹⁷ The garbage piling up on the streets reached epic proportions, with estimates running as high as 10,000 tons accumulating each day. Trash fires increased nearly 750 percent in the first days of the strike as children and young men in poor neighborhoods set it alight.⁹⁸ Other residents organized protests against the trash, part and parcel of ongoing struggles around sanitation in low-income areas.⁹⁹

With negotiations at an impasse, Lindsay called for the harshest solution to the strike: mobilizing the National Guard. While Lindsay had avoided asking the state to mobilize the guard during outbreaks of rioting during the summers of 1966 and 1967, one week into the strike he called on Governor Rockefeller to bring in the troops.¹⁰⁰ For many New York labor leaders, memories of National Guard mobilizations and civil violence during the Depression remained potent. Leaders like Van Arsdale of the AFL-CIO, Joseph Trerotola of the Teamsters, and municipal labor leaders like Gotbaum, whom Lindsay had already alienated during this affair, threatened to strike in response to any guard mobilization.¹⁰¹ While DeLury had alienated other labor leaders in the past, especially other municipal labor leaders, Lindsay had succeeded by complete accident in uniting labor behind the strike.¹⁰²

Lindsay's attempts to put down the strike were an attempt to rewrite municipal labor relations and strike back against organized labor. Amid the negotiating impasse, he told a Rockefeller aide that he rejected settlement recommendations because it was excessively compensatory and violated the principle of negotiating with an illegally striking union.¹⁰³ This position was spurious given that from his very first days in office, he had negotiated with an illegally striking union. More important, the mayor wanted to undo the legacy of the transit strike by any means necessary, and by 1968, in the recollection of Harry W. Albright Jr., Rockefeller's deputy secretary, Lindsay now thought it was "time to break these public employee unions and to draw the line." In order to do this, he pitted unions against the rest of the public, arguing in a press conference on February 9, "My effort here is to do whatever I can to establish the principle that the rights of 8 million people cannot be violated by selfish interests."¹⁰⁴

With Lindsay hoping to put down the strike and transform municipal labor relations, Governor Rockefeller reluctantly intervened. Many historians have rightfully emphasized that Rockefeller opposed bringing in the National Guard because he feared another Ludlow Massacre besmirching the family name. His motivations were more complicated, however. Rockefeller enjoyed the support of organized labor in the state for many years.¹⁰⁵

DeLury campaigned for Rockefeller in 1966, even orchestrating an event in which Rockefeller spoke to USA shop stewards atop a sanitation truck.[106] Van Arsdale and the Central Labor Council equally cultivated a close working relationship with Rockefeller, whom they had endorsed in the 1966 gubernatorial elections.[107]

Given his political entanglements, it was no surprise that Rockefeller, under consideration for nomination as the Republican Party's presidential candidate, rebuked Lindsay for his National Guard demand. Rockefeller instead proposed a state takeover of the sanitation department to end the strike, offering a $425 pay increase as compared to the $400 pay increase the OCB offered. While DeLury, who was in jail for much of the strike, liked the possibility of negotiating directly with Rockefeller, he and other USA negotiators found one major fault with the plan. "The rabbit"—the name given in negotiations for Rockefeller's state takeover—would require approval in the state legislature and offer nothing in the immediate term to strikers. Negotiators were very concerned that the rank and file would not accept such a measure, given their initial rejection of a $400 settlement and the disastrous meeting at city hall a week earlier. DeLury, whom Rockefeller had managed to free from jail to continue negotiations, eventually brought the contract to the sanitationmen, and after nine days on strike, USA members accepted the improved deal.[108]

New Yorkers were delighted that the strike was over, but it left a bitter taste in the mouths of many. For union leaders and many rank-and-file workers, Lindsay's recalcitrance in the face of the sanitationmen's demands and his desire to use the National Guard to bring the strike to an end only seemed to be further evidence of his disdainful attitude toward the city's working class. Many other citizens saw the strike and the mountains of garbage as a disgrace and evidence of labor's disregard for the rest of the city.[109] In fact, many Black antipoverty groups called for breaking the strike in protests against the growing trash piles in neighborhoods like the Lower East Side and Harlem.[110] And though many New Yorkers did not like the garbage accumulation, there were still a number of them who did not agree with the mayor's attempt to use the National Guard, approving instead of Rockefeller's attempts to bring the strike to a peaceful conclusion.[111] In the aftermath, Lindsay would explain that he had to hold out against the USA in order to fight an illegally striking union that rejected the OCB. Lindsay characterized his opposition to the union as a stand of an entire city "against illegality, against violence, against extortion," cementing a divisive legacy concerning labor organizations and union rank and file.[112]

New York City's 1968 sanitation crisis exposed important political developments in the city and reveals much about some workers' political motivations. As Victor Gotbaum of District Council 37 would later declare, "The difficulty in the sanitation strike was a breakdown in many relationships: the Mayor's with the leadership; the leadership at one point with their own men; their own men amongst themselves."[113] Furthermore, by 1968, labor insurgency pushed and was pushed by a growing multilateral polarization in New York City.

While many historians have emphasized that public opinion ultimately turned the tide of the strike, there is also evidence that sentiment among rank-and-file workers played a part. Sanitation worker Joseph J. Chiarelli, one of the shop stewards who had rejected the initial settlement with the city, expressed his thanks to Governor Rockefeller in the aftermath of the strike. Chiarelli considered himself representative of many working people in the city: living in a small apartment with his family and working hard to make ends meet. But Chiarelli resented how maligned his class and line of work were, telling the governor of a death on the job and two severe injuries involving hit-and-run accidents and emphasizing the need for better equipment and better service to the public. While brokering a more favorable settlement was certainly important to his support of Rockefeller, Chiarelli also supported the governor because, unlike Mayor Lindsay, he "understood the working man's feelings more than some people realize."[114] Chiarelli was proud of his hard work and proud of what he had earned, but he felt that politicians rarely connected with the experience of working people. This sense of disempowerment, anger, and alienation among working-class people would remain front and center throughout 1968 as George Wallace made his bid for the presidency.

A Southern Segregationist in New York City

In 1968, George Wallace would try to tap the anger of white working-class New Yorkers, intertwining pervasive sentiments of societal alienation and populist denunciations of the status quo with fears of crime and thinly veiled racism. In fact, one of Wallace's best-attended 1968 rallies was in New York City's Madison Square Garden, where the candidate was met by a ten-minute, standing ovation on the part of 16,000 fervent supporters.[115] Denouncing radicals, criminals, liberals, bureaucrats, and the undeserving poor, Wallace set the crowd to its feet repeatedly throughout the night. Several union officials from Alabama and one from the steam fitters in upstate New York accompanied the candidate on stage. Wallace was in a working-class city, and he went to great lengths to identify himself with the aspirations and fears of working people there.[116]

Wallace's 1968 campaign focused heavily on working-class voters in the industrial North. Wallace's hopes of breaking into this demographic rested on his concrete achievements in the Democratic presidential primary of 1964, in which he polled quite well among white ethnic voters in Wisconsin, Indiana, and parts of Maryland.[117] Wallace's all-volunteer New York City campaigners agreed with this strategy; nineteen-year-old Thomas Stokes argued, "All those ethnic groups that usually vote for Democrats—the Italians, the Irish, the Eastern Europeans—we'll really crack them."[118]

As sociologist Stephen Steinberg has argued, ethnic concerns—of Jews, Irish, and Italian Americans in New York—are often a way of discussing class-based realities. Thus, while ethnicity shaped the responses of New York's different white ethnic groups, a discussion cannot neglect a requisite label: working class.[119] And as Jefferson Cowie has suggested, class was a key dimension in the 1968 election and in the primaries. Robert Kennedy, in spite of his history of investigating unions and union corruption, garnered considerable support from working-class Americans, white and Black.[120]

As Wallace's campaign picked up steam, some New York workers began to contribute financially to the governor's presidential run. In late August, a group of sixteen workers from Pennsylvania Central Railroad's Hudson Division contributed twenty-six dollars to his campaign; most of the men's surnames were Irish, Italian, and German. A transit worker, Paul Petaja, and his wife contributed four dollars to the campaign, while Edward Hudak, an elevator mechanic and member of Teamsters Local 237, contributed an undisclosed amount. Frederick V. Naporlee, a retired shipyard worker who had previously helped organize a union of bookbinders in 1961, donated a fifty-one-dollar check that he had received for jury duty. This was on top of the $216 he had donated prior to that! While the contributions from these working-class New Yorkers did not often contain letters explaining their reasons for supporting Wallace, several other letters of support focused on crime and to a lesser extent welfare.[121]

In September 1968, a story in the *New York Times* indicated high levels of support, with a New Jersey United Auto Workers straw poll resulting in troubling figures for labor leaders: 62 percent of 500 autoworkers polled in Trenton and 73 percent of autoworkers polled in Middlesex County supported George Wallace as their choice for president. Union leaders deplored the polls' results, arguing that their membership was misled and had no appreciation for the gains won in the past. They further feared that their members were no longer thinking in terms of economics.[122] Ironically, the United Auto Workers rank and file was among the most militant in the country, the most willing to walk off the job over grievances concerning speedups, managerial disrespect, or complacent union bosses. In fact, these workers practically represented a vanguard of discontent. That union officials would bring them up as people not thinking about economics demonstrates quite clearly the growing gulf between workers and their representatives, which was to some degree responsible for white workers turning to Wallace.[123]

In New York City's police department, both rank-and-file anger and support for Wallace grew in 1968. Ongoing conflicts with the Brooklyn branch of the Black Panther Party had ironically begun to politicize officers. In August, after a melee involving police and Panthers, in which the radicals were set free without bail, patrol officers founded the Law Enforcement Group of New York (LEG).[124] LEG was a rank-and-file group that argued for a police crackdown on radical groups and crime, the abolition of the police-led Civilian Complaint Review Board, and the prevention of another Warren court.[125]

LEG's rhetoric drew upon long-established right-wing narratives concerning police and the court system, as well as the period's growing law-and-order discourse.[126] Emerging at the national level in the first half of the 1960s as a result of the efforts of both Wallace and Barry Goldwater, law-and-order politics connected the civil rights movement and urban riots to an increase in street crime and lawlessness. Wallace deployed this rhetoric to attack the civil rights movement, which threatened to overturn the racial order in his state, but Goldwater broadened the rhetoric's purview in his 1964 presidential bid to include a more comprehensive critique of liberalism. This rhetoric gained strength from the rise in violent crime in cities across America, and especially in New York.[127] While there are indications that a portion of the city's increased crime rate was due to Lindsay forcing better bookkeeping on the police department, murders grew by the hundreds and robberies grew by the thousands into the 1970s.[128]

In the 1966 battle over the Civilian Complaint Review Board, conservatives and police drew upon law-and-order rhetoric for television commercials and print ads, highlighting the destruction caused by the Harlem riot of 1964 as well as the dangers of armed youths.[129] LEG combined law and order with rank-and-file rebellion, contesting the parameters of police labor, calling for better equipment, improved communications, and superior treatment for injured officers.[130] They spoke with a radical tinge, however, and in the words of LEG spokesman and organizer Lt. Leon Laino, Judge Furey—who had freed the Panthers without bail—was not the problem; rather, "it's the whole system."[131]

In New York, rank-and-file police officers angry with their union leaders and the city government saw Wallace as a vehicle for their aspirations. When LEG and other police officers mobilized for a September 4 court hearing, 150 off-duty cops attacked Black Panthers and their Students for a Democratic Society supporters. Most of the officers were armed, either with pistols on their hips or blackjacks in their hands, as they kicked, punched, and beat their victims. Many officers wore pro-Wallace pins, and some shouted "Win with Wallace" and "White power" before the fighting broke out. Two members of the executive board of LEG were also present at the beating, though they claimed not to have participated. Mayor Lindsay denounced the beatings and called for an investigation. A LEG spokesman tried to distance the organization from the violence, but the attack on the Panthers and Students for a Democratic Society was part of an increasing rightward trend within the New York Police Department, which LEG exemplified.[132] In New York, the Wallace campaign's threats of retribution against protesters and radicals spoke directly to officers' on-the-job experiences, tapping into what the *New York Times* called "the cop vote."[133]

While not all of Wallace's New York supporters were rebel rank-and-filers, he had an undeniable cachet with militant workers in the city. One *New York Times* reporter informally polled attendees at Wallace's Madison Square Garden appearance, finding among them a number of workers who had wrangled with their union heads and the city, including police officers, firefighters, sanitationmen, social workers, and other civil servants. The fall was a time of intense negotiations between the city and the police, firemen, and sanitationmen. Notably, the city's firefighters had battled with the mayor for the last two years, and by the height of Wallace's presidential run, the rank and file rejected a city contract and voted to strike, with one fireman arguing, "I think the threat of a strike is the only thing [Lindsay] understands."[134] To avoid penalties of the newly enacted Taylor Law, the firemen's union called for a partial strike on October 23, with the men continuing only the most basic services while refusing drills, training, hydrant inspections, and court appearances.[135]

While police officers' concern with law and order requires little explanation, law and order had become a concern on the job for many workers in New York City. Uniformed city workers reported increasingly frequent attacks.[136] For example, in July 1968 there were 114 attacks on firefighters, including physical assaults and thrown rocks, bottles, and occasionally Molotov cocktails. Black and Latino areas of the Bronx and Brooklyn were the most dangerous neighborhoods, and in journalist Joe Flood's estimation, growing racial polarization drove these attacks, as "firemen were virtually the only white authority figures left in neighborhoods with little love for white authority figures."[137] But firefighters were not the only ones threatened, as sanitationmen, taxi drivers, and transit and telephone workers recounted similar tales.[138] As one CWA rank-and-filer remembered it, in 1968 many older union men had Wallace stickers on their lunch boxes, though he believed it was primarily confined to suburbanites who were culturally conservative, sometimes racist, but still staunch unionists.[139]

The Ocean Hill–Brownsville strikes in the fall of 1968, which pitted the heavily Jewish UFT against the Black community in New York, raised similar law-and-order concerns. In the face of Black demands for community control of schools, which circumvented union gains, UFT signs proclaimed themselves for teacher safety and "against mob rule."[140] In fact, a local political columnist commented that UFT president Albert Shanker was only "an accent away from George Wallace."[141] The strike was a complicated affair with many rank-and-file teachers only reluctantly supporting it. Many teachers were already organizing against Shanker, spurred by on-the-job mistreatment, desires for more curriculum control, and wider labor militancy in the city.[142] Teachers, however, were divided among themselves, with many white teachers associated with Students for a Democratic Society and the Communist Party crossing the picket lines of their own union.[143] At this very same time, there was widespread talk among teachers that they might vote for Wallace, but this support was fleeting. For many Jews, who were the bulk of the UFT, Wallace was too much of a demagogue, fitting a profile that was too similar to the historical experience of fascism. As one teacher put it, "Being Jewish, I was afraid he would get me next. He was too much like Hitler, and we don't need another Nazi Germany."[144]

Interestingly, racial polarization within teaching also emerged from Black rank-and-file efforts. The most significant teachers opposition group during the 1968 strike was the African-American Teachers Association (ATA). Jerald Podair estimates that by 1967 some 2000 Black teachers in New York were dues-paying members of the ATA, with most joining the organization because of the UFT's failure to significantly oppose racist, antibusing protests. The ATA's beliefs were increasingly nationalist, articulating a cooperativist vision built on an idealized notion of Blackness, which was juxtaposed with a deeply immoral, materialist, and individualist whiteness. According to the ATA, this conglomeration of negative traits was especially manifest among white educators, who were damaging the life opportunities of Black students and inculcating them with a toxic ideology.[145] The ATA's nationalism disregarded the lived reality of class for white New Yorkers, ignoring the white working class's erection of a social democratic polity as well as teachers' constant battles with the educational system and union.[146] But in the face of accusations of racism and complicity in Black oppression, many white teachers sprang to the defense of the values of competition and meritocracy, blaming Black failure on a culture of poverty, an equally stereotypical and damaging reification of Black attributes. Some left-leaning teachers who had participated in the civil rights movement found themselves at odds with this growing strain of Black Nationalism and the way in which it advocated measures that undermined the viability of the UFT.[147] The ATA's vociferous denunciations of white teachers, as well as their unnuanced nationalism, inadvertently helped build a fertile environment for Wallace support among teachers and in the city as a whole.[148]

New York's Wallace surge mimicked the growing fervor outside of the state. Wallace's support grew in September and October 1968 as the candidate crisscrossed the nation giving rousing speeches in the bastions of union power. In Flint, Michigan, 10,000 people came out for Wallace, while Akron, Ohio, and Pittsburgh, Pennsylvania, boasted equally large crowds. By early October Wallace was garnering 21 percent support in national polls.[149] Polls of union members indicated an even greater support for Wallace, with some showing 25 percent support, as compared to 34 percent for Hubert Humphrey and 32 percent for Richard Nixon. These polls also indicated a strong preoccupation on the part of respondents with the Vietnam War, civil rights, and crime but, interestingly, a majority agreement with nondiscrimination in hiring. With one month until the election and with far fewer resources, George Wallace was making a substantial showing in national polls, and some editorials opined that perhaps the Alabamian's dream of achieving a plurality of the popular vote was not so farfetched after all.[150]

New York's labor establishment acknowledged Wallace's broader appeal in the month before the election. On October 10, the Central Labor Council (CLC) held a special meeting to discuss Wallace's third-party presidential campaign and his support within the ranks of labor. Van Arsdale believed that Wallace support was overstated, bordering upon a total figment of the media's imagination. While it was true that no union officials in New York City publicly supported Wallace, Van Arsdale was ignoring the rank-and-file appeal, ironically understating the Wallace influence at an emergency meeting designed to address its very prevalence.[151] In the upper echelons of the

AFL-CIO, there was a strong concern about Wallace's influence, as shown by a private memo to George Meany from the head of the AFL-CIO's Committee on Public Education, but this fear was rarely expressed publicly.[152] Clearly there was more support than Van Arsdale was letting on, but at a news conference later that day, he claimed that "a fraud [was] being perpetrated" because of media misrepresentation of the labor movement and the AFL-CIO's 1.2 million members in New York City.[153] Fundamentally, Van Arsdale's concern with the Wallace voters was not that they would lead to a Wallace victory, but rather, as indicated by many polls, that labor's votes would be split in the incredibly tight election. *New York Times* labor commentator A. H. Raskin went so far as to comment, "As the leaders of organized labor see it, the man to beat in November is George C. Wallace."[154]

While Van Arsdale claimed Wallace support was overstated, New York's CLC undertook a monumental effort to support the Democrats in 1968. On Labor Day 1968, Democratic candidate Hubert Humphrey kicked off his fall drive not in Detroit, which was customary, but in New York City. With the help of local and national resources, the AFL-CIO led a massive parade of over 100,000 participants, with AFL-CIO president George Meany and Democratic presidential nominee Humphrey leading the festivities.[155] The solid show of labor's support was needed more than ever if the Democrats were to win, but parades were not enough. New York's CLC was waging a virtual war for Humphrey's election through the final months of the campaign, mobilizing thousands of members and distributing millions of pieces of literature.

In September the CLC set itself to the task of voter registration, focusing on union members and their families as well as unregistered but likely Democratic voters. Union locals played a large role both in the registration process and the campaign by ensuring that individual members and their families were registered voters, purchasing mobile sound equipment, and organizing stewards, shop chairmen, and the rank and file for the effort.[156] In October, the New York CLC effort shifted into overdrive for the Humphrey blitz. In the final month of the campaign, the labor organization distributed 3.1 million pieces of literature and paraphernalia including posters, buttons, and stickers at homes, subway stations, housing projects, rallies, and union meetings across the five boroughs. Meanwhile thirty sound trucks targeted industrial areas, housing projects, low-income neighborhoods, and shopping districts with the Humphrey message. Over 1,000 union volunteers participated in a phone drive to contact every registered Democrat in the city.[157] The CLC asked individual unions to publicize the campaign in their publications, put up signs in storefronts, and distribute literature to the rank and file.158 Finally, the CLC organized twenty-eight torchlight parades across the city with hundreds of marchers in hopes of highlighting the importance of the election. Ultimately, over 18,000 people contributed to the AFL-CIO's campaign in New York. In the final days before the registration deadline for participation in the November 5 election, the AFL-CIO had registered an incredible 237,773 new voters in New York City, with more than half coming from Brooklyn and Queens.159 This massive number of new registrants in the heavily Democratic city, alongside the parading, phone calls, and literature, helped strengthen the pro-Humphrey forces in the tight race.160

The Committee on Public Education produced important campaign propaganda for Humphrey, some of which helps explain how the national leadership was attempting to deal with the combined Wallace-Nixon threat. One CLC foldout was titled "Warning: Wallace No Friend of Working People or Their Unions" and signed, "An Open Letter from Alabama Unionists." It detailed the mistakes organized labor made in its support for Wallace as Alabama's governor, outlining a series of damning facts, including Alabama's weak per capita income and low educational expenditures and Wallace's connections to antilabor forces. One highlighted portion of the text took on Wallace's law-and-order claims, demonstrating that in 1965 Alabama had the highest per capita murder rate in the country and ranked unusually high for aggravated assaults, too.161 For the most part, Committee on Public Education campaign literature focused on the two main candidates in the race, Hubert Humphrey and Richard Nixon, comparing their congressional records and their parties' political platforms in detail.162 Other propaganda implored working people not to "blow the elections of '68" for fear of not "surviv[ing] the assault of '69."163 As many people across the country seemed fed up with the status quo and were considering a variety of protest votes, the CLC's rhetoric was clear: in spite of the disillusionment many feel, Humphrey was the only vote that would not result in disaster for working people.164

In spite of surging support in the fall, Wallace ultimately won only five states in the Deep South and did quite poorly in New York, winning only 5.3 percent of the vote. The only silver lining to his meager results was his support in white working-class neighborhoods. On the border between Brooklyn and Queens, in neighborhoods such as Greenpoint, Maspeth, Bushwick, and Long Island City, Wallace received between roughly 8 and 10 percent of the vote. Farther south in heavily Italian American Red Hook and downtown Brooklyn, 9 percent of voters came out for Wallace. Not coincidentally, these were some of the very same areas and populations that the AFL-CIO targeted with their pro-Humphrey and anti-Wallace election materials in the run-up to the election. Farther east in another border area of Brooklyn and Queens, which included East New York, Cypress Hills, Ozone Park, and Howard Beach, Wallace received 8 and 9 percent of the vote. In similar areas in the Bronx like Parkchester and Throggs Neck, support was the same. In Astoria and Jackson Heights, Queens, Wallace votes appear to have contributed to a Republican victory with Nixon winning out by a matter of 1 or 2 percentage points. In the Republican areas like Bay Ridge, Wallace's support averaged nearly 7 percent, but on Staten Island, Wallace support reached anywhere from 8.5 to 9.5 percent.[165]

In other parts of the deindustrializing North, Wallace won higher margins: 12 percent in Ohio, 10 percent in Michigan, 8.5 percent in Illinois, 8 percent in Pennsylvania, and 9 percent in New Jersey.[166] Conservative working-class New Yorkers had a more viable option in Nixon, and the ad hoc Wallace campaign had to fight with already established party organizations pushing for the Californian.[167] Republicans held a few strongholds in the city, and the leadership of New York's Conservative Party had fought off a small-scale, pro-Wallace rebellion within its own ranks earlier that year.[168] New York's demographics also disfavored Wallace, with a significant Jewish segment, who in spite of occasionally breaking ranks on particular issues, voted overwhelmingly Democrat in presidential elections. Finally, the AFL-CIO's vast effort, which historians have acknowledged as having played a large role nationally, was also a large factor in keeping down Wallace support in New York City.[169]

A Militant Fracture

By 1968, rank-and-file rebels were challenging union leaders, employers, and politicians across the city, and for many workers, demands ran deeper than bread-and-butter concerns. Long-term anger at their low social rank and growing political polarization drove sanitationmen toward a strike in 1968, leading to a contentious strike that once again saw workers facing off with Mayor Lindsay. Others struck for greater safety on the job. Certainly, some workers were turning or already were conservative on law-and-order issues, but for many more, like firemen, sanitation workers, parking enforcement officers, teachers, and postal workers, crime was a daily, material concern.[170] Other workers flocked to George Wallace as the polity rapidly polarized, helmed by John Lindsay, who rejected or criticized the demands of union members in both the public and private sectors, often repeating and reissuing those demands as racism and white ethnic cretinism on the one hand or as privileged power brokering on the other.

The tumultuous 1968 concluded with a series of rank-and-file-led actions. In mid-November, incinerator stokers wildcatted for eight days, resisting a court injunction and leaving massive lines of trash trucks with no place to dump.[171] At the end of the November, Con Edison employees rejected a union-endorsed contract, initiating a two-week strike—the first in the company's history—that threatened to plunge the city into darkness.[172] The year ended with 3,500 Teamster fuel oil drivers rejecting a leadership-endorsed contract, which deprived hundreds of thousands of people of heat during a virulent flu epidemic.[173] Like the Hong Kong flu of 1968, workers' militancy was circulating around the city, infecting many workplaces but in some cases rapidly fading away.[174]

THREE

Strike Fever

On January 9, 1969, the executive board of the AFL-CIO's New York City Central Labor Council held a special meeting at the Hotel Commodore. The gathering brought together some of the city's and nation's most powerful labor leaders, including Central Labor Council president Harry Van Arsdale Jr., James Beamish of Local 1-2 Utility Workers, Raymond Corbett of the Iron Workers, and Leon Davis of the Drug and Hospital Workers Local 1199, as well as rising stars United Federation of Teachers president Albert Shanker and District Council 37 president Victor Gotbaum. Special guests Joseph Trerotola, Teamster Joint Council 16 president, and New York governor Nelson Rockefeller, a personal friend and political ally of Van Arsdale and the AFL-CIO in New York State, flanked the AFL-CIO leaders.

On that cold January day, the labor leaders discussed what Van Arsdale called "strike fever." Strikes, to highlight only a few, had shut down sanitation service, the city's schools, and construction sites and threatened the provision of electricity and heating. Most AFL-CIO leaders in New York City blamed the strikes on their membership's unrealistic expectations. Trerotola of the Teamsters was "disturbed" by rebellion in his own ranks, which he believed lacked "specifics." Governor Rockefeller blamed inflation and growing insecurity, but he also conceded that "young people want action" and were to blame for the city's strikes just as they were to blame for campus occupations, the growing number of antiwar protests, and urban riots. While the conference did result in any particular plans for dealing with the growing number of strikes, it sent a signal across the leadership strata of New York's labor movement that rank-and-file rebellion had moved front and center.[1]

Van Arsdale's epidemiological comparison was quite apt. Strikes were spreading rapidly from workplace to workplace, crossing the lines of profession, skill, and race. While in many histories the boundaries of white, Black, conservative, and liberal are often hewn in stone—impassable for lack of want and effort—workers in New York often came together fleetingly or exerted a large influence on one another by example. But like a fever, the strike outbreaks were often short-lived. Rank-and-file revolt emerged from long-term grievances but exhibited a high degree of spontaneity, which often lacked longer-term organizing and strategy.[2]

This chapter discusses several important strikes and rank-and-file efforts between 1969 and 1972. The first section looks at contract rejections and strikes within the International Brotherhood of Teamsters (IBT) Local 553. Though Teamster unions are underrepresented in the historical literature, in New York City they experienced rank-and-file rebellion, and their strikes help us understand the inchoate nature of the movement as well as the consequences of its failures. The second section traces the evolving efforts of Joseph Carnegie and the Transport Workers Union's (TWU) Rank and File Committee, which hoped to build its base in the union's growing number of Black members to topple the TWU. The middle portion of the chapter explores an important and as yet unexamined national rank-and-file organizing conference in New York City, which brought together New York leaders and activists such as Carnegie and James Haughton of Harlem Fight Back with Detroit's League of Revolutionary Black Workers, members of opposition caucuses in the United Auto Workers, and representatives from a dozen other rank-and-file struggles. The fourth part examines New York's postal workers, who, emboldened by local strikes in the public sector, pushed their leaders into an illegal strike that grew to national proportions. The final portion of the chapter looks at the complicated events and legacy of the 1970 Hard Hat Riot, which provide an important window into the intertwining of class resentments with the growing political polarization in New York City.

A Rebellion in the Teamsters

In 1968, a multiday fuel oil strike amid freezing temperatures threw the city into disarray.[3] After years of trying, rank-and-file drivers of the IBT Fuel Oil Delivery Drivers Local 553 overcame their leadership, voting down an inadequate contract and winning moderate wage and benefit gains.[4] In December 1970, fuel oil drivers did it again, as members burned copies of the contract and physically attacked union leaders.[5] The Teamsters remain an outlier in historical literature because of widespread corruption and unapologetic embrace of business unionism. But the union was home to powerful rank-and-file activism in the 1960s and 1970s, including a national wildcat by truck drivers in 1970 and successful reform organizations. The contract rejections of fuel oil drivers help us understand worker activism within the Teamsters as well as the way that persistent rank-and-file efforts intertwined with but ultimately were unable to capitalize on growing militancy.[6]

IBT Local 553 began like many Teamsters unions, as drivers of teams of horses, but its members began switching over to trucks in the early twentieth century.[7] The drivers and repairmen who made up the largest portion of IBT Local 553 never numbered more than 3,500 men, but at their peak, they delivered the majority of the city's coal and oil. Prior to the advent of fuel oil, drivers delivered coal for both commercial and home heating use, and union leaders had used strikes to achieve benefits for their members.[8]

Like many other unions, Local 553 members made significant gains in the 1950s, and their wage improvements were higher than those of most other Teamster unions in the city. The importance of fuel oil made the drivers powerful.[9] The union was made up of primarily white ethnics, specifically many Italians, though there were a few Black drivers in the union by the 1950s.[10] While Local 553 negotiations received plentiful coverage in the city's newspapers, presumably because of the threat of fuel and coal strikes, their struggles and internal dynamics do not appear in secondary literature.

Timothy Costello left the only written account of the union's rank and file. Costello, a young Students for a Democratic Society member from Massachusetts, was a fuel driver in New York from 1969 until 1971 while attending the New School for Social Research.[11] He was also involved with a group called Root & Branch, which was inspired by council communist ideas and drew on the works of Paul Mattick. Costello's hopes lay in rank-and-file self-organization against *both* employers and unions, which he argued acted as a force of mediation upon the working class.[12]

In a pseudonymously published piece for the *Root & Branch* journal entitled "Keep on Truckin'," written in the second half of 1970, Costello described the attitudes and work experience of Local 553 fuel oil drivers, giving us an excellent picture of their daily work routines and the manner in which they organized. Unlike factory work, where many people worked in the same space for most of the day and cooperated directly, fuel oil drivers went out on daylong delivery runs, servicing multiple homes and businesses, and for the most part spent the day alone. Costello argues that this isolation produced a strong individual relationship with bosses and led to one-on-one conflicts. Many fuel drivers resisted work individually, commonly taking longer breaks, sabotaging the company-supplied rigs, or parking their trucks and sleeping off part of the day.[13] Costello sometimes called the drivers of Local 553 "little Lenins," strategists within the work environment trying to figure out all of the angles to not be ground down by the boss. While a lone fuel driver might feel powerless in the face of the forces that surrounded him, they still resisted, sometimes individually and sometimes collectively, albeit in ways that the structure of the work allowed.[14]

Despite limitations, drivers managed to find ways to develop solidarity and organize themselves. During the course of a workday, drivers could make multiple small deliveries using the same load of gas or they could make large runs requiring a return to the depot for a refill. While trucks were refilled, workers socialized. More important, drivers would routinely arrive fifteen to twenty minutes early to work. While awaiting their assignments for the day, they would discuss "new outrages of the company, or . . . how they beat the company in some way, or . . . what should be done to change things and how."[15]

While informal relations helped build some of the insurgent energy, Local 553 had small opposition groups. Many had experience in contract fights dating back to the 1940s, and they believed that the union leadership worked in collusion with fuel owners, and as one former driver described it, the union leadership "ran [the union] with the company, and they ran it against the men."[16] Other studies have shown that insurgent groups were active in Teamsters unions large and small during the 1960s and 1970s because of corruption, antidemocratic elections, and racketeering, and some believed that kickbacks and corruption were present in Local 553, though these allegations of corruption did not surface in any public way.[17] Just as fuel depots were scattered across the city's five boroughs, so, too, was the union's opposition divided. The opposition groups were generally groups of five or six men at a single fuel depot, and while these groups tried to work together occasionally, men's personal ambitions sometimes got in the way.[18]

When Costello worked as fuel oil driver, the opposition groups were more united, and he referred to them as a coalition. The opposition coalition was very active in strike votes, and outside of the realm of negotiations they maintained a publication and ran candidates, unsuccessfully, for various posts in the union. Their monthly newsletter was critical of union officials and their unwillingness to properly advocate for their membership. The coalition had gained strength in the late 1960s, and Costello attributed the 1968 contract rejection to their rising prominence, though he does note that their election bids, while sometimes close, always failed.[19]

Politically, the insurgents were staunch unionists advocating for reform and a change of leadership. In Costello's words, "The coalition never transcends trade-unionism, nor does it ever advocate direct action," which he believed would lead to inevitable reincorporation into the union machinery.[20] Estimating the size of the insurgent group is difficult to do, but a walkout from the final contract vote in 1970 points to the existence of some 200 men who were willing to picket a rank-and-file-approved contract as well as the union itself, much like in the 1950s.[21] While the core of the group was perhaps not this large, it serves as an indication of those who were prepared to picket union leaders and points toward a degree of organization and discontent on par with many other insurgent organizations in the city.[22] While the drivers did not often take part in collective action, Costello contended that their attitude was becoming more militant.[23] Union leaders and politicians blamed young workers for much of the labor disorder of the period, but it was the older workers of Local 553 who had waged a protracted struggle for control of the union and better gains in contracts.[24]

The 1970 strike, like the 1968 strike, began at a boisterous meeting, but this vote was an intensely antileadership event that included many drivers verbally assaulting the local president, James McGuire, whom they accused of selling them out.[25] Prior to the contract negotiations, the leadership of Local 553 was in dialogue with the mayor's office, which relayed to Governor Rockefeller's labor adviser Vic Borella that the possibility of a strike in the fuel oil industry was highly unlikely in 1970. Labor advisers to Mayor Lindsay believed that the recent reelection of McGuire and his slate would result in less stormy negotiations, because these officers did not need to prove themselves. City labor advisers grossly miscalculated, and the strike occurred for the exact reasons that they believed it would not: union leadership did not feel the need to deliver a significant contract.26 At the union meeting, drivers burned contracts and hundreds of men shouted and gave the contract a thumbs-down under the impression that the money wasn't enough and that their overtime agreements had been left out of the contract. Beyond that, Local 553 leadership failed to even comment on the agreement other than to say that they had endorsed it.27

Throughout the meeting, McGuire—who had taken the reins of the union in the late 1950s—was the focal point for the anger. Some members, seemingly the insurgent group, claimed that he had been illegitimately re-elected as president. Other men pushed him or shouted him down, while another tried to attack him. As one driver interviewed by the *New York Times* stated, the contract was "ridiculous," saying they "got no cooperation from the leadership" and "deserve $225 dollars now."28 In the face of shouts of "sellout" and "no heat," McGuire backpedaled before the crowd, arguing that the leadership had never agreed with the final offer at all. Once the votes were tallied, drivers voted down the contract 981 against and 433 in favor. The drivers celebrated, throwing unburned contracts in the air.29

The mood of the strike was jubilant and conflictual, as the fuel drivers carried forward the scenes of excitement and violence from the strike vote.30 While some men in the Bronx somberly carried officially printed strike signs, others seen in a photograph of one picket in Queens on the first day of the strike were quite different: a group of six men stood nonchalantly in front of the gate, some laughing and smoking cigarettes, while one read the newspaper and two others carried golf clubs for practicing their swing or defending their picket lines.31 After all, the same day in Brooklyn, strikers attacked a nonunion firm's trucks for scabbing, stopping one in transit and setting it on fire. Strikes attacked another truck entering the depot, smashing its window with a brick; fifty-year-old Anthony Santaro was arrested. On the second day of the strike, *El Diario La Prensa* reported that strikers attacked an office worker delivering fuel for Chevron with "fists and a piece of pipes."32

Three days in, a harried Local 553 leadership announced a new contract proposal, but the union's president warned the news dailies that approval would be difficult. According to McGuire, a "small faction" was using "hoodlum tactics" to get their way, and these same "hoodlums" had taken advantage of the larger restive rank and file.33 This was clearly a topic of intense conversation at the negotiations, which involved the chairman of the state mediation board, Vincent McDonnell.34 After the negotiations, McDonnell publicly decried a "faction that had strike signs up without knowing the conditions of the offer."[35] In order to avoid a potential repeat of the first strike vote in which McGuire was assaulted by the membership, Local 553 leadership mailed out a plea to its members, calling for calm and asking, "Are we rabble-rousers and rioters or are we responsible citizens?" The union was attempting to draw a comparison between their men's violence and that of the New Left and Black rioters. Hoping to further shame the fuel drivers and cause a division in their ranks, the letter opined that "our officers were insulted, abused and attacked by a seemingly well-organized small group of men whose conduct was a disgrace to the American labor movement."[36]

The 1970 strike could not reproduce the social crisis the fuel oil drivers had caused in 1968. City administrators and many private landlords had learned from their earlier mistakes and either stockpiled fuel or had their buildings' tanks refilled before the strike.[37] By 1969, the city's Emergency Control Board–Civil Defense, an interdepartmental coordinating agency, was working with the employers group, the New York Oil Heating Association, to develop plans to deter fuel shortages caused by emergency conditions. The board outlined a strict set of actions to be followed in case of a fuel emergency, which employed a systematic verification and delivery process that included the Department of Health, Department of Rent and Housing Maintenance, the Local 553 bureaucracy, New York Oil Heating Association representatives, and, if necessary, police. These emergency fuel deliveries would be brought to both public institutions and private homes and paid for by the city. While one could make a humanitarian argument for delivering the fuel, the simple fact of the matter is that the emergency deliveries amounted to a breaking of the strike on the part of the union itself. Once the Department of Health verified a public or private emergency, the Department of Purchase would then procure the fuel and the joint committee of labor and management would determine which particular fuel depot to use and who would drive the truck. Additionally, the labor-management committee would determine the threat level of violence or other "obstructionist tactics," and if such a threat existed they would then arrange for the police to accompany the delivery.[38]

The emergency system reduced the strikes' impact alongside mild winter weather. During their 1968 strike, the city received tens of thousands of calls per hour concerning fuel shortages and lack of heat, but in 1970, there were fewer than 200. Hospitals maintained heat and the majority of homeowners and private tenants had no problems. Ultimately the only city institution to run out of fuel oil was public housing, resulting in 200,000 people without heat and another 100,000 more on rationed fuel.[39]

On Monday, December 21, roughly 1,300 members of Local 553 gathered at the High School of Fashion Industries in midtown Manhattan to vote on the new contract. In spite of the pleas for calm, there was still a large and vocal opposition. Drivers shouted their disapproval, hoping to dissuade others from voting in favor of a contract whose only modification was reducing from fifteen to twelve months the amount of time necessary to grant new raises.[40] One man draped himself in a sign that read, "The owners got their $$$$, let's get ours." In spite of the opposition's best efforts, drivers overwhelmingly approved the contract, 901–415.[41]

A group of some 200 drivers challenged the vote, calling for a recount and picketing the decision outside. Carrying signs like "Scrooge McGuire Killed Our Christmas," "Cost of Living Clause Now," "Vote No!" and "McGuire Uses Gas Heat," the oppositionists manifested their continuing disapproval of the contract *and* leadership, while one man simply wore his old sign, proclaiming that he was still "on strike."[42] While some drivers protested outside, the strike had already broken down the night before, and the 1970 strike ended with a small but vocal opposition group divided from the rest of fuel drivers who were ready to get back to work.[43] To date, the union has not gone on strike again.[44]

As one former driver remembered it, fuel oil drivers found themselves opposed on all sides by powerful institutions, including their own union, and the 1970 strike yielded no material gains. While he remembered the job with fondness, arguing that he liked its challenges and that his real major concerns at the time were the Yankees and the fight for the working class to better itself, the lesson he learned in battling the union was that nothing could be done. The asymmetry of power, held in the hands of unions, politicians, business owners, and the like, was far too great to be overcome. His strategy was to turn inward, to step away from fighting and close his eyes to what he could not change. Only in the context of a broader strike wave sweeping the city could Local 553's small and divided opposition groups spur their fellow drivers to strike against their own union, but like a fever, rank-and-file power seemed to rise quickly but dissipate rapidly, especially when easy victories did not emerge.[45]

Transit Battles and the Shift to Dual Unionism

While smaller unions like Local 553 underwent their own rank-and-file rebellion, larger unions like the TWU were home to more persistent and public insurgent efforts. The Rank and File Committee for a Democratic Union, which helped focus some of the anti-Quill energy in the 1966 strike, pushed for greater, lasting power outside of the more ephemeral strikes that characterized the labor upheaval in New York during this time. Transit rank-and-file activity was embedded in the broader insurgent energy of the 1960s, and the committee focused on issues important to Black and Latino workers. Unlike in many of the city's unions, the racial makeup of the TWU was changing rapidly, and basing one's group on the concerns of Black workers situated the organization in an emerging majority.

In the years immediately following the 1966 strike, the committee took part in the same relatively small activities as before: picketing the union over changes in the workplace—the implementation of radios in buses for example—pushing back against the "kangaroo court," and organizing to overturn the use of mail-in ballots, which the committee felt was a way the TWU bureaucracy maintained its power. The 1967 "mass picket" against mail-in ballots only gathered a dismal eight rank-and-filers for the protest.[46]

The committee's power would grow significantly after 1967, when the union negotiated an agreement allowing transit workers to retire at age fifty with 50 percent of their pay after twenty years. For many older workers, this was music to their ears, and a slew of retirements quickly followed.[47] This resulted in a swift demographic shift in the union, as many older, white workers accepted retirement and the Transit Authority (TA) hired many Blacks and Puerto Ricans to replace them. In fact within two years, nearly 40 percent of the union was Black, according to TWU statistics. Joseph Carnegie believed that the union was closer to 70 percent Black by 1970 and that the union deflated the number in order to hide the demographic shift.[48] In spite of the fact that Blacks were approaching majority representation in the union, long-standing issues plagued them: lower-level assignments, less defense before the TA disciplinary board, and underrepresentation in the highest ranks of leadership.[49]

Just as it had in the past, the committee mobilized to denounce discrimination in the union. In July 1968, a white TA cop beat a Black conductor, John Wharton, when he defended a group of Black men and women who had stood up against the harassment of a drunk white passenger. The officer wanted them ejected from the train and Wharton disagreed. When an argument ensued, the TA officer detained the conductor and severely beat him, leaving him hospitalized for days. When Wharton awoke, he found himself charged with the crime of harassment and maligned as a victim of his own inability to control himself.[50]

The committee jumped to Wharton's aid, producing leaflets in his favor and organizing people to attend court dates. In spite of the resistance put up to Wharton's mistreatment, he was convicted of harassment and eventually fired from his position in the subway system. Out of the Wharton case and out of the racial transformation of the union, the committee felt itself poised to take its fight to a much bigger level, bringing to the forefront the fight against discrimination and systematic inequality within the TWU's ranks.[51]

The committee hoped that forefronting the fight against racism would recruit more Black TWU workers dissatisfied with their union leaders. The increased focus on racism and specifically organizing Black workers can be seen in a shift in rhetoric and focus in the committee's irregularly published *Rank and File News*. In its November-December 1968 issue, the main articles were dedicated not to the travails of transit work but to the politics of the teachers strike, which the committee argued was a powerful example of racism in the ranks of organized labor.[52] Carnegie's public rhetoric had become less conciliatory on race as the TWU's makeup shifted. As he put it in a 1969 interview: "For the first time . . . nearly 20,000 black transit workers have the opportunity to be involved in a struggle in which their numerical strength can decide whether transit workers will be represented by a union in which they have no real voice (no other workers do, for that matter) or whether we will be represented by an independent union that is not tied to management and the rotten, racist power structure of this city." Carnegie believed that with racial turnover in the TWU, Blacks would be able to decide the direction of labor struggles in the subway, which Carnegie hoped would translate to the decline of the TWU and the rise of the Rank and File Committee in its place.[53]

While the committee increased its focus on racism in the transit system, it also changed its organizational focus in two key ways. In October 1968, the committee began organizing public meetings to draw on the increasing number of Black transit workers, experiencing some growth.[54] And as before, meetings were primarily held in the offices of the Harlem Unemployment Center (HUC), which was in the process of changing its name to the more militant Fight Back Center.[55]

Though records of their meetings are not archived, a white worker sympathetic to the union recorded the events of one in December 1969. According to his report, more than seventy people attended the meeting, including five white workers and six women, but the rest of the attendees were primarily Black members of the TWU. At this particular meeting, Carnegie spoke on the goals of the committee, and David Lubash, the group's lawyer, spoke about upcoming motions to have the TWU decertified through the New York State Public Employees Relations Board (PERB).[56]

After failing in the election of 1965, the committee believed strongly that the mail-in ballot would always prevent them from winning an election. The committee hoped a PERB election would be fairer. Like the 1950s Motormen's Benevolent Association, which hoped to build on the motormen's grievances as well as their critical place in the subway system to split the union, the Rank and File Committee hoped to build an alternative organization but one based on Black union members' grievances and growing demographic power.[57]

In order to decertify the TWU, the Rank and File Committee needed to demonstrate to the PERB that 30 percent of the nearly 30,000 employees across the industry's different divisions supported the decertification drive. A petition was the key to demonstrating this support, and committee members needed to organize where their fellow workers were most likely to congregate in order to gather that number of signatures. Unions themselves had already broken into the workplace against the wishes of most employers, but an insurgent group's efforts were perhaps more difficult: both employers and the union often opposed them. After all, the committee's decertification challenge called for the end of the TWU, and small insurgent groups had disrupted the subway system more often than the union.[58]

During the petition drive throughout 1969, the TA and the TWU harassed rank-and-filers, sometimes calling the police. When committee members tried petitioning outside of the Surface Line Operators Fraternal Organization, its directors sent a memo banning committee members from the premises and promising to expel members involved in such activities.[59] After much harassment, the committee challenged the TWU and the TA at the New York Supreme Court in Queens for the right to distribute printed material. Committee members argued they were poorly represented by the TWU and needed to have their voices heard, alleging endemic racism within the ranks of the union's leadership. Secretary-treasurer Ellis F. Van Riper countered with Martin Luther King Jr.'s positive remarks about the union, casting Carnegie as a racist who wanted to "peddle his divisive, poisonous and utterly untruthful racist propaganda."[60] In October, the court upheld the committee's right to petition, but when the committee submitted signatures, the PERB rejected the petition.[61]

In spite of these setbacks, the committee's activity remained steady, and in an interview with *New York* magazine in 1970, Carnegie argued that workers faced the same problems as ever. Safety issues and tight schedules particularly concerned TWU members and were harmful to both workers and commuters. In fact, a May 1970 crash on the subway's IRT line (now the 7 line), which killed two people and injured seventy-one, prompted *New York*'s article in the first place. Carnegie went on to argue that the TWU leadership was just as conservative in negotiations as ever. Though the twenty-year retirement package gladdened some workers, many wanted better gains than leaders were willing to ask for, let alone deliver. In Carnegie's words, the 1969 negotiations yielded little: "They asked for a 30 per cent increase, and actually got an 11 per cent increase over two years. The workers wanted 20-year retirement pay at any age; they didn't even ask for it. The shorter work week? We never got that. Management still has the prerogative of drawing up schedules; that question has never been settled." By 1970—with the help of much-improved retirement packages—the union had become perhaps as high as 70 percent Black and Puerto Rican. The committee promised that the confluence of these changes with such lingering problems would eventually lead to an outburst of anger the TWU could not control.[62]

With their right to collect signatures and distribute literature affirmed by the lawsuit during their 1969 decertification drive, committee members went to work in April 1971 to gather signatures, and after months of work the committee submitted 9,110 signatures to the PERB in late September, demonstrating support from 30 percent of the union.[63] In the first days of November, however, the PERB rejected the committee's petition on the grounds that the signatures were not accompanied by dates, which made it impossible to determine whether the application was timely.[64]

While timeliness was a long-standing evaluative criterion, at the time of the committee's filing, dated signatures were not required, and it was only in October 1971, weeks *after* the committee's submission, that the PERB amended its own rules to require such dates. To Carnegie and the rest of the committee, the PERB's attempt to retroactively apply the dating rule was evidence that the board stood on the side of both the TWU and the TA. The militants believed that a fair election ought to determine who represented the city's transit workers, but the board wanted to refuse them their chance.[65]

When the committee challenged the PERB's dismissal, a New York Supreme Court judge agreed with the rank-and-filers. Because of a subpar contract, a transit wildcat of more than 1,000 bus drivers broke out only a few days before the court ruling, and the time seemed ripe for an electoral challenge. Carnegie believed that there was insufficient leadership for the wildcat to continue, and he hoped his election challenge could provide a constructive outlet for the anger.[66]

Unhappy with the state supreme court ruling, PERB officials appealed the decision. Before an appellate court in July 1972, the PERB failed for a second time to strike down the rank-and-file effort, with the court affirming the early ruling and sending the hearing back to the PERB.[67] While Carnegie and the committee remained positive about these court outcomes, a second PERB hearing did not mean the board would approve of the petition, and on August 31, 1972, when the PERB again convened to decide on the Rank and File Committee's application, it rejected the petition because it both was untimely and did not show sufficient interest.[68] Though estimates of the union's size varied wildly, with the union presenting itself as having 38,000 members, the most commonly agreed upon number was closer to 30,000, which would have allowed the committee's petition to overcome the 30 percent sufficient interest bar.

After this second denial, PERB rules barred Carnegie's group from petitioning for decertification for another four years, a lengthy prohibition that would leave the Rank and File Committee no viable route to power. For some members this was the end of their activism in the workplace. Years of agitation brought them into conflict with both management and the union, and as an autonomous labor organization with no legal right to defend its members, the committee had limited power to protect leadership opponents from retaliation. As one former committee organizer remembered it, "I came to the realization that I had to cover my own ass."[69]

Within the ranks of the TWU, the committee made a concerted effort to try and channel the inchoate discontent of the rank-and-filers into a longer-term political program. Over several years of organizing, Carnegie and the committee came close to obtaining a decertification vote within the TWU, but the PERB's repeated denial of the Rank and File Committee begs the question: Did its decertification challenges stand a chance of being approved?

New York State had created the PERB in order to stabilize labor relations in the aftermath of the 1966 transit strike, and a rank-and-file challenge for control over the very same union threatened to seat an untested and more militant leadership. The PERB existed within a broader institutional matrix that favored power players like the TWU and its president, Matthew Guinan. Big Labor ally Governor Rockefeller, with whom the TWU had an on-again, off-again relationship, had appointed the three-member board, and Rockefeller had been on hand at Central Labor Council discussions about stemming the city's strike fever. While there is no smoking gun, preventing the committee's election drive was certainly in line with the PERB's goals.[70]

Rank-and-File Radicals Gather

While the committee and its supporters battled for control of the TWU, Carnegie was equally involved in broader attempts to capitalize on the renewed militancy of American workers. Alongside his ally James Haughton, he and others pushed for greater communication and coordination among rank-and-file rebels, participating in long-distance discussions and supporting efforts to organize a national conference on rank-and-file struggles in 1969. Thus, while union leaders and politicians were organizing themselves to deal with the unleashing of rank-and-file energy in New York City, militant workers, left-wing political groups, and rank-and-file organizations across the country were planning their own gathering to discuss what should be done with labor's increasingly combative mood.

Initial meetings and discussions were held in the industrial heartland around Detroit to determine the participation and focus of the conference, bringing together a variety of United Auto Workers rank-and-file groups as well as many small, left-wing political organizations installed in the city. Initially scheduled for February 8–9, the conference's first day was to involve discussions of rank-and-file revolts, the situation of Black workers and Black caucuses within unions, and the situation of white workers and the issue of George Wallace, racism, and rebellion. The second half of the conference was to be dedicated to a discussion of building up working-class consciousness, interfacing with the student movement, and taking practical steps, in particular establishing a publication. Connecting workers with students was a key goal of groups like Students for a Democratic Society and the many small left-wing socialist parties of the period and is indicative of the New Left influence on the conference's organization. But due to a series of planning errors, the Detroit conference organizers were unable to host the conference.[71]

Haughton, Carnegie, and Silvio Mello of the longshoremen salvaged the conference, pushing for a smaller and more limited gathering in New York in early April 1969. Building on the initial proposals for the Detroit conference, Haughton and others maintained most of the important debates but refined their focus. Under their watch, the first major discussion addressed racism in the rank-and-file movement, and the final discussion included solutions from workers by workers. Most important, Haughton and allies placed themselves in the role of keynote speakers on both days, with the opening speech given by Mello, a longtime militant of the International Longshoremen's Association. The second day included Haughton's organizational proposals, as well as a closing session about ongoing struggles in different areas of the country. Stepping back from a massive come-one, come-all approach, Haughton and Carnegie pushed for a tighter conference that would act as a foundation for rank-and-file efforts in the years to come.[72]

A variety of highly politicized rank-and-file organizers from some of America's biggest cities attended this hastily organized conference. There were United Auto Workers members from Cleveland and Detroit; transit workers from New York City and Chicago; longshoremen and sailors from Berkeley and Baltimore; and a host of rank-and-filers including long-haul drivers, packinghouse workers, machinists, and teachers from places as diverse as New Haven, Connecticut, and Fremont, California. Organizers from New York and Detroit played a central, and highly vocal, role in the conference. New Yorkers included longtime organizers such as Carnegie, Haughton, Mello, and Steve Zeluck of the American Federation of Teachers. Some of the city's largest and most militant unions such as the United Federation of Teachers and Uniformed Sanitationmen's Association as well as many smaller, primarily white unions were unrepresented at the conference.[73] Many organizers came from Detroit, including Chuck Wooten and John Watson of the League of Revolutionary Black Workers (LRBW), a Marxist-Leninist and Black Nationalist organization that operated at the intersection of autoworker wildcats and militant Black mobilization. Also from Detroit were Arthur and Edith Fox, left organizers active in the United Caucus, an opposition group within United Auto Workers Local 600 in Dearborn, Michigan. Wayne King, founder and editor of the *New Rank and Filer*, also came from the Motor City. The New Yorkers and Detroiters would guide the conference's agenda and set the debates over the course of the two days, opening major discussions on both the problems and prospects of a rank-and-file workers movement.[74]

The conference began at the Hotel Diplomat on the morning of April 12 with a keynote speech from Mello of the International Longshoremen's Association. His opening remarks, "Toward a Rank and File Movement," outlined some of the necessary characteristics and problems for the emerging movement, including the need for militant caucuses within unions, Black and white unity, and independent political candidates. For Mello, an older communist, the heart of the issue was that unions in America no longer believed in class struggle but rather had reached a position of total accommodation of business interests. The International Longshoremen's Association militant had developed his ideas based on the day-to-day struggle of longshoremen against their own union, the federal government, and shippers, a rank-and-file battle that had declined by the mid-1960s in spite of some continued wildcats. While his speech was mostly well received, the majority of the discussion on the first day of the conference took place around the question of racism.[75]

Many rank-and-file organizers identified racism as the main problem in the struggle for workers' power. Some, such as Ed Topp of the painters union in New York as well as Haughton, argued that opening jobs in the construction trades was an essential element of the struggle against racism. John Watson of the LRBW argued a much broader position, that racism was in fact the linchpin of the revolutionary struggle. Citing white betrayal of Blacks at various points in American history, including in the populist movement of the nineteenth century, Watson, Wooten, and other participants like white radical Noel Ignatiev argued that whites not only were racist but also benefited directly from racism, constantly acting in defense of their "privileges." Ignatiev went so far as to suggest that the seniority system had to be torn down because it was structurally racist—keeping older whites in better, higher-paying jobs and confining Blacks to lower-paid positions—and ultimately forwarding the notion that white workers were "white supremacy scabs."[76]

Others, like Edie and Arthur Fox, strongly countered this position, arguing that white workers did not benefit from racism and any assertion that they did was part of a ruling-class fiction and certainly not a conscious and calculated reality in the workplace. Arthur Fox added that missteps by the LRBW had helped contribute to racial divisions in the workplace in Detroit and that unity in the face of racism and continued dialogue was the only way forward for workers. Carnegie, of the TWU Rank and File Committee, intervened in the debate, arguing that union bureaucracy found its base in white membership, a point that mostly agreed with the position of the league without necessarily saying so.[77]

Deep political divisions undergirded the debate on racism in the workplace. While many argued that educational events and classes for white workers would help build an understanding of the historical role of racism and illuminate the degree to which it was an impediment to rank-and-file efforts, some, like the LRBW, thought that independent Black political organizing was paramount. The LRBW's argument was fairly straightforward: due to the legacy of racism, whites and Blacks had to organize in separate organizations, and also due to the legacy of racism and the widespread nature of broader social movements like civil rights and Black Power, Black workers constituted the vanguard of any workers movement in America. This leadership position was so absolute, the league argued, that no one had the right to question it. Many in attendance agreed that the league was the best-organized group of any rank-and-file organization in the country—rapidly expanding in 1968 and 1969 to various auto plants but also to a United Parcel Service center—but they challenged the extension of vanguard status to Blacks as a whole and the necessity of always organizing separately. Gary Beneson, a New Haven hospital worker trying to unionize his workplace, countered the Black vanguard theory with his own experiences in which two white organizers pushed for unionization while the majority-Black staff was seemingly uninterested. Others argued that such tactics would further divide workers and that joint struggle, not separate race-based workplace organizing, was essential. Ultimately, the main discussion of the first day was an Old Left–versus–New Left debate of whether working-class unity would be forged through broad class-based demands or whether antiracism and independent organizing were the beginning point for class struggle. While participants did not arrive at a consensus position on the question of racism in the broader working class, the divisions were not such that the conference devolved into sectarian denunciations. After all, the conference's goals and organization were such that jockeying for position was unnecessary; there were no positions in a new national organization to fill, no media attention to garner, or even, at that point, no practical proposals to vote on.[78]

The second and final day of the conference opened with James Haughton presenting the history of HUC and proposing three plans for extending and strengthening the rank-and-file movement throughout the country. Haughton asked, "How can rank and file workers organize a power base from which to conduct struggle against trade union bureaucrats who have national and international connections . . . [and] become the appendages of the employer class?"[79] In response, he forwarded three key proposals to build rank-and-file power. His first was the extension of the workers' center model, which he had pioneered, to cities across the country. Such centers provided workers with a space outside of work to organize themselves for "struggle against trade union bureaucrats, employers, and government." The fact that the centers were based in particular communities meant that workers would have not only a space outside of union or government interference but also one in which their struggles could interrelate with forms of resistance outside of the workplace. Haughton confirmed the powerful effect that Black militancy outside of the workplace had on rank-and-file Blacks; drawing on this energy and building support within it was key. While he emphasized that workers' centers would bridge the gap between workplace and neighborhood struggles, he argued that they would just as importantly bridge the gap between different kinds of workplaces, providing space for different autonomous workers' groups to organize and interact. While workers' rebellious actions influenced one another in New York City, there were rarely organizational ties between rank-and-file insurgents. Haughton, unlike members of the LRBW, argued that such organizing spaces could be interracial, as was the case in the HUC. Though Haughton proposed a broad form of organizing in the workers' centers, he did not propose a broad program of activity for them because he felt that local conditions were so varied that each city, and by extension each rank-and-file group, had to develop its own tactics and goals. Furthermore, Haughton was strongly committed to the notion that it was only workers themselves who should guide and shape their struggles and that workers' autonomy vis-à-vis the unions, government, and any outside group was necessary.[80]

Haughton's final two proposals spoke directly to the need for national coordination. According to him, one impediment to expanding action was the lack of information concerning workers' activities across the country. To top it off, any information that was available rarely came from the workers themselves; it tended to be *about* workers but not by workers. To fill this gap, he proposed a nationwide publication to gather and disseminate information on rank-and-file activities, demands, and programs to inspire and promote greater self-activity across the United States. Haughton's call for a nationwide publication, like the workers' center proposal, emerged from his experiences with the HUC and its bulletin, *Fight Back!* In this case, however, a key goal of this new periodical was "to overcome a deep sense of isolation that afflicts most rank and file struggles and in overcoming this isolation to consciously instill in rank and file activity a sense of direction toward building a nationwide rank and file movement."[81] The third and final proposal was for the creation of regional rank-and-file workers conferences. Haughton argued that they had limited the size of this particular conference in order to help set in motion a wider process. In the future, Haughton hoped that conferences in other regions of the country would open up in participation to a wider number of workers.

Haughton was aware of the strong ideological divisions in the conference, and as a result he focused on very broad goals for this first-ever gathering of rank-and-file militants. In each of Haughton's proposals he left the definition of the rank-and-file movement wide open, neither ascribing to it any particular political goals nor forwarding any particular set of tactics. It was clear even before the conference was organized that certain ideological differences would not be overcome and that any organizational initiatives would have to succeed in spite of those differences. After all, implicit in most of the discussion throughout the conference were several other questions, including whether to work within or outside of the unions for rank-and-file power, which workers constituted the most advanced section of struggle, and what the nature of the ongoing struggles really was: Was it to reform the system or put an end to it through revolution? Attendees had mixed reactions to Haughton's proposals, in particular the workers' centers. Many had a strong ideological aversion to the idea because it invoked the specter of dual unionism, establishing a force outside of the unions rather than within their framework. The Communist Party had advocated such activities in the past, and many socialist organizations denounced dual unionism as a tactic that divided workers and therefore weakened their political struggle. Others felt that struggling within unions was a dead end: American unions were only husks of their formerly combative selves and what remained was an accommodationist bureaucracy. Organizations like the Rank and File Committee and the LRBW both pursued this strategy, though at various points in time they ran candidates within the union framework. Meanwhile, other conference participants insisted on using the unions' own frameworks with elections and opposition caucuses to push for more rank-and-file power. With this deep division, the workers' center proposal failed. On the other hand, attendees unanimously supported Haughton's national publication proposal. Ironically, due to the costs and commitments necessary to write, edit, fund, and publish any periodical, conference delegates decided to empower the HUC's *Fight Back!* as the national publication.

While Haughton and the HUC may have forwarded particular tactical and strategic positions on the movement—starting a national publication, organizing labor centers, fighting job discrimination, and facilitating rank-and-file organizing—they never moved to establish an organization or install themselves as the vanguard at the conference. On the one hand, this was perhaps a result of their long-standing experiences fighting for more workers' power and democracy within unions. They had experienced what they thought of as dictatorial behavior on the part of union leaders for the better part of their working lives and were loath to raise themselves up to such a position. Their democratic mode of organizing boasted a consistency between both their means and their ends. On the other hand, their refusal to assume leadership represented an impasse in the rank-and-file movement as a whole. Though common experiences—battles, conditions of labor, and similar or shared enemies—brought them together to make a class, workers were divided. While racial division was a key topic at the conference, American workers were also divided among thousands of different workplaces with different concerns and realities, and to boot, they were geographically dispersed across a country that spans a continent. Any rank-and-file movement would have to take up this geographic and economic terrain, but it was not within the ability of any of them to do so. Later in his life, Haughton would discuss the persistence of the problem, citing the failure of the Negro American Labor Council as perhaps the greatest missed opportunity for militant workers. In his view, workers never had "organizational strength . . . that could do battle with racism as A. Philip Randolph used to call it, within the house of labor, racism in government, and in industry."[82]

The 1970 Postal Wildcat

In March 1970, what was once unthinkable had finally happened. In New York City, tens of thousands of letter carriers, mail sorters, and postal clerks collectively walked off the job and shut down the largest mail facilities of the world's most powerful nation, an act that went against their leadership, the law, and a legacy of weakness that overshadowed decades of bargaining. Other public-sector workers had paved the way in the preceding years, illegally shutting down essential services against the wishes of their elected representatives—both in the union and in the government—and winning impressive gains. Deteriorating work conditions, low pay, speedups, and a lack of respect motivated the postal workers, but only a risky strike could change their situation.

New York City was home to a huge number of postal workers, all of whom were organized into different and sometimes conflicting labor organizations during the 1960s and 1970s. There was the National Association of Letter Carriers (NALC), a craft union that organized those who delivered and cased the mail, whose most prominent local was the 7,000-member Branch 36 in the Bronx and Manhattan. The city was also home to Branch 41 in Brooklyn and Branch 79 in Queens. Then there was the Manhattan-Bronx Postal Union (MBPU), which boasted some 25,000 members.[83] The more industrial MBPU brought together the thousands of maintenance workers, mail sorters, and clerks. In the 1950s it had seceded from a more conservative parent union, the National Federation of Post Office Clerks, and on its own was one of the largest and most influential postal unions in the country.[84] In addition to the MBPU and the NALC branches, a large number of Black postal workers in New York City and elsewhere were members of the

National Alliance of Postal Employees, a sort of dual union that had lobbied heavily on behalf of Blacks since the Progressive Era.[85]

In spite of the high levels of unionization, postal workers did not have the right to collectively bargain. Though the federal government had recognized the right of workers in the private sector to form unions during the Great Depression, it kept a tight leash on its own employees, leaving them in a sort of limbo state that weakened their ability to shape contract outcomes. Relegated to lobbying Congress—what many members called "collective begging"—the unions developed political connections that they could leverage for some gains, but they failed ultimately to improve the lives of the many postal workers in urban areas like New York City who faced high costs of living.[86]

For the postal workers who formed the vanguard of the national walkout, the issue of pay was paramount. In 1969, first-year postal employees made roughly $6,100 and were required to work twenty-one years to make it to the maximum pay of just over $8,000. Postal workers made less than almost every other government employee, sometimes as much as 25 to 30 percent less.[87] For example, newly minted sanitationmen were making $9,871 a year, while new police officers and firefighters were making $10,950.[88] In New York City and other large cities, pay rates were so low that some letters carriers and clerks qualified for public assistance.[89]

Increasing inflation in the city at the end of the 1960s made pay raises even more pressing.[90] Consumer prices had risen at 2.7 percent annually for most of the 1960s, but in 1969 and 1970, prices spiked 7.4 percent and 5.8 percent, respectively.[91] Not only were postal workers' wages behind many other workers', but they were increasingly falling behind as inflation outpaced their pay raises. Some workers quit postal work altogether, complaining that the importance of their job was in no way reflected in their compensation.[92] The unions similarly argued that postal work's centrality to American business—delivering checks, contracts, products, and so on—ought to warrant their members significant pay raises, with NALC president Joseph Rademacher claiming, "The economy literally rides on our back."[93]

Abysmal work conditions added to the indignity of low pay. Manhattan's General Post Office's exterior boasted a beautiful neoclassical facade, but its interior bordered on medieval, with broken and exposed flooring, intermittent heat and air conditioning, and complete filth to boot. Workers dragged bags of mail across the ground and, amid a beehive of activity, still hand-sorted most of the mail.[94] Some of the work was monotonous, and its pace intensified in the 1960s. Mail volume increased significantly, requiring a massive speedup and leading to declining service quality and itinerant hires at lower pay grades. And with daily conflicts with post office managers—who union leaders argued were undertrained and overcompensated with dictatorial behavior tyranny—the situation was ripe for an outbreak of anger.[95]

Ironically, it was a pay increase that prompted New York City's postal workers to action. In the spring of 1969, union leaders were "begging" for a 10 to 15 percent raise, but the Nixon administration agreed only to 4 percent, slated to take effect on July 1. In response, NALC members picketed in front of the central Brooklyn post office on June 20, blocking traffic. The police moved in to clear the strikers from the road and a melee ensued, with two strikers arrested and two police officers sent to the hospital. In Manhattan, a protest of some 2,000 postal workers chanted for a strike and held signs calling for sick-outs and the disruption of mail delivery.[96] Meanwhile some postal workers posted pro-strike flyers on union bulletin boards, calling for a "Postal Clerks Independence Day" sick-out on July 4. Tensions became so high that union officials in the city met with postal management on June 30 to discuss contingencies for a wildcat strike.[97]

On July 1, workers at the Kingsbridge station in the Bronx staged a sick-out. Seventy-two postal workers, both letter carriers and clerks, called in sick at the station, sparking another dozen more sick-outs at a station in Throggs Neck. The postal service immediately suspended the wildcatters without pay, accusing them of disrupting the delivery of checks to the elderly and to the impoverished on public assistance.[98] The MBPU paid its suspended members' salaries, but the NALC only did the same after a groundswell of pressure from letter carriers. In fact, the NALC president had gone so far as to denounce the strikers, only changing course in the face of much rank-and-file pressure.[99] Though the MBPU more quickly defended the militants, rank-and-filers across the city called union headquarters demanding action, and a handful sent letters to MBPU president Moe Biller expressing their support for their comrades, but some questioned why more militant action was not taken.[100]

The summer walkout resulted in increased rank-and-file activism in NALC locals in the city. Members began attending regular union meetings, defining their own sets of demands. Militant members of Queens NALC Branch 41 forefronted pay increases that would make the 1969 top rate of $8,500 a year the new *starting rate* for postal employees. They also demanded reaching the top rate in five years and retirement after twenty years with a full pension paid for by the federal government.[101] Other letter carriers issued similar demands but called for a thirty-five-hour workweek, the right to strike, and rank-and-file ratification of all pay-related agreements.[102] These demands were much more militant than those sought by the NALC leadership in concert with the Nixon administration at the end of 1969, which included a 5.4 percent increase in pay, top pay reached in eight years, and binding arbitration for disputes, all of which were contingent upon a reorganization of the post office.[103] In January 1970, NALC rank-and-filers rejected their leadership's endorsement of the Nixon plan, calling instead for a strike survey among the membership to assess possibilities for further militant action.[104]

For New York City's postal workers, the surrounding environment of labor upheaval was paramount in helping to transform anger into action. Illegal public-sector strikes had produced significant wage gains in the city: the TWU's strike in 1966 resulted in a 15 percent pay increase, teachers won union recognition and similarly large pay increases with several illegal strikes, and other unions used threats of walkouts to do the same.[105] As one postal worker put it during the 1970 wildcat: "The teachers, sanitationmen and transit workers all struck in violation of the law and got big increases. Why shouldn't we?"[106] Some militant postal workers circulated flyers that criticized union leaders and drew even wider comparisons: "Window Washers won themselves a $60 raise over three years, Longshoreman won $5 over three years, Private Sanitation won an immediate $20 raise plus $20 over the next two years, the President got himself a $100,000 raise, Senators and Congressman got themselves $20,000 raises."[107]

Historian Philip F. Rubio's excellent *Undelivered: From the Great Postal Strike of 1970 to the Manufactured Crisis of the U.S. Postal Service* notes that many of New York's postal workers were heavily influenced by the strikes around them. But Rubio asserts that strikes were illegal for federal employees but not for public-sector workers in New York State or New York City. The 1947 Condon-Wadlin Act and later the 1967 Taylor Act barred public-sector workers from striking. In fact, this is a key parallel between the postal strike and the municipal strikes. For New Yorkers by 1970, in many cases, direct action got the goods, the law be damned. Like the subway and sanitation strikes, the postal strike was illegal, and like scores of private-sector strikes, it was a movement from below.[108]

Postal workers had reached a breaking point, and on March 12, in a general membership meeting, NALC Branch 36 letter carriers excoriated their union leaders. Branch 36 president Gus Johnson was concerned that the militant workers attending NALC meetings would outvote the opposition; thus, he recommended tabling strike discussion and a private vote. The meeting revolted, rejecting both the call for a mail ballot and passing a motion forcing the leadership to hold a strike vote. Biller, fearful of a strike, wrote to President Nixon about the growing anger among postal workers, warning him that the inadequacy of current offers might result in a walkout.[109]

At the Manhattan Center on March 17, the NALC held its strike vote meeting, with the leadership working in the background to manufacture a no vote. Militant rank-and-file letter carriers practically invaded the meeting, chanting for a strike and refusing to leave until the results of the vote were read. Interestingly, the NALC members were rebelling not only against their own leaders but against the heads of the MBPU, who attended the meeting in support of NALC leaders. Biller adamantly wanted to avoid a strike, and in hopes of undermining the growing anger appealed to the letter carriers to wait for the outcome of the MBPU membership meeting the following month. NALC rank-and-filers booed the MBPU president, and after hours of voting, NALC Branch 36 leaders announced a final tally of 1,555–1,055 to strike. NALC president Gus Johnson, who had been booed repeatedly throughout the meeting, announced that the union was on strike, disappointing the MBPU leaders who believed he should have refused the illegal maneuver.[110]

In prior discussions with Johnson and the NALC leaders, Biller had agreed to hold an emergency strike vote meeting of the MBPU should the NALC rank and file vote to strike. The MBPU leadership immediately released a statement in the aftermath of the strike vote saying that the NALC members had rebelled against their own leaders but the MBPU would not be following their lead into a strike, choosing instead to take a survey on attitudes toward the strike.[111] But postal workers had already taken the initiative, and as the clock struck twelve, the largest work stoppage against the federal government in history began. Letter carriers and mail sorters picketed at post offices across the city, carrying signs for higher pay and manning police barricades to prevent scabbing. Mail handlers and clerks who reported to work honored the picket lines though they themselves had not voted to strike, joining the pickets and calling on their leaders to strike.[112]

That same night, the rank and file took over the MBPU's emergency meeting, refusing the union leadership's pressures to follow by-laws and adhere to a secret ballot rather than a voice vote. Members chanted "Power to the people," and Biller described the more than 6,000 members as being in an "angry and hostile mood." When a vote finally did come, the margin was overwhelming, 8,242–940 in favor of a strike, giving a formal stamp to what was already a fact.[113]

The joint rank-and-file votes in favor of striking resonated across the country. By the afternoon of March 18, postal workers in Detroit walked off the job as well, and the wildcat spread up and down the East Coast to Newark, Philadelphia, and Boston. Days later the strike spread to Chicago as rank-and-file workers pushed through union channels to vote for a strike, and the factionalized postal unions either stood aside or recommended honoring picket lines. Across the country, the postal strike ebbed and flowed, with various cities and towns alternately striking or returning to work. In total, some 200,000 workers struck the federal government.[114]

The strike caused massive disruption of the postal system. On the first day alone, the New York Police Department and the US postal inspectors chased problems back and forth across the city, including trucks that blocked delivery bays or that were abandoned in roadways after spontaneous walk-offs. Picket lines were huge at many stations, and picketers climbed atop postal vehicles and organized themselves to block entrance into major post offices. Confusing matters even more, postal rank-and-filers called in dozens of bomb hoaxes, shutting down even more facilities.[115] Some of this activity was probably coordinated, with some militants in the Manhattan's General Post Office having circulated flyers in the run-up to the strike calling for sabotaging the postal system with phone complaints, letters without stamps, and boxes of onions and ice cubes shipped to warmer areas of the country.[116]

By the morning of March 19, strikers had completely paralyzed New York City's post offices. One of the largest impacts of the strike was halting the delivery of checks by mail, which damaged a variety of businesses and economic sectors. For example, the strike interrupted Con Edison's ability to gather $3 million in payments on a daily basis, a number that is paltry in comparison to the disruption inflicted on banks, who were prevented from garnering their usual $300 million a day in payments by mail.[117] The rest of the financial sector was affected as well, and several days into the strike the president of the New York Stock Exchange feared a market shutdown as a result of the walkout.[118]

While the post office sought an injunction to end the strike, the Nixon administration opted to break the strike with the National Guard. When New York City mayor John Lindsay had tried to muster the National Guard to end the 1968 sanitation strike, Governor Rockefeller nixed the plan. President Nixon had no such check, and on March 23, he ordered the New York National Guard to go to picket-guarded post offices across the city. By that time, postal workers in many other states had returned to work, but New York's postal workers scoffed at calls to do so.[119] Nixon hoped to use the guardsmen to both intimidate the strikers and deliver the mail, but the intricacies of postal work and the mountains of accumulated mail baffled the guard members. Some historians describe a degree of solidarity between troops and strikers, because it was not uncommon for letter carriers or postal clerks at the time to join the guard to make up for their paltry wages.[120] Leaders like Biller, however, reported that they were frightened by the troops and felt that they must order the rank and file back to work.[121]

Local labor leaders denounced Nixon's actions. The Uniformed Sanitationmen's Association president condemned Nixon's attempt to "Vietnamize relationships with Federal employees." Further-removed leaders like George Meany, president of the AFL-CIO, were more lukewarm, opposing the use of troops but advocating the end of the strike. Though the troops were not able to deliver the mail, they certainly changed the tone of the strike and helped speed its end.[122]

On the first day of National Guard mobilization, NALC president Rademacher brought word of an offer from the federal government, with 12 percent pay increases, wage adjustments for large cities, amnesty for strikers, and collective bargaining rights.[123] Biller was initially skeptical, both wanting verification of the deal's authenticity and arguing that New Yorkers needed a much higher pay increase to get them back to work. Rademacher, who claimed to have brokered the deal, had his local proxy, Branch 36 president Gus Johnson, assure Biller that it was a legitimate deal but only if the strike ended. With many postal workers in other cities returning to work and because of fear of the National Guard, Biller acceded to Rademacher's plan. But in reality, Rademacher had completely lied, receiving no agreement from Nixon.[124]

Nationally, many strikers were less resolute than their New York counterparts, and by March 23, most postal workers in Boston, Pittsburgh, and San Francisco were back on the job and many had begun to return to work in Chicago, Philadelphia, and Detroit.[125] In New York City and nearby Newark, most postal workers remained on strike the day the National Guard arrived, but picketing had decreased.[126] Some workers became concerned that continuing the walkout might endanger the viability of their unions, which could face massive fines and the revocation of automatic dues check off, which allowed union membership fees to be paid directly from paychecks. Some workers were also intimidated by the National Guard mobilization, and after a week, many were unsure whether staying off the job longer would yield any benefits.[127] On March 25, some carriers in Jamaica and Flushing, Queens, voted to return to work, while in the Bronx, some postal workers simply reported for duty. After a week-long walkout that had grown to national proportions, New York City's postal strike rapidly faded away.[128]

Just as its end came from both above and below, the 1970 strike's results were mixed. The strike led to serious victories, such as the recognition of full collective bargaining rights for postal workers as well as retroactive pay raises and full amnesty. What the workers had imposed, in fact—a force of collective bargaining—would be legally inscribed in law by 1971, putting an end to the era of collective begging that had for so long defined the plight of mailmen and women.[129] Postal workers also threw less militant leaders out of office: rank-and-file leader Vincent Sombrotto became NALC Branch 36 president following the strike and ultimately president of the entire NALC.[130]

On the other hand, the union leadership won these demands at the bargaining table in the months *after* the strike. Biller, who strongly advocated against the strike, claimed all positive settlements and blamed losses on Rademacher. Like the government, union leadership was fearful of another wildcat, and when negotiations stalled, the NALC placed Branch 36 into trusteeship in order to prevent it and its allies in the MBPU from organizing another strike. Ultimately, the strike led to the 1971 merger of several national unions into the newly formed American Postal Workers Union, which would represent the majority of postal workers for years to come.[131] In subsequent negotiations, a Rank and File Bargaining Advisory Committee would take part in decision-making, yet the complaints of a feeble and nonmilitant leadership continued, and Biller, who initially opposed the strike, would go on to lead the American Postal Workers Union for many years.[132]

Hard Hat Riot

In the city's financial district, just before noon on Friday, May 8, 1970, about 200 longshoremen and construction workers, carrying American flags and gathering a crowd of supporters as they marched, violently confronted students protesting Nixon's expansion of the Vietnam War and the killing of four students at Kent State University in Ohio. Lines of police did little to hold the workers back as they drove their way into the thousand or so students, who either retreated or stood their ground and fought with their fists. Bystanders intervened on both sides, finding themselves bloodied by construction workers if they came to the students' aid. After breaking up the antiwar protest on Wall Street, the growing crowd and its vanguard of construction workers wound its way up to city hall, where it overturned barricades and stormed the inner halls, forcing city officials (Mayor Lindsay was not present) to raise the

American flag back to full mast from half, to which it had been lowered in honor of the four dead in Ohio.[133] In the following days, rank-and-filers took efforts into their own hands, resulting in weeks of demonstrations primarily involving construction workers.[134] Swiftly thereafter, the hard hat emerged as a symbol of the silent majority and, in the words of historian Jeffrey Bloodworth, "add[ed] to the nascent class war within the Democratic Party."[135]

Workers' motivations for participating were diverse, but support of the Vietnam War and support of American troops was a major, albeit complicated, motivation. According to some estimates, construction workers opposed the expansion of the war into Cambodia just as much as students did, and in this period, a working-class person was actually more likely to be against the war than someone from the class background of most university students.[136] Powerful union bureaucracies stoked pro-war sentiment among their members, with Local 3's *Electrical Union World* featuring pro-war letters and articles. Some issues of the publication had letters from drafted members of the union, who received a ten-dollar contribution from the union each month, along with a letter from the leadership about antiwar opposition and encouragement. Some letters simply expressed thanks while others expressed hatred of the draft's opponents. As one Local 3 GI put it in 1968, "I wish they draft them HIPPIES, they are a group of sick people!"[137] Some construction workers came from much more conservative backgrounds and supported the war as an effort to prevent communist subversion worldwide.[138]

While support for the troops was sometimes inspired by conservative political leanings, sometimes it represented respect for sacrifice and fulfillment of duty and a disdain for those protesting the war.[139] In fact, in many interviews during and after the Hard Hat mobilizations, construction workers expressed significant disgust for students. Several days before the Hard Hat Riot, violence had already broken out between construction workers and students multiple times across Manhattan. In an immediate response to the killings at Kent State, thousands of students shut down both public and private colleges. At City College, construction workers building a new science facility attacked a student on the way to the protest on May 5, with one worker shouting, "I was in Vietnam and I love to kill Gooks"; the student defended himself with none other than a conch shell.[140] On May 7, shoving matches broke out between protesting students and construction workers in downtown Manhattan, prompting some workers to participate in the riot the following day.[141]

Opposition to students mixed class resentment and envy. As Robert Romano, a foreman at the World Trade Center, argued, students had "been with the silver spoon in their mouth too long."[142] When interviewed on the subject, older workers often expressed dismay at the "kids" who seemed to them to be ungrateful, self-righteous, or confused. They further lamented the destruction of property and rioting on college campuses the previous year, identifying it as a breakdown of law and order. Ironically, though many construction workers resented the students, they yearned for their own children to attend college and leave behind demanding physical labor.[143]

The Vietnam War and resentment of student protesters were important drivers for the Hard Hat Riot, but Mayor Lindsay was a focal point of the anger both for the initial violence and in the weeks of protest that followed. The first Monday after the riot, some 2,000 construction workers and longshoremen from docks on the city's west side mobilized. The group marched for nearly two hours, chanting "Lindsay is a bum," carrying signs that read "Impeach the Red Mayor," and attacking a handful of bystanders.[144] In the week that followed, several hundred construction workers marched around the Financial District at lunchtime waving flags and singing songs like "The Star-Spangled Banner." On the one-week anniversary of the original riot, some 5,000 workers marched through the Financial District, carrying, among other signs and symbols, a coffin with an epitaph that read, "Here Lies the City of New York, Killed by Commissar Lindsay."[145]

While conservative, anti-communist rhetoric dominated the signage, even some conservative New Yorkers had voted for Lindsay in his 1965 electoral run because he was a member of the Republican Party. By 1970, though, a large number of working-class whites living in the city's outer boroughs questioned the mayor's ability to comprehend their struggles and concerns, abandoning him in the 1969 mayoral race for either conservative Democrat Mario Procaccino or Republican John Marchi.[146] In one plumber's estimation, construction workers "feel they're getting stepped on. We built this country, and I don't think we have a say now."[147] In 1969, Procaccino gave working-class whites a verbal vehicle for their anger, labeling Lindsay and his elite supporters "limousine liberals."[148]

With some notable exceptions—Black carpenters and drillers and Mohawks among the ironworkers—construction work in New York City persisted as a socially isolated enclave for white working-class men. It was particularly tight-knit because unions and contractors relied on familial, ethnic, and religious ties to recruit workers and because unions were strong enough to back up a degree of workers' autonomy on the job and stave off outside attempts to enforce nondiscriminatory hiring.[149] In New York, protests had brought major attention to exclusionary practices, and in the second half of the 1960s, the battle over hiring had gone national, with Nixon pushing his own version of the Philadelphia Plan to promote increased hiring of racial minorities in the building trades. In the summer and fall of 1969, protests took place across the country against the slow, or in some cases nonexistent, integration of building trades unions, and violent street clashes took place in Chicago, St. Louis, and Buffalo.[150] In Chicago, construction workers even clashed with a group protesting the trial of the Chicago Eight.[151]

In New York City, Lindsay strongly supported affirmative action attempts, and historians have argued that the Building and Construction Trades Council (BCTC) and its president, Peter J. Brennan, organized the protests to fight affirmative action measures. On the day of the initial violence, many reported the presence of men in suits—presumably union officials—directing the construction workers' violence, but the identities of anyone engaged in such action was never confirmed. Brennan denied union involvement, but he did little to denounce the violence, arguing that the antiwar protesters deserved what they got and that hopefully the beatings knocked some sense into them. While initially not claiming involvement in any of the protests, the BCTC held a special meeting on May 13 and announced plans for a large rally to show "love of country and love and respect for our country's flag."[152] On the day of the march, 150,000 people inundated downtown Manhattan, with many construction unions marching with banners and flags. Construction workers working in downtown Manhattan who took part were compensated for their missed time at work, but some reported that they felt forced to participate.[153] The week following the massive patriotic demonstration, Brennan met with President Nixon at the White House, pledging his support and the support of construction workers everywhere for the war and their commander in chief.[154]

Historians have focused on the riots, but they have given little attention to the fact that the large protest and work interruptions fit a formal pattern of BCTC threats that had occurred over the preceding seven years. At a 1964 BCTC executive board meeting, Brennan threatened a "holiday" and march on city hall against what he saw as mayor Robert Wagner's administration's undue interference with the rollout of various city projects.[155] Again in February 1966, Brennan addressed a BCTC meeting and threatened to "strik[e] the whole city" because Mayor Lindsay wanted to force fair hiring concessions by delaying projects like the World Trade Center and Richmond Expressway.[156] In April 1966, carpenters union vice president Charles Johnson denounced Lindsay for "paying more attention to the minority groups than to the majority of the people," calling on the BCTC to declare a strike and march on city hall, and by May the organization's executive board voted unanimously to organize a mass march.[157] Brennan's and the BCTC's threats ultimately led to negotiations with the mayor, and though conflicts with Lindsay continued, for a time the threats subsided.[158]

After protests in the summer of 1969 and battles over the Revised Philadelphia Plan reached a fever pitch, Brennan met with Lindsay, who told the union leader he would issue an executive order on nondiscriminatory hiring.[159] In response, Brennan told a BCTC membership meeting that the mayor's plan "might call for a complete shut-down."[160] In March, Mayor Lindsay, in concert with the BCTC, announced the New York Plan, which many civil rights activists immediately denounced because they believed it created a lower trainee tier for Black hires while whites would move directly into apprenticeships.[161] Later that month, the city obtained compliance on minority hiring by withholding funds from elevator contractors who pledged to work in concert with Local 1 Elevator Constructors.[162] In mid-April, Lindsay announced an improved New York Plan that would require 25 percent minority hiring on all construction jobs that were financed with city money, which Brennan adamantly opposed.[163] Three weeks later, the BCTC was orchestrating attacks on student protesters, capitalizing on their popularity with a mass march to both attack Lindsay and cozy up to the Nixon administration.

The Hard Hat Riot left a complicated legacy in the city. Municipally, the riot and protests served as a rallying point for many who were anti-Lindsay and led to increased organized labor endorsement of conservative candidates like James L. Buckley.[164] Nationally, the hard hat would become synonymous with a conservative turn, as Brennan both courted and was courted by the Nixon administration, becoming secretary of labor after supporting Nixon's reelection run in 1972.[165]

While the Hard Hat Riot signaled some unity of purpose between construction workers and their leaders—many feared the Revised Philadelphia Plan's threat to their economic livelihood—many construction workers opposed Nixon's anti-inflationary measures, especially as inflation in New York City ate into wage gains.[166] In 1972, more than 60,000 construction workers would strike in the city, asking for a variety of changes including wage increases, more shop stewards, stronger seniority protections, and protection of overtime opportunities. In nearly every case, construction workers fought for contract gains opposed by Nixon's anti-inflation measures.[167] And like their support of the war, their support for Nixon was not overwhelming. In the 1972 presidential election, more than 50 percent of union households—and manual laborers—did go over to Nixon, but their levels of support were dwarfed by support for Nixon among white-collar workers and professionals.[168]

An Inflection Point for Rank-and-File Struggle

By the end of 1968, a rank-and-file-driven strike fever gripped the city, with a broad range of workers continuing to influence one another across lines of race, occupation, and skill. In many cases, new organizing and new insurgent energies impelled big changes within unions, with young and Black militancy infusing the strikes. This political environment spurred militancy nationwide, but both union leaders and left-wing rank-and-file activists at the time believed that the upheaval was inchoate and lacking in long-term strategy. Union leaders were particularly concerned about the long-term damage that could be done to labor's public image while activists found the rebellions to be fleeting and insufficiently revolutionary or antiracist in character. But workers encountered other obstacles to their demands beyond the categorical prescriptions of aspiring left-wing leaders. Institutional opposition from unions, employers, and politicians killed off significant campaigns. Some workers saw their failed efforts as fruitless, and many militants focused on their own economic survival and moved away from the constant campaigning and conflict. Such norms would become more common in the early 1970s, and in the years that followed, other important rank-and-file movements would flounder.

FOUR

Fading Fires

In the early 1970s, some of the city's rank-and-file rebellions began to take on a darker tone, with localized inflation and the beginnings of nationwide stagnation undermining workers' confidence and economic stability. In 1971, telephone workers hoped to push their employers into further concessions, as they had done several times in years prior. But after a seven-month strike, New York Telephone (NYT) roundly defeated the rank-and-filers, nullifying their pattern-breaking wage demands and crushing their militancy.

This chapter examines the defeat of one of the city's most militant unions: Communications Workers of America (CWA) Local 1101. From the mid-1960s to 1972, Local 1101 members engaged in wildcat strikes, workplace sabotage, electoral rejection of their leaders, and solidarity gestures with other striking unions, making them a problem for their employers and union leaders. To push for greater economic gains than the international leadership obtained in nationwide bargaining, Local 1101 rejected a contract and struck on its own in 1971. With the help of strikebreakers and an automated workplace, employers held the line, defeating insurgent workers. In the strike's aftermath, managerial revenge and union reprisals shut the door on militancy, ending Local 1101's rank-and-file rebellion. Finally, this important strike showed a changing attitude among workers. Whereas many rebellions were once optimistic, amid a localized inflationary spike and declining economic vitality in the city, this strike signaled increasing desperation.

Local 1101's militancy had contributed to the era's broader restiveness, and its members' defiance against their employers and union leadership resonated within the ranks of the CWA nationally. But from 1971 to 1972, this celebrated, militant union would find itself in a protracted struggle with employers and union officials, both local and national. What began as an exuberant rank-and-file rejection of the union hierarchy ended as a devastating defeat that closed the door on rebellion. This dramatic struggle, culminating in an equally dramatic defeat, explains why the efforts of some of New York's most militant workers failed, what concerns and desires drove them, and how their loss contributed to a declining field of struggle in the city.[1]

New York City's plant telephone workers joined the CWA in 1961 after a hotly contested three-way election among their former organization, United Telephone Organizations, the powerful International Brotherhood of Electrical Workers, and the CWA.[2] Local members dissatisfied with United Telephone Organizations' leadership had led the charge, but immediately after winning representation rights to the largest telephone local in the country, the CWA, too, came under threat. Several powerful stewards worked with the Teamsters to try to leave the CWA, and there was intense political jockeying among various stewards in different plants across the city. Throughout the 1960s, leadership turnover was high and various internal opposition groups threatened to take the massive local out of the CWA.[3]

Behind the internal tumult was a craft-based militancy infused with citywide class consciousness. Plant workers had intimate knowledge of the prone-to-breakdown telephone equipment. Older workers were the real experts within the industry, and most managers lacked a real understanding of how the system functioned.[4] Skilled, older workers tended to be stewards and chief stewards, and in some locales, like northern Manhattan, they led militant action. For example in 1961, when four men took off work to celebrate Columbus Day, NYT suspended them, and some 3,000 men wildcatted to protest the suspension.[5] CWA militants had a broader class consciousness and were willing to defend it: in 1961, a chief steward in Brooklyn's Local 1109—which later merged with Local 1101—refused to cross a United Auto Workers picket line at the Intertype Company. He was suspended, and the threat of a citywide strike led the company to reinstate him and submit the issue to arbitration.[6] Solidarity with other strikes was but one component, and many CWA workers stayed abreast of labor politics in the city, comparing their pay and work conditions to skilled trades like plumbing and electrical work.[7]

Stewards also played an important part negotiating with managers on the job. When NYT hired new workers, they first trained them for several weeks and kept them on probation for an entire year. In this time period, small infractions, including being a few minutes late to work, could result in dismissal. Stewards could often speak with managers in order to smooth over problems, while in other cases they used formal grievance procedures to challenge decisions. They also threatened strikes, walkouts, and slowdowns.[8]

The CWA allowed for a large number of stewards, and within the union the stewards organization was a mobilizing body that often outflanked leadership. The ratio of members to stewards was roughly ten to one, and these stewards in turn elected chief stewards, who no longer worked full-time but rather attended to union business, including a large number of grievance hearings. Stewards were largely "stand up to management guys who had proven themselves as reliable leaders," and that reliability often meant they could lead highly effective actions. According to an oral history, the stewards organization in CWA Local 1101 was the site of intense "political jockeying," some of it ethnically or socially defined, and stewardship could be a pathway to real power in the union hierarchy. The union hierarchy also reached down into the stewards organization because the vice presidents of Local 1101, who represented distinct geographical districts in the union, wielded the power to certify or decertify a steward. Such power sometimes contributed to what one former rank-and-filer called a "feudal hierarchy" wherein loyalty was owed to a chief steward or a vice president. Regardless, the stewards organization was one of the critical, formal mobilizing spaces and was made up of staunch union men with a strong class consciousness, like many other members of the CWA.[9]

This militancy and the fact that Local 1101 was the largest CWA local in the United States, with some 20,000 members in 1970, brought conflict between the local and the international. Local 1101's size gave it greater representation within international elections and negotiations, and in the early 1960s the international amended representational rules to limit the local's influence. In response, Local 1101's then president Hank Habel and the rest of the executive board voted to take the union out of the CWA and into the Teamsters.[10] While Habel and others initially had rank-and-file support, many rank-and-filers soured on their former leaders, believing them to be self-serving and power hungry. In fact, some younger workers who opposed

Habel and the Teamsters' Telephone Employee Company Union made pins for their coworkers that read, "FU TECU."[11] Local 1101 went through a series of leaders in the late 1960s and early 1970s, with cliques falling in and out of favor, leading to a contested election in 1971 in which opposition candidate Ricky Carnivale eked out a win. Carnivale had relatively little leadership experience, often finding himself outflanked by his own members.[12]

The influx of young working-class New Yorkers in the second half of the 1960s dramatically helped further increase the union's militancy. Some were fresh from high school and ready to be in control of their own lives. Some were influenced by the period's cultural and political tumult: they wore their hair longer, had mustaches and beards, and saw themselves as rebelling against a series of authoritarian institutions in their lives. Many of their older coworkers viewed them with suspicion, if not shock, for both their aesthetic and political differences. One CWA rank-and-filer in Brooklyn remembered a cafeteria conversation that turned into a brawl as older workers remarked that the Chicago police should have shot the protesters at the 1968 Democratic National Convention.[13] Another in Manhattan recalled a chief steward pulling him aside to find out if he was part of Students for a Democratic Society. Finally, some younger workers were newly returned veterans of the Vietnam War, many of whom brought with them a dislike for excessive authority, which put them into continual conflict with what one former CWA member called the "stupid authoritarians in lower management."[14]

Underlying some of the confidence of the youth was that they were born and raised in an economy with plentiful employment.[15] This fact was strongly reflected in NYT's abysmal 50 percent retention rate, though some of that could be attributed to its mass hiring practices.[16] Young workers bucked against some controls, causing some changes in the workplace. For example, in the blazing summer months when air conditioners failed, managers would order workers to simply suffer through the heat. But in the late 1960s, younger workers rejected these conditions and walked off the job, calling other men out. Challenging workplace discipline and unfairness on the job, young workers grieved the company on issue after issue, becoming so obstinate in the face of their employers that it would "make the pope kick in a stained-glass window."[17] In 1969, a series of wildcats broke out, and in November of that year CWA members struck over a wage-scale progression. Rank-and-filers in Brooklyn, many of them young, led the walkout, and their efforts resonated with other CWA members in the state who walked off in solidarity. Only threats of massive fines and the company's agreement to negotiate the issue brought the men back to work, with both sides claiming victory. While these wildcats did not disrupt service in any major way, the company was willing to negotiate in order to get the men back on the job to continue expanding and repairing its system.[18]

Though New York's population was changing, the CWA was a largely white male union because of the stratified nature of NYT's hiring practices. Though there is a long history of Black and female employment in the industry, there was also long-standing discrimination against both women and Black people that either sorted them into particular jobs or barred them from employment altogether. The combination of expansion of service and civil rights struggles led to increased Black hiring in the industry by the second half of the 1960s. In 1967, 92 percent of the Black employees of NYT were women, the vast majority of whom were operators and thus not members of CWA Local 1101, who were primarily skilled plant workers.[19] In that same year, only 2.1 percent of all craft workers in New York were Black, and they were mostly framemen, the lowest-paid craft rank. In the words of an Equal Employment Opportunity Commission report, "black employment was being concentrated in the lowest-paying, least-desirable, dead-end jobs in the Bell System."[20] That being said, younger Black women found the initial wages desirable, and in many cases they represented a step up, albeit a small one, in an environment of diminished choices.

Historian Venus Green argues that in many cases white CWA leaders across the country did not want to organize Black workers and feared Black voting blocs that could upset internal electoral coalitions.[21] The New York situation was different given the union's battle over crime and safety. In 1966 in response to attacks on its workers in poor Black neighborhoods, District 1 president Morton Bahr called on NYT to hire and train more Black workers, stating that the "CWA recognizes its responsibility to both our membership and the community" and that the organization "fully appreciates the anxieties, desires, frustrations, and hopes of the Negro Community."[22]

In 1967 after the shooting of a coin collector, CWA International leaders called on NYT to create a jobs program to train residents of the city's poorer neighborhoods for telephone work, which they hoped would solve some of the underlying economic problems that the union believed motivated the robberies and attacks.[23] Local 1101's union hierarchy and stewards were also keenly aware that a large influx of Black workers into the ranks was inevitable given both the city's changing demographics and the demand for more robust telephone service. While that would mean upheaval within the union as Green suggests, some stewards believed they needed to accept Blacks so as to not create a bloc of workers loyal more to the company than the union.[24]

Though it is difficult to determine just how pervasive racism within the ranks was, it was certainly present.[25]

In 1967, NYT did begin to hire more Black and Latino New Yorkers as part of a broad attempt to expand and improve its service and perhaps because of union pressure. While the hiring of Black employees in the crafts accelerated, they largely remained framemen and were often "at a disadvantage in respect of skills, diversified overtime, and opportunities for promotion and advancement."[26] In 1970, the anger boiled over at two plants when all Black craft workers, led by Harlem-born switchman Dennis Serrette, wildcatted against the continued stratification of the workplace. When the strike ended, the issue went to arbitration between the union and the company, with upgrading improvements coming in 1972. Serrette became one of Local 1101's vice presidents in 1970 and would be involved in some of the militant action during the 1971 strike.[27]

Local 1101's restiveness attracted left-wing activists to the union. International Socialists, a small leftist organization, founded an opposition caucus within Local 1101 called United Action (UA) consisting of some twelve members. A former UA member, Rust Gilbert, was motivated to organize within the union after seeing a young Black man wearing a Bell Telephone work jacket with a copy of the Black Panthers newspaper stuffed in his back pocket.[28] Like their coworkers, the UA opposed the CWA leadership's complacency and lack of militancy, but unlike their coworkers they advocated an expansion of the union's turf. NYT's female operators—many of whom were Black or Puerto Rican—were organized by the Telephone Traffic Union (TTU), which was practically a company union. Though critical of the CWA leadership, UA wanted to include operators in Local 1101 to not only provide better material gains for the operators but also unify workers through a multigender, multiracial union covering all of New York City's telephone workers.[29]

While UA worked within Local 1101's caucus framework, the Progressive Labor Party founded the Bell Workers Action Committee (BWAC). While the Progressive Labor Party had played an important role in the decline of Students for a Democratic Society during its 1969 national convention, BWAC included Progressive Labor Party members, nonaffiliated New Left militants, and former Students for a Democratic Society members who had cut their teeth in antiwar and civil rights activism. Like UA, BWAC promoted the addition of TTU's operators to Local 1101, but their program also included organizational efforts outside of the union's control such as independent plant committees and cross-union building committees, which were largely unsuccessful.[30]

Aware of long-standing discontent within its ranks, especially in New York, the CWA International leadership approached Bell in 1970 for a discussion of "Big City problems," with the union identifying crime, racial turnover, drug use, housing costs, transportation, and taxes as key problems for its workers in large cities.[31] Company representatives agreed with the union that there were specific problems for workers in the country's biggest cities, but they preferred to focus on their inability to hire or retain a productive labor force. While the CWA ranked economic problems low the bottom of its list of Big City problems, New York's rank-and-filers prioritized them, especially as inflation increased.[32]

In the past, the CWA had used its Western Electric ranks to set the bargaining pattern for its entire union, calling them out on strike in 1968. Among Bell System workers, however, CWA president Joseph Beirne had garnered a reputation as a sellout who was afraid of strikes. In November 1970, Beirne sent a timid letter to the national bargaining committee assessing the possibility of an "effective strike against the Bell System."[33] Many committee members called on Beirne to lead a nationwide strike to unify the ranks and achieve much needed pay raises. Even those against striking cited the need for major contract improvements, though they doubted the CWA's ability to dramatically disrupt services due to automation. As one of Beirne's assistants wrote, "Regardless of how high Bell's offer may be, we will almost have to strike to convince our members that blood has indeed been squeezed from a stone."[34]

While Beirne and others considered the possibility of a strike, conflict broke out between NYT and Local 1101 in January 1971. As part of a "Service Improvement Program," NYT began bringing out-of-state workers to conduct system repairs. CWA Local 1101 president Howard Banker denounced the program for violating an earlier agreement to use locals, and many rank-and-filers suspected that NYT's efforts were designed to make the system resilient in case of a strike. On January 11, Local 1101 members walked off the job, and in many parts of the city the largely Black female operators honored their picket lines. The operators were undertaking a decertification drive, but were divided among themselves about whether to join the CWA or District 65. With the walkout solid in the city, the rest of New York followed, and the strike lasted for two weeks until arbitration was agreed upon; arbitrators ultimately sided with NYT and the program continued into the spring.[35]

In May 1971, as talks between the international and Bell Telephone were reaching an impasse, regional leader Morton Bahr wrote to Beirne to emphasize that inflation was hitting the New York–New Jersey metro area hard.[36] Food prices had increased 15 percent, apparel by 16.1 percent, and medical care by 20 percent. Rent was up by 10 percent in the city, with Governor Rockefeller's rollback on rent control regulations in 1971 only making rents higher. Even the subway fare was up to thirty cents by the beginning of 1970.[37] On top of that, New York's unemployment hit a ten-year high at 6 percent.[38] The accelerating deindustrialization of the city was partially to blame. In the 1950s, the five boroughs lost around 90,000 factory jobs; in the 1960s, they lost another 117,000. But between 1970 and 1972 alone, the city shed another 100,000 more manufacturing jobs. A flood of cheap imports hit the city's garment district incredibly hard, with the industry losing 50,000 jobs in 1970.[39] Manufacturing profits were down nationally and many firms went under while others had begun to relocate in order to take advantage of more conservative areas of the country where unionization and taxes were lower.[40] This shake-up began to color workers' anger, with inflation becoming an ineluctable force that dragged workers down no matter how hard they fought.[41]

With growing restiveness in the ranks and inflation threatening to rise both nationally and especially in New York City, Beirne and the executive council moved to strike. The CWA demanded an immediate 30 percent raise, with Bell's negotiators willing to concede to a 26 percent increase, with the pay hike evenly divided over a three-year period.[42] Many telephone workers feared that the roughly 8 percent increases per year would amount to very little real income gain in the face of inflation.[43]

On July 14, in a well-coordinated event, the international led a strike of 500,000 telephone workers across the United States, and within days they had a new contract offer.[44] It outlined a 27.4 percent raise over a three-year period with just over half of the raise in the first year, an increase higher than the automotive or steel industries were seeing.[45] The contract also included an agency shop provision, which would allow the CWA to collect representation fees from all employees. Such agreements were a financial windfall for unions, giving them greater stability and increasing their war chests significantly. With an agency shop agreement and raises in hand, the executive board voted unanimously to end the strike on July 19, ordering its men back to work by July 20 before rank-and-file approval of the contract.[46]

In New York, strikers refused the executive board's back-to-work order, as did rank-and-filers in New Jersey, Pennsylvania, and Florida, leaving more than 100,000 strikers on picket lines nationwide.[47] The CWA Executive

Council feared that New York locals and Local 1101 would spearhead a special convention to renew the strike, and within a week New York locals and many others across the country did call for a convention, but the executive board denied the motion on the grounds that it did not meet the 20 percent membership threshold.[48] With no means of reopening a national strike, every other local in the CWA voted to accept the contract except for Local 1101. Leftists in BWAC and UA praised the local's militancy and disobedience in the face of the CWA International, hoping the New Yorkers would lead a nationwide wildcat like the postal workers had the year before.[49]

In both the run-up to and aftermath of the nationwide strike, leftist activists in Local 1101 pushed for militant demands and cross-union organizing. BWAC, alongside UA, advocated a resolution declaring support for any TTU members who honored the CWA's picket lines. They had worked in the months before the strike to build connections between operators and CWA members who worked in the same buildings, which made economic sense to some TTU workers because their gains were often tied to the gains of CWA workers. Through months of organizing at the NYT Second Avenue plant in Manhattan where some UA and BWAC members worked, strike activity briefly crossed organizational lines.[50]

But all was not immediately well in the effort. In fact, organizing with TTU members only happened where militants like themselves worked and often did not involve most TTU members.[51] BWAC felt that it was incumbent on the men of Local 1101 to create the possibility of cross-union solidarity, and when most CWA members did not heed their call, BWAC attacked the white male members of the CWA for undermining their own strike. BWAC primarily blamed the men's sexism and racism, which was certainly present in the ranks, but many members' lack of interest was more complicated than prejudice.[52]

Rank-and-file militants' rejection of the BWAC strategy was indicative of a broader rejection of the group as well as practical limitations of the strategy and groups proposing it. Many of the older workers in the union were put off by avowedly socialist organizations.[53] During the 1971 strike, BWAC's publication featured multiple pages dedicated to an antiwar march, which called for solidarity with the riot in the Attica prison and with Vietnamese communists. Like the hard hats, many telephone workers would have been hard pressed to engage in dialogue with, let alone follow, those who proudly carried the label of socialist or communist or who praised the North Vietnamese and Viet Cong.[54] During the early days of the 1971 strike, members of the Socialist Workers Party intervened in Brooklyn picket lines, giving directions to the men and selling newspapers. Local 1101 members were skeptical, and after a few days—and socialist pretentions to leadership—they were beaten up and thrown out of the picket lines.[55]

Another difficulty with the UA and BWAC strategy was that the vast majority of Local 1101 members did not work with TTU members. Their solidarity with their fellow telephone workers was built not only on a commitment to their union but also on day-to-day interactions and short-term walkouts and grievances. In plants that actually had both operators and plant workers, the cafeteria was one of the few common spaces, though many workers would opt to eat instead in any number of the city's working-class restaurants or bars. UA was more astute than BWAC in its assessment of its fellow workers, and in the months before the strike, UA decreased its emphasis on a single union and emphasized economic demands instead.[56]

While leftists promoted cross-union organizing, NYT had progressively made its system less susceptible to disruption. The company had long used technology to undermine workers' power, and the company's introduction of the dial system undermined the need for operators, and a nationwide strike in 1947 for a closed shop, wages, and paid holidays lost when the phone system's functionality remained mostly intact.[57] By the late 1960s, most phone lines in the New York area were equipped with sensors that could monitor their functionality and diagnose problems, and much of the phone system, if properly serviced, could be maintained and run by supervisors in case of a strike. The CWA's international leadership recognized this fact, with the union's head Joseph Beirne stating that "it is not a very satisfactory discovery for a union to realize that the direct impact of its strike weapon is quite moderate."[58]

With an increasingly automated and strike-proof system, workers fought scabs and sabotaged company equipment and phone lines in various parts of the city. In one case, several cut lines left nearly 2,000 people without phone service. NYT decried the sabotage but was just as concerned during the strike about the intimidation and property destruction at its facilities.[59] Strikers harassed and roughed up scabs and supervisors working to break the strike, damaging facilities by throwing eggs and paint.[60]

While a powerful spirit marked the strike's early days, CWA members sank into a malaise after weeks of stalemate. Early in the strike most of the picket lines dissipated as President Carnivale and the union leadership stopped organizing them. Men who had spent the majority of their waking hours at work among a large group of coworkers with whom they often shared strong bonds now found themselves isolated. Many stayed at home, often without any activity to orient themselves around and occasionally in the company of spouses they were not used to spending so much time with. As one militant worker described it, the feeling that pervaded the strikers was something like depression.[61]

By late fall, talks between the union and NYT had reached an absolute impasse; the company was not willing to budge, and the longer the strike dragged on, the more difficult it was for the ranks to give in and return to work empty-handed. The strike was slowing the rate of repairs—leaving 100,000 customers in the New York area without service—but it was not causing major outages, and fewer than 1,000 out-of-state strikebreakers held the telephone network together.[62] Workers appealed to the Lindsay administration to apply a New York City law that made it illegal to bring in out-of-state strikebreakers, but no action was forthcoming from the mayor.[63]

Meanwhile, the international gave little support to the strike. After all, if a strike that defied their authority could produce a better contract, the international might lose control of many more locals. With little initial help from the city government or the union international (as defense funds were only disbursed in November), Local 1101 had to rely on its own devices.[64] Many rank-and-filers applied for unemployment, and many younger workers took it upon themselves to help older members navigate the application process. For many of the male plant workers, their working wives' supplementary incomes bolstered their position.[65] In other cases, Local 1101 members used their personal and familial connections to work part-time elsewhere.[66] Twenty-three weeks in, when Local 1101 president Carnivale presented a new contract, the membership rejected it by a massive 3–1 margin. The militant telephone workers were down but not out.[67]

The show of unity in November temporarily broke the malaise, leading to a short-lived coalition between militants, leftists, stewards, and Local 1101 vice presidents, including Dennis Serrette and Ed Dempsey. Together they organized renewed picket lines in the city and out-of-state pickets at CWA-organized Bell Telephone facilities.[68] UA members had initially proposed this tactic in August along with the creation of a strike committee, and though the strike committee had been created under the aegis of Serrette, UA's out-of-state picketing strategy had been ignored. In December however, desperation had grown and elections within the local loomed. Carnivale opposed much of the out-of-state picketing, refusing to disburse funds until some chief stewards proposed funding the effort without his help.[69]

From December to January, Local 1101 militants traveled to cities in New Jersey and Connecticut, Washington, DC, and as far as away as Detroit. In every city, local telephone workers honored the pickets in solidarity with Local 1101. UA hoped these actions would become the springboard for rank-and-file coordination within the CWA that could bypass union bureaucracy.[70] Local 1101 vice presidents like Dempsey—a militant and former chief steward in Manhattan—were ambivalent about the out-of-state picketing. With the combination of UA and rank-and-filers from around the city, they might potentially lose control of the pickets and the loyalty of the ranks. Furthermore, the fact that the technique was largely experimental and sought to bypass union hierarchies within the CWA as a whole also posed a contradiction to those who sought to jockey for control of the union. Dempsey was forced to concede to the tactic, however, and when Local 1101 picketed in Washington, DC, he didn't participate and some of the chief stewards associated with him went to CWA headquarters instead.[71]

Even though the Local 1101 rank and file was mobilizing again, NYT operations were running smoothly. The combination of recently upgraded supervisors from the ranks, out-of-state supervisors, and increased automation held the system together. The out-of-state picketing, while certainly a way to bring temporary pause at other AT&T plants around the country, was neither widespread enough nor disruptive enough to do much damage to the company. Frustration mounted within CWA Local 1101, and in mid-January, at a rally of some 1,000 workers at city hall, CWA strikers began an impromptu march, blocking traffic, destroying telephone equipment, and fighting with police. The following week another rally against out-of-state scabs resulted in more arrests.[72] In the face of ineffectual resistance, NYT offered the same deal as before with two insubstantial improvements: a one-dollar raise for employees who had reached the top tier and 15 percent extra pay for Saturday work.[73]

By mid-February the telephone strike had run its course, failing to cause major outages or hinder the company. The Carnivale leadership attempted to get the men back on the job by conducting a mail-ballot election, and by that point demoralization was rampant in the union.[74] Strikers voted 13,769–9,193 to accept the new contract.[75] After nearly seven months, the militancy of CWA workers in New York was unable to garner a significant local settlement and demonstrated an almost complete failure to impact the company. In its aftermath, rank-and-filers would refer to the defeat as the "dollar strike."[76]

While Aaron Brenner also argues that the 1971 strike was a defeat, he does not adequately underscore either the degree of the defeat or its long-term effects.[77] Immediately following the strike, NYT fired one UA and two

BWAC members and a handful of other militant unionists. But within two months, company reprisals expanded, and somewhere between 250 and 300 plant workers were fired, including shop stewards who helped lead the strike and entire gangs of workers. The company fired thirteen for strike-related actions and used small-scale disciplinary measures to fire others, for reasons as varied as leaving five minutes early, absences, lateness, and managerial metrics for reliability and production.[78] With hundreds fired and a freeze on hiring the previous year, NYT also punished its workers with a productivity drive, forcing those who remained to shoulder the increasing load of expanding service.[79]

Another major reprisal came from the international. Amid defeat, several Brooklyn leaders who had been voted out of the Local 1101 bureaucracy in the 1970 elections pushed to secede from Local 1101. Many Brooklyn members of Local 1101 backed the drive because they were disappointed in Carnivale's strike leadership.[80] Carnivale killed the proposal in the local, but the secessionists appealed to the CWA International for support.[81] International vice president Morton Bahr, who had for many years overseen the Northeast's District 1, backed their drive because he believed radical fringe groups controlled the organization because of inept local leadership.[82] Bahr believed that a stable and effective leadership capable of reining in the ranks was nowhere in sight and that "a Brooklyn Local could serve to bring about a desired balance within the New York plant bargaining unit. At present Local 1101 has a real stranglehold."[83] The international ultimately approved the secession, and Brooklyn's exit took away nearly a fifth of Local 1101's members.[84]

Local 1101's defeat was an important public rebuke of militant rank-and-file action. In the words of UA militant Joseph Nabach, "The telephone strike [was] the first major industrial strike in recent memory which has ended in undeniable defeat for the labor movement."[85] More than just a defeat for the labor movement, it was a defeat of rank-and-file workers. After all, Beirne had led a strike, delivered a sizable contract, and obtained an agency shop agreement. While the strike perhaps confirmed Beirne's reputation as fearful of strikes, it also resulted in a major gain for the union's organizational stability. For rebellious workers in the CWA, the story was much different. Seven months of challenges had led to relatively little gains, and the resistance came at great economic cost. All eyes were on New York City for leadership in the 1971 contract battle, and the local went down in flames. Unlike the 1970 postal strike, which was remembered by and large as a victory—in spite of the limitations and problems discussed in the previous chapter—the Local 1101 strike was a disaster for rank-and-file militants.[86]

A Lost Era

The failed telephone strike helps explain workers' changing attitudes in 1970s New York. A malaise had set in relatively early on in the strike as workers found themselves isolated from one another as well as from the rest of the CWA. The end of the strike brought a combination of defeat and relief, with many so disheartened that they were simply ready to get back to work. Though the battle had bound many people together and created some camaraderie in the aftermath, many were no longer interested in fighting. In the strike's aftermath, a new mindset emerged among Local 1101 members in which they gave up on collective struggle and focused primarily on their individual survival.[87] In fact, the following year, when many women began to enter the ranks of Local 1101—as well as a new set of leftist militants who wanted to challenge the gender stratification in the workforce—they described a widespread state of apathy in the union.[88] In 1974, amid national negotiations and nationwide stagflation, New York's militancy was neither a beacon of hope to other rank-and-filers nor a source of significant fear among union leaders.[89] Workers increasingly focused on their own economic survival, and as one CWA militant described it, "The era was lost."[90]

FIVE

Taxi Drivers' Rage

For most of the twentieth century, New York's taxi drivers struggled for increased pay, greater stability, and public dignity, eventually achieving some of those goals and union recognition with the help of Harry Van Arsdale Jr. and the AFL-CIO in the mid-1960s. Shortly after the unionization drive, Van Arsdale would become the focal point of fury over weak contracts, lack of internal democracy, and fare raises that hurt many drivers. Driver anger was volatile and directed at many adversaries, and though union leaders bore much of it, the rising threat of the livery cab industry—often colloquially referred to as gypsies—brought yellow cab drivers into a racially polarized conflict with Mayor John Lindsay and the city's primarily Black and Puerto Rican livery cab drivers. Amid the discord, the Taxi Rank and File Coalition emerged, bringing together long-term anger and the organizing energy of young radicals. Left-wing activists would struggle to situate themselves amid the anger, leading a powerful but short-lived insurgency against the leadership.[1]

In spite of years of anger and frustration with the Taxi Drivers Union (TDU), opposition never coalesced enough to defeat the union leadership, overcome stiff employer resistance, or deal with the livery threat. Union heads went to great lengths to maintain their power, including canceling elections and putting the union into trusteeship at one point, but they also directed driver anger at the livery industry, embroiling yellow cab rank-and-filers in a racially divisive battle. Though anger was widespread, drivers were divided. They fought one another and were increasingly angry at nearly everything and everyone in the city, reflecting the darkening political mood toward the end of John Lindsay's second term.[2]

Rank-and-file discontent within the TDU in the mid-1960s revolved around two specific issues: the conduct of the union bureaucracy and the inadequacy of union gains. When Van Arsdale and the Central Labor Council intervened to organize the taxi drivers, their rhetoric promised great changes, including "Industrial Democracy and a Better Life."[3] Quite early on, however, taxi drivers began to resent the newly formed union. The union bureaucracy excluded many original campaign organizers, and some taxi rank-and-filers considered Van Arsdale, who had never driven a cab, a paternalistic ruler with little faith in the taxi drivers' ability to run their own affairs.[4]

There was certainly some truth to this claim. After staving off some initial electoral challenges in 1966—some of which were pro–Van Arsdale and others anti—the union lengthened the tenure of office for many elected positions, which both ensured steadiness at the top but also stoked resentment from below. In the union's second year, drivers wildcatted in hopes of pressing fleet owners into a better commission, and in order to get the drivers back to work, Van Arsdale called a membership meeting to vote on continuing negotiations. When it came time for the vote, Van Arsdale refused to hold a yay or nay vote, choosing instead to only ask for yays![5]

The anger at the new union's conduct was always intertwined with a disappointment in the speed of contract gains. The union had achieved some early successes, including an increase in driver commissions from 44 to 47 percent, a pension for those who retired after twenty-five years of full-time driving, vacation pay, and some benefits paid by the fleets. But because they were only recently unionized, taxi drivers were far behind many other workers, looking on in envy at unions that had won health insurance, pension plans, a credit union, and even co-op buying programs. While the union sought to prove its worth, the city's wider labor militancy began to influence the taxi drivers. In 1969, an opposition candidate appealed to his fellow hacks: "We have been called public servants, as are the police, the firemen and the sanitationmen (although they are all under Civil Service). Do they have unions where the leaders make the decisions or where the members make the decisions? When they were dissatisfied with their contracts, did the leaders listen to them? You bet they did!"[6] Though the TDU was very new, it faced a restive membership: taxi drivers both wanted what other workers had and felt impelled by their rank-and-file struggles.

While there was widespread anger at the union leadership, drivers never formed a unified opposition, and divisions in the workplace contributed to this disunity. The majority of the city's taxi drivers were fleet drivers, meaning they worked for a fleet owner who supplied and maintained the yellow cabs. Unlike their counterparts in other industries, fleet drivers did not work for wages but rather for a cut of the fares: the more fares they booked, the more money they made.[7] In doling out the work, employers used a shape-up system in which they chose those who booked more over those who booked less, encouraging drivers to try and outproduce one another.[8] In some garages, workers would take to bribing the dispatcher, sometimes placing dollars under their licenses, in hopes of being given a better-condition cab or assigned one quicker than their fellow hacks. Some suspected that the union was aware of such activity and was actively taking its cut of the bribes.[9]

Demand for cabs was up in the postwar era, but the number of cabs had not grown, leaving drivers to fight for assignments. This competition manifested itself on the streets, with drivers cruising the same busy thoroughfares in search of customers, often racing with one another to win a fare. To make ends meet, some drivers would negotiate a decreased price with a customer without turning on the meter, thus cutting out the fleet owners. One driver remembered trying to not "throw the flag" as often as possible, at least once per shift, with customers often initiating the negotiation.[10] This was a widespread practice with some degree of tolerance among the owners, though by the late 1960s, owners installed sensors, or hot seats, to automatically turn on the meter when a customer sat down.[11]

While they sometimes used disciplinary techniques to achieve driver obedience, fleet owners also used more dubious methods, with older rank-and-filers alleging the widespread use of bribery to ensure loyalty and division in the workplace.[12] The constant competitiveness led to some skepticism about collective action, and though many older drivers who had lived through one or more unionization drives had their gripes with the new leadership, internal divisions and a predilection for individual survival practices kept many divided.[13] Though the nature of the industry encouraged competition, there was certainly a sense of commonality among drivers, with many older drivers congregating at places like Belmore Cafeteria, famously depicted in the film *Taxi Driver*, and Katz's Delicatessen. There they took a break from the job, grabbing a cheap dinner and coffee, swapping stories, exchanging tips and complaints, and finding much needed relief in the cafeterias' bathrooms.[14] When the Belmore closed in 1981, a driver called it "an oasis in the jungle," while in typical fashion other cabbies complained about everything from the coffee quality, lack of free seltzer water, and overpriced Danishes.[15]

Another source of division among the ranks of taxi drivers was the fact that nearly 5,000 drivers owned their own cabs. Like the fleet owners, these owner-drivers held a medallion, the license to cruise and pick up passengers for a fare. Medallions were becoming increasingly expensive in the 1950s and 1960s. In fact, the average owner-driver medallion cost nearly $25,000, and new owner-drivers had to take out large loans to pay for them. While they incurred their own costs, owner-drivers worked for themselves and kept the entirety of each fare. This distinction also brought owner-drivers' interests in line with fleet owners' in that fare hikes benefited them, outside competition threatened them, and regulation from the city was unwelcome.[16]

In the aftermath of unionization, fleet owners brought in thousands of part-time drivers and lowered the minimum driver age to eighteen. These part-time drivers drove for supplementary incomes, temporary stints between other work, and summer employment. The influx of part-timers swelled the ranks with drivers who were committed to improving neither the industry nor the rank-and-file condition.[17] Large numbers of countercultural youth flocked to the industry for this purpose, and as one longtime driver remembered it, "All they wanted to do was make money and get high."[18] The major exception to this trend was the many young radicals who would form the core of the union's opposition, the Taxi Rank and File Coalition.[19]

The relationship between younger and older drivers was often strained. Just like in the telephone industry, shifting attitudes toward hairstyles, drug use, and clothing caused a cultural divide between the older drivers who "chewed cigars" and the students, hippies, and aspiring actors who had recently joined their ranks.[20] Some drivers resented the increased competition for fares, and others felt a degree of superiority to those who had yet to prove themselves and learn the tricks of the trade. According to one driver who started in the late 1960s, the older drivers were not particularly helpful, and their ethos was "We're not passing our knowledge around; you've got to learn that yourself, motherfucker."[21]

By the end of the 1960s, crime and violence was a growing concern for all taxi drivers, and five drivers were murdered in 1969. Crime had long been a problem for cabbies because they carried cash and picked up strangers at all hours of the day, but violent crime was growing and cabbies were increasingly targets. During the 1965 unionization drive, two drivers, one white and one Black, were murdered in Brownsville and Bedford-Stuyvesant, and in the first three years of the union's existence, eight cabbies were murdered.[22] Murders and crime against taxi drivers grew significantly in the final five months of 1969, with four cabbie murders and 660 robberies. The robberies themselves were often quite violent, with drivers recounting knives put to their throats, punches to the face, and threats. When 1970 began, two more drivers were murdered, and there were 3,000 robberies in the first six months of the year.[23]

Rank-and-file taxi drivers complained about the increasing prevalence of crime, and they connected it to the demographic and spatial transformation of the city. By 1970, New York's Black population had grown to more than 1.6 million people—roughly 20 percent of the city's population—expanding from the older ghettoes of Harlem and Bedford-Stuyvesant to adjacent areas.[24] Attempts to stave off white outmigration, either through liberal planning efforts or violent neighborhood defense, were mostly unsuccessful, and as most whites left neighborhoods like Brownsville, East New York, Bushwick, and the South Bronx, larger and larger portions of the city became almost exclusively Black or Latino.[25]

White drivers openly discussed their refusal to pick up Black fares. Racist white drivers used slurs and racial stereotypes to describe Black fares, but others who began skipping over Black fares had a more nuanced position.[26] Some made quick decisions about the physical appearance and dress of the customer or simply their "vibe."[27] For some, tennis shoes were a tip-off that the rider might try to run away or rob them. Age, too, was a significant factor, and many new drivers learned quickly not to pick up young people. Drivers were often wary of particular neighborhoods and refused to service potential patrons on that basis. But race, too, played a role but sometimes not based on stereotypes. In the words of one younger driver who was robbed more than ten times in his three-year stint as a cabbie, "More times than not I was robbed by African Americans or Hispanics, but that isn't to say I wasn't robbed by white guys."[28]

Such experiences shaped the behaviors of drivers, regardless of their political leanings. A white veteran driver and longtime Communist Party member who had been involved in antiracist activism argued that after 1968, there was growing racial hostility in the city from both whites and Blacks. After a Black rider robbed him at gunpoint—his second robbery by a Black customer—he began to skip more Black fares. Though he understood what he was doing was discriminatory, he believed himself to be making a life-preserving decision in an increasingly polarized city.[29]

Though Black taxi drivers complained that they often had problems hailing a cab because of driver discrimination, they too admitted to sometimes avoiding Black fares, making their own judgments about who appeared dangerous or likely not to pay.[30] While the issue was wrapped up in driver racism and the refusal to pick up Blacks, as Van Arsdale would argue in the early 1970s, the majority of cab drivers who were murdered were themselves Black and Latino, and most of them were killed in the city's poorer, non-white neighborhoods like Brownsville, Bedford-Stuyvesant, and East New York. Van Arsdale, however, used this as evidence that taxi union men did not discriminate against riders, which was untrue.[31] Many Black customers complained that they had long had difficulties hailing a cab, and increased crime only worsened an ongoing practice among drivers. Another important consequence of discriminating against Black fares was the rise of the livery cab industry.[32]

Livery cabs, often referred to as gypsy cabs, became commonplace in the 1960s in response to the transportation and work needs of the city's Black and Latino populations. Unlike yellow cabs, the law confined liveries to phoned-in pickups, though they often cruised for fares illegally. Their exponential growth confirms their popularity and usefulness, numbering perhaps as high as 10,000 in 1970.[33] Though less archival material is available from livery cab drivers, livery cab fleet owners spoke repeatedly about their aspirations and beliefs, including Calvin Williams, a short-term New York state assemblyman representing Bedford-Stuyvesant and the owner of Black Pearl Car Service. Williams couched his enterprise in the language of Black liberation and empowerment, claiming that he was providing a much-needed service to an underserved community, even deploying the slogan "Black Pearl Means Black Power."[34]

While many major Black Power advocates were anticapitalist and would have been critical of Williams's identification of Black Power with business, there existed broad grassroots support for his position.[35] In the memory of one Black yellow cab driver, many Black people in New York City would wait for a livery cab even if a yellow cab was available, making clear their preference. While there was some difference in price—liveries were often cheaper—many Black people also used livery cabs out of racial solidarity with the institution.[36] With employment discrimination and the unemployment rate much higher than the national average, many Blacks felt that the attack on livery cabs was a racist attack on people trying to earn a living.[37]

In the face of union campaigning, livery cab drivers organized with their employers in the name of serving their community, sometimes using force to protect their turf. There were myriad accounts of attacks on yellow cab drivers—white and Black—and yellow cabs being surrounded by livery cabs and "escorted" out of neighborhoods.[38] Many white drivers thought they were protecting themselves when refusing to pick up Black fares, and as gypsy cabs grew in popularity, they believed themselves under threat from two directions: Black people were not only robbing taxi drivers but also stealing their livelihoods.[39]

The union had publicly opposed livery cabs since the initial unionization drive in 1966, but their growing prevalence, cab driver complaints, and the need to shore up internal support led the TDU leadership to take a stronger stand. During the 1969 union election, the Van Arsdale administration set the terms of the new debate, arguing, "The greatest threat to the owner-drivers and taxi drivers' future is the widespread failure of the Mayor to enforce laws and regulations pertaining to the illegal taxi racket which is victimizing bona-fide men and women in our industry and the citizens."[40] As described above, livery cab service was growing across the city, but equally threatening to the union was its growing acceptance under Mayor Lindsay. Lindsay was sympathetic to the livery cab services as befit his broader political goals, and he wanted to provide a means for them to be regulated by the city.[41]

Lindsay's support of liveries earned him the ire of the primarily white TDU owner-drivers, who would challenge their union leaders to do more to stop the liveries. Owner-drivers were the steadiest portion of the union because they had each invested thousands of dollars in their own medallions; they were not in the industry as a side job, and the size of their investment meant that they would not move on from driving a taxi until they were ready to retire. The basis of their stability for the union—the large cash investment in the right to pick up fares—was also why owner-drivers were so threatened by livery drivers: while livery drivers' illegal cruising "stole" fares from yellow cabs, it also rendered meaningless the medallions owner-drivers had often worked years for.[42] Catering more strongly to owner-drivers and organizing more actively against the livery cab industry provided the union a basis to manage a "union membership [that] stands divided, frustrated, and in deep doubt of what our future will be in this industry," and immediately after winning the 1969 elections, the union set to the task, organizing a major meeting with over 1,000 taxi drivers denouncing the growing phenomenon, with owner-drivers at the forefront.[43]

While the union's focus on the livery cab issue would help build some support within the ranks, especially from owner-drivers, fleet drivers wanted much more than the reining in of competition, and anger simmered all throughout the year. When negotiations opened with the fleet owners in 1970, Van Arsdale promised the many dissatisfied yellow cab drivers that the union would win them benefits and pay that rivaled the Transport Workers Union's.[44] Alongside this vital economic demand were increased pension payments, a medical center, and stronger protection for drivers in the form of bulletproof dividers in cabs.[45] Fleet owners nominally agreed to some of these demands but argued that they ought to be funded by increased fares and not by a cut into the fleets' profits. Van Arsdale was initially opposed, but in spite of many meetings and even state mediation, employers would not agree to any demands without a fare hike. Angry drivers stormed a union meeting in late November calling for a strike.[46]

The tension finally broke in December 1970 when the union led its drivers off the job. The TDU organized pickets across the city but primarily in front of hotels and travel hubs. Picket lines brought drivers into direct and often violent confrontation with the police and with livery drivers looking to make money off of the strike. The city's transit system and livery drivers absorbed much of the impact, and employers held the line.[47] Union leaders began backing the calls for a fare increase, as did many of the owner-drivers.[48] Fleet drivers opposed the increases because they believed they would decrease ridership and tips. The strike dragged on for more than two weeks, and taxi drivers failed to gain parity with transit workers. Knowing that he would never gain approval of the contract, Van Arsdale never put it before a membership vote. The defeat was palpable, and one taxi rank-and-filer would go on to call the whole strike "fruitless."[49]

After the strike, Van Arsdale conceded to fare hikes, a lower commission rate for drivers with less experience, and a dime taken from the driver's percentage of each fare toward the union benefit funds.[50] Perhaps taking a page from the expansion of the apprenticeship program in Local 3, Van Arsdale solidified the division between new and old drivers, with the former receiving a smaller, 42 percent commission on fares and becoming eligible for increases after 200 days of work. In this contract, owners avoided the cost of wage increases by pegging all demands to fare increases and creating a second tier of new part-time drivers, whom they would come to increasingly rely on.[51]

Newer fleet drivers considered the two-tier percentage unfair, but older drivers were more enraged by the dime taken out of each of their fares. Taxi drivers were paying for benefits out of their money, not employers', leading many to believe that Local 3036 was nothing more than a racketeer union making money off its members.[52] As the union and fleet owners came to terms, the Lindsay administration used the city's power to authorize the fare hikes to push through a regulatory shift in the industry, creating the Taxi and Limousine Commission on the back of the failed strike. Established in March 1971, after using dilatory tactics to hold back fare hikes and thus wage gains, the new commission regulated both yellow cabs and livery cabs, giving greater legitimacy to the latter, albeit not the right to cruise.[53] When the city finally granted fare hikes, it led to a weeks-long crash in ridership. By that time, many hacks were fed up with Lindsay, and as one TDU official put it, "The men are disgusted with City Hall. . . . They are disgusted with the City Council and the Mayor."[54]

On April 14, thousands of drivers gathered for the union's semiannual membership meeting to discuss the effects of the fares and renewed negotiations with the Metropolitan Taxicab Board of Trade. Drivers flooded the hall, pushing past union security that tried to check their dues-payment status. Boos and whistles filled the auditorium as Van Arsdale tried to explain the need for compromise on the fare hikes. Suddenly, a young driver jumped onstage and grabbed the microphone and the meeting's attention, but the union leadership quickly cut power.[55] Workers stormed the stage, union delegates threw their presentation table down into the crowd, and taxi drivers began throwing chairs at Van Arsdale as he and the rest of the leadership escaped out a side door of the Manhattan Center. Workers took over the meeting hall, and only the police put an end to the chaos.[56] While the union called the attack a product of subversive elements bent on destroying the union, it was a spontaneous boiling over of anger about fare hikes, the dime, and the city government.[57]

The day following the attack on the union leadership, sixty fleet drivers met to discuss the need for a rank-and-file organization to fight within the union, founding the Taxi Rank and File Coalition. Some were energized by the previous day's events, some were informally organized groups of politicized young people, and others were older workers who had sought to unseat Van Arsdale's leadership in 1969. During their first meeting, drivers decided on three key avenues of activity. The first was bringing together more drivers out of the some 30,000 represented by the union. Their second major task was launching a petition drive among taxi drivers around the losing contract of 1970. Among its demands was equity in fare shares for all drivers regardless of their hire date, benefits for full- and part-time drivers, a decrease in the fare, and benefits paid for by owners and not from the drivers' fares. Their third task was starting their own publication, *Hot Seat*, which took its name from the sensor in the back seat that activated the fare meter.[58] The publication's first issue, which was distributed by hand at various garages across the city, denounced the union-negotiated contract, laid out the group's purpose and composition, and encouraged members to sign their petition.[59] After gathering 6,000 signatures in a matter of weeks, the coalition took things a step further, organizing a protest against the union itself, in which 300 taxi drivers participated. As its influence grew, the coalition immediately began pursuing a takeover of the union through electoral channels.[60]

Elections in the taxi union took place in individual garages where taxi drivers worked and within the union's leadership structure, and in the summer of 1971, the coalition planned to move on both fronts. Due to union regulations stipulating that one had to have more than two years of continuous service in the industry before holding office, many of the rank-and-file organization's members found themselves ineligible, signaling the degree to which their ranks were made up of young drivers. Meanwhile, some of the older, more politically active workers fought among themselves, refusing to accept any position other than president, leaving the coalition without a full slate of candidates.[61]

In spite of these internal problems, the group's agitation was beginning to yield results, as some of Van Arsdale's former supporters began to oppose parts of the contract, jumping ship to form the Watchdog Committee, which parroted the style and claims of the coalition. The coalition allied with the Watchdog Committee, and the two endorsed each other's candidates at the garage level. In the September 1971 garage elections, a handful of Taxi Rank and File Coalition members were elected, as were a handful of nonaligned anti–Van Arsdale advocates.[62]

Hoping to capitalize on these gains, the coalition mounted an unsuccessful challenge for union control in the November leadership elections. By election time, the Watchdog Committee abandoned its partnership with the Rank and File Coalition, publicly making their peace with Van Arsdale.[63] While the coalition's candidate Leo Lazarus made a good showing by winning 3,073 votes, Van Arsdale remained in power, winning 5,207. With their hopes for an early victory dashed, coalition members began the difficult project of long-term organizing in what was becoming an increasingly divided union and city.[64]

With the Taxi and Limousine Commission now regulating the industry, livery cab legalization was becoming an ever more pressing issue for the taxi rank and file. During the 1971 electoral challenges, the union published many articles on livery cab drivers, arguing that they were at once a criminal enterprise and a regression to segregated locals of the Jim Crow South. As the union rightfully argued, livery drivers had no benefits and made less money on average than their yellow cab counterparts. What the union did not discuss was that in spite of the industry's low wages, it provided gainful employment to thousands of Blacks and Latinos.[65]

The city council began discussions to license livery drivers for work in Manhattan in late January 1972, with Mayor Lindsay arguing that the industry already existed and that bringing it under greater government regulation would only improve it. The union and fleet owners countered that regulation was but a step toward allowing livery cabs to cruise for fares and that the livery cab industry only flourished because of Lindsay's unwillingness to enforce the law.[66] Dozens of the city's Black and Puerto Rican livery drivers rallied outside city hearings, shutting down traffic, and the union mobilized owner-drivers for the hearings while the drivers organized pickets against the livery industry.[67] The Taxi Rank and File Coalition stood with angry cab drivers against the regularization of the livery cab industry, though many of them considered it to be scapegoating by the union and racism on the part of many drivers.[68]

On the last day of January, another licensing hearing brought out owners and union heads, with Van Arsdale making a defiant speech and threatening a citywide strike.[69] Though this was an idle threat, he was still the city's most powerful labor leader and held sway through important political connections to the Democratic and Republican Parties in the city. During the hearing, the union made sure to mobilize and forefront Black owner-drivers. The combined effort of the union and the fleet owners staved off livery cab legalization in Manhattan, and though drivers backed the union's antilivery position, it did little to quell discontent within the ranks of fleet drivers.[70]

With the threat of livery drivers' legalization minimized, the union had to once again face its many internal problems, not having the power to either impose better terms with employers or gain the consent of its membership. In mid-February 1972, the union organized a series of spontaneous strikes against the 42 percent shares that it had negotiated for newer drivers.[71] On a Friday afternoon, several dozen drivers at two garages, one in Manhattan and one in the Bronx, walked off the job, forming picket lines, shutting down operations, and paralyzing hundreds of taxis.[72] The strikes continued for four days with the union publicly denying its involvement, and on the fifth day two more garages were hit by strikes as well. Since the taxi drivers had never approved the contract, Van Arsdale hoped the pressure would bring the fleet owners back to the table for a renegotiation of commissions for newer drivers. As one driver put it, "Van Arsdale can't admit he's wrong so he handles it this way. They pretend to be trying to stop the strike but they're hoping it will spread."[73]

The plan backfired miserably. Owner-drivers refused to honor the picket lines—their income was not determined by commission percentages—and many older drivers crossed the lines as well since they were already working at the top rate. At one garage, older drivers voted down a strike move by younger drivers. When the union tried this selective strike strategy again the following month, to no one's surprise the move was equally ineffective.[74]

When the April 1972 membership meeting approached, taxi drivers and union leaders expected conflict. The union hoped to use the meeting as a venue to build support for upcoming negotiations and to double down on the improvements made since the union began in 1966. Opposite them was the Taxi Rank and File Coalition, which hoped to use the event as a stage for undermining the leadership and building support for future electoral efforts.[75] As the meeting began and the agenda was announced, members of the Rank and File Coalition called for a vote on restructuring the meeting to discuss the lack of a contract and the issue of smaller driver percentages in the aftermath of the disastrous 1970 strike. Roars of approval filled the Manhattan Center, forcing the union to consider the proposal with a hand vote. But when the leadership said the count indicated that the coalition's motion had failed, all hell broke loose in the meeting, with shouting, chair throwing, and fistfighting between taxi drivers and union stewards and among taxi drivers. For the second year in a row, the meeting completely devolved, and Van Arsdale and the union leadership fled the room, summoning the police to restore order.[76]

The union blamed the brawl on a small group of agitators. While they were in some ways correct that there were agitators within the union, the anger was more widespread than the union was willing to publicly admit. The union even went so far as to say that the membership-meeting melee did a disservice to the union by showing that there was disunity in the ranks, when according to the union, there was in fact none at all![77] Despite these propagandistic claims of unity, the taxi drivers were increasingly divided and like New York City in miniature: drivers were fighting their elected leaders, the young fought the old, full-timers fought part-timers, and the primarily white owner-drivers fought the primarily Black and Latino livery and gypsy cab drivers. Growing anger had catalyzed rank-and-file rebellion but the anger had difficulty coalescing.[78]

With TDU leadership gearing up for another round of talks and shoring up its position, it brought the increasingly rancorous debate around livery cab drivers to the forefront once again. In mid-June 1972, the union called an owner-driver meeting, with AFL-CIO regional director Michael Mann as keynote speaker. While there were some Black TDU members present at the meeting of over 3,000 owner-drivers, Mann denounced the liveries and Mayor Lindsay, who he claimed was prioritizing welfare recipients and criminal livery drivers over the honest, hardworking owner-drivers of Local 3036.[79] Though the union would always supplement its anti-gypsy rhetoric with claims of racial equality, such imagery was common in its denunciations.[80]

To differentiate liveries from taxis, the Taxi and Limousine Commission called for an end to the livery drivers' usage of meters, setting an October 1 deadline for police enforcement. In mid-September, livery companies and their drivers responded by organizing protests that blocked intersections and caused massive traffic jams across the Bronx. When the police arrived, a riot ensued involving a crowd of over 500 people in a Puerto Rican area of the South Bronx. Protesters attacked several yellow cabs and the police, preventing them from making arrests. The situation took a deadly turn when police chased a man to the roof of a five-story building, where, according to witnesses, they threw him to his death. In spite of the arrests and one death, the violence subsided for a short time, picking up again on the October 1 deadline with more traffic blockades and groups of people attacking yellow cabs in the Bronx.[81]

As with many Black riders who supported the likes of Black Pearl and its claims of Black community service, many Puerto Ricans strongly supported the livery cab industry as providers of much needed jobs and transportation. Some Puerto Rican livery cab drivers preferred the flexibility and self-managed nature of the work to the supervision and regimentation of factory work, and in a parallel to Calvin Williams, José Rivera, a prominent advocate for gypsy cab drivers, would use the struggle as a springboard to political power in the early 1980s.[82] While there was widespread community support, the violence only confirmed the beliefs of the industry and union officials, with the taxi industry denouncing the police and the city for lax enforcement during the protests, claiming that their workers and cars "once again . . . have been exposed to the terror, violence, and destructive tactics of thugs."[83]

Internal divisions in the Taxi Rank and File Coalition over the anti–gypsy cab fight give us some insight into the difficulty of addressing the issue. To some members, it seemed clear that the union used the anti-gypsy campaign to divert anger from itself. The union leadership was failing to deliver in contract negotiations and they could shore up their own support by blaming wage and work issues on liveries. Racial invective was evident in the union's rhetoric, and some coalition members felt that racism played a primary role in the average driver's anti-gypsy sentiment, which prevented yellow cab drivers from understanding that gypsy drivers were also struggling for their rights and safety, with livery cab drivers also subject to robberies and murders.[84]

Other members took issue with statements like these, arguing that the coalition underplayed the very real threat to drivers' livelihoods that the gypsies posed. After all, with the fare hikes, livery cabs had a competitive advantage, and they illegally cruised for fares. Coalition members skeptical of the livery cab struggle also argued that gypsy owners were heavily involved in coordinating the protests and stood to gain much more than the average driver; thus it was not strictly a workers' struggle against the bosses or bureaucrats. In retrospect, some coalition members felt that the *Hot Seat* underplayed the real physical dangers that crime posed for taxi drivers, which they argued came mostly from Black fares. While some members looked back, arguing that they should have tried to organize with livery cab drivers to form their own driver-led groups, others remained uncertain whether it was ever in their power to get out in front of the issue at all. The internal debate was difficult, presupposing that there was a viable rank-and-file solution to the problem, and for some members, the coalition's inability to confront this problem effectively became emblematic of the group's broader racial problems: while more Black drivers became involved in the taxi industry and joined the ranks of Local 3036, the Taxi Rank and File Coalition in no way reflected this growing demographic.[85]

By the beginning of 1973 the coalition was made up of highly politicized—mostly young—members who had been active in civil rights and antiwar struggles in the 1960s. Though the coalition was able to work in the presence of broader driver anger at the 1972 membership meeting, when they called for a picket later that year, only two dozen drivers were involved, the majority of whom were young.[86] A year earlier, a similar rally drew some 300 drivers, and the coalition was consolidating around an activist core made up of leftwing activists with experience in the broader political upheaval of the era. With the exception of a handful of older drivers, who came out of the Old Left, the Taxi Rank and File Coalition's members were young socialists who were more hopeful than many of their fellow drivers.[87]

Though the coalition was able to muster only a small number of people for demonstrations, the Local 3036 leadership still believed that the Rank and File Coalition posed a potential electoral threat. In the fall of 1972, Van Arsdale shut down elections at the garage level under the premise that the union did not have enough money. Rumors circulated that the taxi union could even be placed in trusteeship.[88] There was some truth to the union's financial woes, as many angry members had begun refusing to pay dues. While there was some uproar over the lack of elections at the union's October membership meeting, alongside some calls for strike and booing of Van Arsdale, the response was subdued compared to earlier meetings. The meeting was rather poorly attended, with only 800 drivers taking part.[89] While some coalition members felt that winning elections could potentially put them in a compromised position, without elections to contest, the Rank and File Coalition was ultimately confined to an agitational group.[90]

In the last days of December 1972 and after two years without a contract agreement, the TDU leadership and taxi fleet owners agreed to binding arbitration. While sources do not indicate what brought on the arbitration agreement, in early 1973 the state mediation board's Vincent McDonnell increased the 42 percent fare share for new drivers to 43 percent, but he did not significantly alter the time it would take to get to the top percentage of 49, effectively providing a middle-ground decision that would please both union leadership and fleet owners.[91] Van Arsdale never brought the contract to a vote in the TDU, and the coalition challenged the union in a multiyear legal battle that would eventually force the TDU to put the contract to a vote, albeit two years later.[92]

The coalition also continued to fight to get garage elections reopened, when in September 1973 the union canceled them yet again. In March 1974, the coalition delivered 2,500 signatures for elections.[93] At the end of 1974, the Taxi Rank and File Coalition made a final electoral challenge, but just before that, the TDU leadership put the union into trusteeship in case of an upset. This safeguard was ultimately unnecessary, as the coalition won only 1,400 votes out of some 7,500, a significant decline from 1971. The election only made official what was already a fact: rank-and-file rebellion within the ranks of the taxi union was ending.[94]

Members of the Taxi Rank and File Coalition maintained some influence at a handful of garages until the organization belatedly folded in 1977. Their largest base was in the Dover garage in Greenwich Village, which employed many young white workers, many of them as bohemian or left leaning as the Taxi Rank and File Coalition. At Dover, coalition members were able to dispute daily concerns of drivers and even led a short-lived wildcat in 1974. But the story was mostly the same: the coalition was a small activist core that had a hard time building any lasting power with the other workers.[95]

In self-criticism sessions, coalition members wanted to understand why so few Black workers had joined the coalition. Some blamed their own failure to adequately address the gypsy issue, yellow cab driver racism, and "white skin privilege."[96] One member of the Taxi Rank and File Coalition believed that "the contradiction between white and third-world people in the industry was the primary contradiction."[97] Some coalition members argued that the livery threat to drivers' economic livelihood pushed Black drivers to support the union's anti-gypsy campaign, and some related their experiences in primarily Black garages where leading Black workers were involved in the union.[98] In fact, the union's main publication, *Taxi Drivers Voice*, continually emphasized the multiracial composition of the union in both the semiregular feature "Keeping the Cab Rolling"—which included photographs and interviews with its many Black and Latino members who worked in garages servicing and repairing the city's taxis—and in driver interviews, which featured statements and photographs of often very diverse groups of drivers.[99] While Black drivers did not flood the ranks of the TDU, neither did many whites after the first years of tumult, with the organization shrinking to its left-wing activist core.[100] As recounted by some cab drivers who were never involved in rank-and-file activism but who did participate in union-led strikes, young people without families who were planning to move into other careers or who were attending college felt that the money was good enough for their short-term needs. Fighting the union, which they believed was a racket, was not worth their time, yet some members of the coalition rejected such simple answers in favor of complicated theoretical lessons on the nature of race and class in the United States.[101]

The internal divisions and multisided battles with fleet owners' liveries and union leadership made the taxi union a portrait in miniature of a fracturing city and declining hope. While the livery battle was not strictly white versus Black, on the stage of city politics and in union meetings it was deeply racialized, and taxi drivers' antilivery fight pitted them against Mayor Lindsay, Black civil rights organizations and businesses, and portions of the city's Black and Latino communities.[102] Drivers also fought with one another, competing as always for fares and assignments, and worse than that, union-led strikes saw drivers crossing the picket lines and a rank-and-file opposition never coalesced. In the estimation of one Taxi Rank and File Coalition member, some drivers had begun to despise their jobs, feeling that the work, in spite of some union gains, had become "lousy."[103] While the anger was palpable, many were increasingly cynical about the union, with some vocal opponents not bothering to attend meetings to challenge it. After years of agitation, a close election, and boisterous meetings, taxi rank-and-file efforts had made relatively little headway, with a rank-and-file activist claiming in the late 1970s, "I don't think that taxi drivers believe that any form of common effort will result in anything . . . and justifiably so."[104]

Darker Horizons

As Joshua Freeman argues in his seminal *Working-Class New York*, "At the end of 1973, a darker, defensive, parochial mood pervaded the city and its working class."[105] While he largely focuses on political polarization and economic decline, rank-and-file defeats were a critical part of this social transformation. While the development, articulation, and course of their militancy was different, taxi drivers along with so many other workers in New York were largely defeated. Some challenges had proven effective, but employer recalcitrance in the face of greater demands and union attacks on militant workers proved too powerful.

The 1970s are often portrayed as the "Me Decade" of selfishness, self-fulfillment, and retreat.[106] The story of rank-and-filers in New York suggests an alternative understanding of this inward turn. Rather than a crass individualism, the focus on the self was more about keeping one's head above water. By 1973, the aggressive confidence of the latter of the half of the 1960s was gone; in its place were defeat, frustration, and a turn away from rank-and-file mobilization. In deeply class-conscious city in which militancy provoked further militancy, such dramatic public defeats contributed to a general state shift, fostering new working-class norms in the city.

SIX

Rank-and-File Resistance to Fiscal Austerity

In 1975, New York City stood at the precipice of fiscal default. After years of growing expenditures, increasing short-term borrowing, and snowballing debt servicing, financial institutions refused to purchase any more city bonds, demanding that the city government and its labor supporters dismantle the municipality's social democratic infrastructures. Months of back-and-forth negotiations saw bitter denunciations of overpaid union members, lazy welfare recipients, and greedy bankers. Unions and community groups organized large demonstrations, and major strikes broke out as the city's "normally opaque class relations became shockingly visible."[1] Threats of a city default increasingly frightened politicians and business elites, and the fiscal crisis became the subject of national and even international attention. Though strikes were on the decline and many rank-and-file struggles had petered out, because of the fiscal crisis many public-sector union members found themselves in conflict with labor leaders, politicians, and business elites.

While traditional narratives, including Kim Phillips-Fein's much lauded work, focus primarily on politicians such as Mayor Abraham Beame and union leaders such as Victor Gotbaum of District Council (DC) 37 or Albert Shanker of the United Federation of Teachers (UFT), rank-and-file workers were a far more significant font of resistance to the business elite's political agenda. In the Social Service Employees Union (SSEU) Local 371, a member of DC 37, social workers—white and Black, male and female—advocated a general strike of public employees to oppose fiscal austerity measures and routinely denounced the fiscal crisis as an attack by the city's big banks. In the Uniformed Sanitationmen's Association (USA), whose ranks had forced a strike in 1968, workers led the way in early summer with work slowdowns, sabotage, and a multiday wildcat strike. Laid-off roadway workers led a shorter-lived wildcat, and fired police officers sparked violent confrontations at city hall. The city's teachers took up the campaign in the summer and fall, organizing opposition groups, rejecting Shanker's contract recommendation, and forcing a strike that was only put down by electoral subterfuge. Repeatedly workers championed militant action while their leaders negotiated givebacks. Their resistance failed, however, and by the end of 1975, New York's social democratic polity was seriously undermined.[2]

Rank-and-file opposition lends credence to the left historiography of New York City's 1975 fiscal crisis, as workers themselves challenged the conservative narrative of overinflated budgets, welfare scammers, and overpaid municipal employees; they repeatedly advocated exposing the economic interests of the city's business elite and the degree to which the 1975 fiscal crisis was a politically contestable event. The fiscal crisis rebellions also demonstrate the ongoing gap between union members and their leaders in the mid-1970s. Though insurgent workers in the city were mostly defeated, they still advocated a more militant stance than their leaders, and as early as the spring of 1975, Gotbaum told his fellow DC 37 executive board members that his initial willingness to accede to layoffs and benefit payment deferrals had only whet the financial elite's appetite. Like many other rank-and-file insurgencies, though, these worker-led efforts to fight fiscal austerity failed, exhibiting some of the same problems as earlier rebellions. Social workers hoped that meetings and resolutions would transform their union into a vehicle for struggle, but the layers of bureaucracy within their own union and DC 37 defeated their efforts. Meanwhile other workers engaged in powerful strikes, but these efforts were short-lived, relying on union leaders to negotiate in an increasingly difficult situation.

Fiscal Crisis

By the spring of 1974, the upper echelons of the labor movement and city hall began discussing the budgetary shortfalls New York would experience in the 1975 fiscal year.[3] The city had accumulated billions in debt over the prior decade, both from financing the city's day-to-day operations, including its growing municipal workforce and generous social democratic institutions, and financing its massive capital projects budget, which had helped to reshape parts of the city into a white-collar financial hub.[4] Meanwhile, deindustrialization, job loss, and white outmigration had damaged the city's tax base, as had years of tax incentives to the real estate industry. As city comptroller during John Lindsay's mayoralty, Abraham Beame had known about the budget crisis for quite some time. In order to make ends meet, the city increasingly relied on short-term notes, and as a result was allocating an ever-growing portion of its budget to debt servicing.[5]

In initial discussions, the mayor suggested that the solution was increased taxes, layoffs, and service cuts, but labor leaders like Harry Van Arsdale Jr. wanted to maintain the city's free higher educational system and low subway fare. Municipal labor unions opposed layoffs and wanted to avoid the friction with their membership. In following months, the heads of the AFL-CIO would discuss the crisis's effects at length, and in particular the possibility of fare hikes on public transit, but their understanding of the city's fiscal problems was so bound up in the broader economic downturn that they could not see the budgetary crisis as a contestable issue. Van Arsdale and others believed that tough economic times necessitated cutbacks, and labor was one player among many who had to do its part. The city's business elites, however, did not view it that way.[6]

New York's elites had decried increased city spending well before 1975. During Mayor Robert Wagner's third term, the city sought to cover a $250 million budget gap with future real estate taxes. Business elites in the Real Estate Board of New York and Morgan Guaranty Trust cried foul, and bond raters wanted the city to abandon its low transit fare and to cut back other social spending.[7] In 1971, then mayor Lindsay and city comptroller Beame publicly attacked Standard and Poor's and Moody's for their refusal to increase the city's bond ratings because of negative publicity around crime, strikes, and deteriorating public services. Low bond ratings forced the city to guarantee interest rates of roughly 7 percent on nearly $400 million in tax-free bonds.[8]

Before making their 1975 demands, major financial lenders silently offloaded their New York City municipal bonds from the summer of 1974 through the spring of 1975, divesting themselves of the possibility of major losses. With billions in short-term debts due and the city looking to borrow in order to pay back its creditors and maintain daily operations, the city's business elite was poised to advocate for a new order, reflecting the increasing organization and assertiveness of business elites nationwide.[9]

While initial discussions suggested an understanding of the problem as one of simple economics, the budget problems became increasingly politicized from late 1974 through 1975 as the city's business elite used short-term debt obligations as political leverage against social democratic New York.[10] In January 1975, David Rockefeller of Chase Manhattan, William T. Spence of First National City Bank, and Ellmore Patterson of JP Morgan formed the Financial Community Liaison Group. The organization developed a broader strategy for demanding wage freezes, implementing service cuts, and creating a state agency to issue long-term debts and purchase short-term debts. Significantly, almost all of their demands would ultimately be implemented by the end of the year.[11]

Attacks on municipal services and workers appalled union leaders like Gotbaum, but from the outset they were prepared to negotiate away past gains in order to survive. Angered by rhetoric from the financial community and from the city's newspapers, DC 37 paid to take out its own column in the *Daily News*, attacking fiscal austerity plans, the financial elite, and the media.[12] In February 1975, DC 37 printed thousands of copies of "The Big Bank Holdup," a pamphlet that denounced the banks for putting undue pressure on the city, but which ultimately asked the banks and other major corporations to shoulder their fair share of cutbacks.[13] Mayor Beame came around to this position as well, and in public hearings in June 1975, in addition to denouncing the debilitating effects of the recession and inflation, he called out the "conservative elements within the financial community that took advantage . . . to dictate the social and economic policies of our City government."[14] Alongside labor, community groups across the city also mobilized en masse to protest cuts.[15]

While Gotbaum would employ confrontational rhetoric in fiscal crisis negotiations, his main goals were avoiding a strike and preserving collective bargaining.[16] Gotbaum was such a prominent figure in negotiations because he not only spoke for DC 37's more than 100,000 members but also spoke on behalf of many other municipal unions as the head of the Municipal Labor Committee (MLC), a joint organization of city unions including those of the firefighters, police, nurses, and several others.[17] As Joshua Freeman has argued, over the course of the negotiations Gotbaum would become not only more conciliatory but also "entranced by the power elite," whom he began to regard as his friends.[18] In later interviews, he would tout his influence with the very same people who forced his union into thousands of layoffs and the investment of pension funds into city bonds. He would begin to see himself as a partner to the business elite, in a time when the business elite's power, especially that of financiers, was growing at the expense of the very labor organizations Gotbaum oversaw.[19]

In May 1975, events forced Gotbaum, the MLC, and other municipal unions into public contestation. The city was facing another budgetary shortfall. The situation was compounded in early April when Standard and Poor's cut the city's credit rating yet again, though its competitor Moody's kept rates level. With banks withholding money, Beame looked to the state and federal government for aid, and neither was forthcoming.[20] The situation devolved quickly, and in May 1975 Mayor Beame announced an austerity budget that required cutting 67,000 jobs from municipal payrolls, alongside pay and hiring freezes.[21] From the outset, organized labor, both in the public and private sector, may have accepted layoffs as inevitable, but the catastrophic nature of the forthcoming 1975–76 fiscal year budget was unanticipated. Business elites were increasing pressure on the city to lay off workers, and in order for organized labor to maintain collective bargaining, it would have to openly fight them.[22] But when unions finally decided to fight back, the response was uneven and uninspiring. While union leaders were quick to negotiate but late to fight, some rank-and-file workers organized and resisted the fiscal crisis agenda, proposing alternative explanations for the city's fiscal crisis and formulating alternative demands to austerity.

Meeting Resistance in SSEU Local 371

Internal debate within SSEU Local 371, a member of DC 37, gives us important insight into how some rank-and-filers attempted to use their union as a platform to resist fiscal austerity, but it also shows us how union leaders controlled that resistance. From the fall of 1974 through the end of 1975, members and delegates repeatedly forced the union's leadership to not only oppose fiscal austerity but also demand militant action within the framework of DC 37's executive council and delegates' assembly.[23] In fact, Patrick Knight, president of SSEU Local 371, was the leading voice for militant action within DC 37's executive council because of his members' resolutions. The social workers' opposition to fiscal austerity also shows us the limitations of their union representatives and their own organizational weakness. While members repeatedly supported calls for opposing layoffs and organizing a citywide strike of public employees, they never moved to militant action; their efforts remained confined to working within their union and DC 37 parliamentary mechanisms, which were thoroughly bureaucratized. In spite of militant resolutions, their calls for confrontation with the "businessmen's coup" went completely unheeded.[24]

Unionized social work in New York City has a long and contentious history. While left-wing social work organizations emerged in the 1930s, the Red Scare saw the destruction of the communist-led United Public Workers. In its place, the American Federation of State, County, and Municipal Employees Local 371, a member of DC 37, emerged as the main organization for Department of Welfare workers. Local 371 was noted for its leadership's focus on legislative and political matters, often at the expense of its members' on-the-job needs, and in the late 1950s rank-and-file activists started a new organization, the SSEU, to challenge Local 371's supremacy. The SSEU was in part a revival of the older left-wing United Public Workers, but the union also attracted a growing number of socially committed young people.[25]

Unlike the Old Left's industrial unions, SSEU organized around the increasingly professionalized identity of caseworkers in the Department of Welfare (later the Department of Social Services), leaving out clerical staff and campaigning against the introduction of lower-paid case aids. In spite of the narrowing of the types of members it represented, the SSEU was known for high member participation, strong internal democracy, and powerful advocacy for welfare clients. But after failed strikes in 1967, internal factionalism, DC 37's increasing influence with Mayor John Lindsay, and a restructuring of city labor negotiations under the auspices of the Office of Collective Bargaining, the SSEU voted to merge with Local 371. The tradition of advocacy remained alive, as did that of membership participation, two factors that would inform resistance to the fiscal crisis.[26]

Social work was much more integrated than many other industries, and by 1960 social work in New York City was 11 percent Black. Amid ongoing demographic changes in the city, by the mid-1970s Local 371 was one-quarter Black.[27] Importantly, social work was a primarily female profession, and though more men began to enter social work in the 1960s, by the mid-1970s, the majority of SSEU Local 371's 11,500 members were still women. As in other unions, a growing number of young people entered the SSEU's ranks.

Many were committed liberals and leftists who saw their profession as a means to make a difference by alleviating social inequality.[28]

While the union was both racially and sexually integrated, these relations were sometimes contentious, with Black members organizing for better representation within the ranks of leadership. In 1970, a multiracial opposition slate was elected with the union's first Black, albeit male, president, Stanley Hill.[29] Women, who made up the bulk of social workers in New York City, also organized for their own representation, and many had opposed merging with Local 371 because older men dominated it. While by 1975 there was no coherent rank-and-file movement in SSEU Local 371, social workers were by and large a politicized group whose experiences, identities, and past political activism would help them in their opposition to the fiscal crisis.[30]

With the initial discussions of the budgetary gaps, municipal workers across the city were frightened, but SSEU Local 371 members initiated a quick response because of the already heightened political nature of their work. After all, the fiscal austerity was a multipronged attack on SSEU Local 371. First it sought to attack social workers as overpaid public employees, though in fact New York City municipal employees' rising wages were similar to other large cities'.[31] Second, it attacked the services they provided and the mission of social relief to which they dedicated their lives. Third, the fiscal crisis rhetoric attacked the clients to whom social workers increasingly provided those services.[32] Welfare rolls had become increasingly Black and Latino in the postwar era, and the numbers on welfare had increase dramatically both as a result of increasing activism through the National Welfare Rights Organization and growing economic stagnation in the 1970s. Because of this, the welfare budget expanded rapidly, with $1 billion being spent each year by the beginning of the decade.[33] For Black and Latino social workers in particular, these racist attacks on welfare recipients would certainly hit close to home, especially for those who embraced racial nationalism.[34]

Social workers, including the union leadership, believed that layoffs and service cuts would only worsen a stagnating economic situation that average workers could not be blamed for. Many rank-and-file social workers, in the estimation of one insurgent candidate, also believed that the fiscal crisis was not inevitable and that banks would not in fact allow the city to default given the massive economic chaos that would ensue.[35]

With initial announcements of layoffs and budget problems in late 1974, both union leaders and rank-and-file delegates from various work sites opposed budget cuts and firings, but they generally disagreed on the appropriate course of action to take. While some of his advisers had recommended more than 16,000 layoffs to balance the books, in November 1974 Mayor Beame announced the imminent layoff of nearly 1,600 city employees.³⁶ In Local 371, members of the executive committee opposed layoffs and discussed a strike possibility, but in the delegates' assembly, rank-and-file members took a firm stand against the layoffs after the city gave nearly 150 SSEU members pink slips. Delegates resolved that their union was against all layoffs, mandating that their union president, who was a member of the DC 37 executive board, call for an emergency meeting of DC 37 delegates to discuss the possibility of a public employee general strike in the event of layoffs.³⁷ President Knight, as directed by the rank-and-file delegates, motioned at the DC 37 delegates' meeting for an emergency discussion of a citywide strike in the event of layoffs. While his motion was seconded and some discussion followed, delegates from the Queens Library Guild and Local 420 of municipal hospital employees motioned to table the discussion, and a vote put the issue to rest.³⁸

While Local 371 members forced their leader into taking a public stand, Knight told his members that the decisions were increasingly out of his hands as Gotbaum took charge of negotiations not only as head of DC 37 but also as the head of the MLC.³⁹ While wary of fiscal austerity's negative effects, Gotbaum was willing to negotiate cost-cutting measures with Mayor Beame, and in late 1974, he pushed for the use of attrition to help ease budgetary gaps. Several thousand New York City municipal workers retired each year, and Gotbaum hoped that their departure would cut costs enough to prevent layoffs. Gotbaum also argued for the elimination of provisional employees or those who had entered either through appointment or without the civil service exams that DC 37 members underwent. Thus unlike rank-and-file members of Local 371, who took a stand against all layoffs, Gotbaum was willing to sacrifice provisional employees—who were not union members—relatively early in negotiations.⁴⁰

In late January 1975, another Local 371 delegates' assembly revolved around strategy, with Knight putting forward a motion that the union should hold press conferences and issue public statements attacking the crisis measures. He wanted to reframe the budget debates by arguing that unemployment was the city's biggest problem and that layoff plans would only worsen it by adding to the number of people out of work and hindering social workers' ability to serve them.⁴¹ Though this motion was seconded, Michael Padwee, a longtime rank-and-file organizer, put forth an alternative motion, arguing for SSEU Local 371 representatives in DC 37 to once again advocate a citywide public employee general strike in the face of any layoffs.⁴² Furthermore, this countermotion demanded no layoffs of any workers, an increase of taxes on commercial real estate and corporate profits, rent and price freezes, and the examination of the city budget by consumer advocate Ralph Nader.[43]

The motion triggered considerable internal debate, with another countermotion calling for a complete rejection of austerity negotiations and an immediate SSEU Local 371 strike referendum. In response to these countermotions, President Knight radicalized his strategy's language but not its methods. Knight then called for a public relations campaign to denounce the bankers' blackmail, the exorbitant interest rates they exacted from the city, and decreasing city revenues due to low corporate and real estate taxes. With the previous strike call shot down in the DC 37 delegates' meeting, a majority of the 124 social worker delegates voted to go along with the public relations strategy and its more oppositional language. While militant action did not result from Padwee's and others' motions, opposition forced Knight to take on a more adversarial public stance than he had initially proposed.[44]

In the early months of 1975, union leaders began to develop a more multifaceted strategy for dealing with the fiscal crisis, combining both virulent denunciations of banks and conceding union benefits and gains. At a DC 37 delegates meeting in late February, Gotbaum let it be known that upcoming budget gaps looked to be severe, and to help the city, the union was giving up one week of summer hours—municipal workers in New York City worked one hour less each day during the summer months—and forgoing two months of health and security fund benefits for new employees. While Gotbaum worked out these smaller cost-cutting measures, he also warned that the budget gaps might call for 50,000 to 80,000 layoffs.[45] In the face of such threats, Gotbaum advocated that funds from the Comprehensive Employment and Training Act (CETA)—a Nixon program to train and employ minorities and the unemployed for civil service—ought to be used to rehire any fired union members. Though he in effect conceded to firings, Gotbaum hoped that CETA block grants, which allowed significant leeway for spending, could be used as a safety net.[46]

DC 37 was also ramping up its rhetoric at the very same moment as it was making these concessions. That February, the council issued thousands of copies of a pamphlet titled "The Big Bank Holdup," which decried the banks' refusal to lend and questioned why police, firefighters, librarians, and sanitation workers had to tighten their belts while banks were making more than ever off the city. The pamphlet concluded with a challenge: "Why don't we ask all the companies making money off of New York City to tighten their belts, to make a little less for a while. It's their city, too. Let's ask them to help out. Ask the banks to the cut the interest rates to the city. Let's ask Con Ed to charge less for city hospitals, day care centers, schools and other institutions. Same for the phone company. Same for everybody doing business with the city of New York."[47] Though rhetorically combative, DC 37 was simply asking the city's business elite to make some concessions as well, to meet in the middle as was routine in collective bargaining. Months later, as Gotbaum came to recognize, labor's conciliatory attitude in the beginning of the crisis only whetted the appetite of the city's business elites.[48]

There is a gap in SSEU Local 371's records between February and April, but opposition to fiscal austerity became more militant during this time. While delegates had not supported Padwee's January motion calling for a strike in case of layoffs, by the spring a slightly modified position had won the day. In early April, the union's position was that no layoffs were acceptable and that any layoff of *permanent* workers was grounds for a citywide strike.[49]

While social workers were closer to the DC 37 leadership on who should be fired, Gotbaum's support of attrition irked older workers, and members of the hospital corporations chapter passed their own resolution against the forced retirement, calling banks "the real enemy" of city workers.[50] These members brought their angry resolution before SSEU Local 371's executive board, but the leadership pared down the statement's language, eliminating the "real enemy" phrase, and agreed to pass this sanitized objection on to the rest of DC 37.[51]

At that month's delegates' assembly, another argument took place within the union when members made a call for the union to take its own vote for authorizing strike action rather than waiting on DC 37. Knight defeated this call, insisting on unity with the rest of DC 37 and going so far as to argue that mandating a strike vote within the local could undermine a potential strike call from Gotbaum and the executive board of DC 37.[52] Knight was more interested in promoting a DC 37–sponsored march in Washington, DC, than advocating militant action.[53] Rank-and-file social workers supported and participated in DC 37 actions in large numbers, but they did not see the marching and lobbying as a substitute for more militant organizing on the part of their leaders. Well aware that concessions were already underway, the ranks passed a motion in April calling for any DC 37–negotiated agreements to be put to a citywide vote. In effect, SSEU Local 371 members wanted any deals to face the entire membership of DC 37 as a single unit rather than on a local-by-local basis, which could lead to isolation and distrust between various locals.[54]

As the fiscal crisis mounted in June and opposition to austerity grew among many workers, so too did Gotbaum's opposition to independent action. SSEU Local 371 members participated in a boisterous June 4 rally against First National City Bank. But many thought that with the July 1 deadline looming, more action was warranted. To achieve this, they distributed leaflets and tried to question the union's strategy at the DC 37 delegates' assembly, but Gotbaum loyalists ejected some of them from the meeting and prevented others from asking questions and trying to influence the debate.[55]

At the leadership level, Knight's oppositional stance within DC 37 led to short-lived organizing efforts with David Beasley, president of Local 1930 of the New York Library Guild. In late June, the two unions organized their own fiscal crisis protest, which sought community support, but Gotbaum ally Lillian Roberts attacked these efforts by pressuring community organizations to pull out.[56] On June 19 at an emergency meeting of DC 37 delegates, Local 371 delegates sent their president to once again call for a strike. Knight first motioned that CETA funds were an unacceptable solution to firings and that laying off any permanent DC 37 member ought to be sufficient grounds for action. Second, Knight motioned that alongside the mobilization and rallies DC 37 had organized or participated in, they should immediately begin to prepare for a strike, and if any permanent employee were terminated, the executive board should implement strike plans. Once again, Knight was the only union leader in DC 37 proposing militant action and not of his own volition.[57]

The discussion of Knight's strike proposal carried over to a regular meeting on June 25. Rather than directly oppose the strike, Gotbaum told delegates that DC 37 was not currently organizing a strike because the July 4 weekend would be an inopportune moment to get the public's attention. When paired with his opposition to independent rallies and silencing of members that opposed his strategy, it becomes clear that Gotbaum played a critical role in preventing rank-and-file opposition to the crisis from coalescing. As such, when thousands of workers from non–DC 37 unions would go on strike on July 1, DC 37 members were left to their own devices and for the most part failed to take part in any substantial way.[58]

In July Gotbaum publicly agreed to accept a pay freeze, pay raise deferrals from earlier contracts, and excuse millions in city contributions to the unions' welfare funds. Though he had argued in months prior that no agreement he made was binding for any member local, the July agreement was to be imposed whether members approved or not.[59]

At the August 20 SSEU Local 371 delegates' assembly, where most of the rank-and-file opposition to the fiscal crisis had occurred, delegates rejected their leadership's recommendations, voting down the agreement. In hopes of delivering a yes vote, the Local 371 executive committee called for a mail-in ballot of all members to vote on the agreement.[60] At the following delegates' assembly in mid-September, which took place before votes were counted, the union's executive committee urged the delegates to reconsider the issue. Debate and questions went on for more than an hour, and the discussion became so contentious that the leadership ended the meeting. While members fought over whether to endorse the agreement or not, bigger problems emerged as the city reached a critical budget gap, prompting unions to invest billions in pension funds to save the city. Gotbaum's July agreement looked quaint.[61]

While dissension and disruption reigned in SSEU Local 371, oppositional activity remained parliamentarian in nature. DC 37's executive committee shot down months of resolutions, leaving rank-and-filers with few alternatives. Though rank-and-file delegates proposed and voted for many oppositional resolutions, their lack of militant action suggests that many members were afraid of striking without the rest of DC 37. In fact, SSEU's last strike in 1967 failed due to its isolation, bringing about the merger with the more acquiescent Local 371.[62]

Michael Spear has pointed out that DC 37 united a variety of different workers who could be incredibly distrustful of one another. For example, many of DC 37's blue-collar workers were rooted in communities that were increasingly skeptical of educated, white-collar professionals and the left-wing politics that were common in SSEU Local 371.[63] Furthermore, social workers' profession tied them to an institution that increasingly large swaths of white, working-class New York had begun to question, especially as stories of welfare fraud circulated and welfare rolls became increasingly Black and Latino in New York City.[64] According to available archival sources, it is unclear to what degree rank-and-filers tried to independently organize outside of union channels and whether such divisions and other obstacles were even reached.

The social workers' battle to push DC 37 toward a more militant posture is also indicative of both the bureaucratic nature of DC 37 and fiscal crisis negotiations. Not only were SSEU Local 371 members trying to influence their own union leaders, but they were forcing those leaders to make a stand in DC 37's leadership bodies, which in turn were mediated through the figure of Gotbaum in the MLC. In spite of claims that DC 37 was a very democratic organization, its structure insulated its highest echelons from the ranks, with the executive director chosen by the DC 37 delegates' assembly.[65] In turn, Gotbaum curried favor with enough local presidents to not only maintain his position but also deny opposition motions and quash independent action. Given Gotbaum's willingness to compromise, independent action was essential to opposing fiscal austerity, but DC 37's structure made it incredibly difficult.[66]

Worker Resistance to the Municipal Assistance Corporation

At midday on June 4, the MLC mobilized a crowd of some 10,000 workers to protest First National City Bank and the rest of the financial elite. Claiming that the banks were the cause of the crisis, extorting the city for both high interest rates and actively refusing to lend without political concessions, union leaders vehemently denounced the potential cutbacks and the undue harm that would be inflicted upon the city.[67] According to Jewel and Bernard Bellush, historians of DC 37, the June 4 rally on Wall Street sought to flush out the banks and to make them take a public position for austerity rather than allowing them to remain behind the scenes and exert pressure through refusing funds on the grounds of uncontestable market logic.[68] Investment banker and future Municipal Assistance Corporation (MAC) chairman Felix Rohatyn recalled this event as a particularly frightening manifestation of public anger.[69]

While organized labor seemed to be on the attack, the June demonstrations marked the only truly confrontational move Gotbaum and the MLC would make throughout the remainder of the fiscal crisis. The rally showed just how angry workers were and just how deep the opposition to the fiscal crisis ran.[70] Like many other labor leaders, Gotbaum feared a failed strike and had already experienced several months of proposals for a citywide strike, and after June 4, he pulled back from further escalation. Despite mobilizing 10,000 members for a midday rally, Gotbaum would urge labor leaders to focus all of their efforts on lobbying, hoping that a last-ditch effort to sway Albany would result in fiscal relief.[71]

While Gotbaum pulled back from militant mobilization, other labor leaders in the city tried alternative, sometimes provocative, methods. In hopes of proving their importance over other city workers, the police and firefighters organized the notorious "Fear City" campaign, which involved passing out pamphlets at hotels, train stations, and airports to scare tourists with tips for avoiding muggers and murderers.[72] Beame denounced the pamphlets, obtaining a restraining order to prevent their dissemination. Much legal wrangling ensued, and the police and firefighters union eventually desisted, giving both the city and the labor movement a black eye.[73]

In late June, the UFT organized a "Day of Mourning" alongside the Board of Education in hopes of protecting educational funding and, as a result, teachers' and paraprofessionals' jobs.[74] Smaller demonstrations proliferated as well, with 1,000 crossing guards protesting outside of city hall in the middle of the month; 1,000 had already been laid off, and the other 1,400 were scheduled be laid off by the end of the same school year.[75] Some voices would still target the business elite, like Beasley, president of Local 1930 of the New York Library Guild, who in a joint rally with SSEU Local 371, decried the firings, proclaiming that New Yorkers were "being crushed by the giant hand of corporate finance, poor administration and bad politics."[76] Beasley had backed the SSEU Local 371 strike call that same month and, unlike other DC 37 presidents, pushed for action independent of the rest of the union.

Amid the days of protest, the state passed legislation creating the MAC, a business-backed plan for cutting New York's budget expenditures.[77] The state appointed eight of nine members to the board and invested them with the power to lend $3 billion in state bonds to help replace city bond obligations that the municipality could no longer meet. Prominent members included William M. Ellinghaus, president of New York Telephone, finance lawyer Simon Rifkin, and Felix Rohatyn, financial adviser for Lazard Frères.[78] Not only were business interests involved in writing the legislation, but they were also given the authority over lending state money under conditions of their own design, including a balanced budget that would require layoffs and service cutbacks. As such, in one fell swoop, a new and completely unelected force had formal decision-making power over New York City's fate.[79]

Though Beame originally opposed it, he was forced to concede to the MAC's demands, pushing through a harsh austerity budget.[80] Seeing that the city would follow through with tens of thousands of layoffs in July, the MAC offered $1 billion in bonds but managed initially to only sell some $650 million of them, a sign that in spite of many assurances of guaranteed bond repayment, investors and the business elite wanted even more stringent measures to be taken. With layoffs imminent, some of the more militant city workers began to take action.[81]

In late June, the city's sanitation workers led the first militant rank-and-file opposition to new austerity measures. In many boroughs, USA members implemented a work-to-rule strike, where they observed safety and productivity measures to the letter, which slowed down the pace of their work immensely. Others simply refused to do their work in any orderly way, picking up trash only on one side of the street or randomly skipping pickup spots. As a result, several thousand tons of trash accumulated, giving a visual sign of both the sanitationmen's willingness to take action and their anger at austerity measures.[82]

In the Lower East Side, sanitation workers initiated a wildcat strike that completely shut down trash removal on Manhattan's east side. Younger sanitation workers led the wildcat because they were most vulnerable to layoffs, but older workers stood beside them. Together they shut down operations and sabotaged nearly thirty trash trucks, breaking windshields and disabling wiring.[83] The city swiftly responded, suspending more than 200 USA members.[84] Joseph DeLury intervened to get the men reinstated, putting an end to the wildcat and resuming regular trash pickup. He also seized the moment to warn the city that these small actions were only the beginning, arguing that "the mayor is sitting on a volcano that could erupt into a general strike."[85]

On the morning of July 1, all 10,000 of New York's sanitation workers walked off the job in the largest disruption since the 1968 rank-and-file strike.[86] The threats, slowdowns, and wildcats of the previous days had not forestalled the austerity budget, and on the first day of July, 3,000 sanitationmen were laid off, and those not fired lost promotions and higher pay; some who had qualified for indoor work would now find themselves back in a truck, while others who were in supervisory positions would be downgraded. The cutbacks also insulted sanitationmen's pride. Echoing long-standing anger that surfaced in the 1968 sanitation strike, one fired worker argued, "Just because we pick up garbage doesn't mean we are garbage."[87] Adding to this disrespect was that sanitation was slated for a much higher percentage of firings than the city's other uniformed services; with a decreasing budget, sanitation work was judged to be less essential to public safety and order than firefighting and police work.[88]

While rank-and-filers forced the 1968 sanitation strike on DeLury, he and the rest of the USA leadership ultimately led the men out. The 1975 walkout was different, with small groups of sanitation workers taking the initiative and organizing their own militant actions.[89] In a later interview, labor negotiator Jack Bigel, a close ally of DeLury, confirmed that it was the men who organized the walkout.[90] Additionally, the mayor's office was in direct contact with DeLury from the very beginning, relaying its potential course of action and even discussing the best time to deploy an injunction against the wildcat.[91]

While DeLury made no formal claim to leading the illegal strike, he was able to end the strike and convince the city to rehire all of the fired sanitation workers by guaranteeing their wages with union money.[92] While the plan forestalled firings with union funds, two weeks later 1,500 sanitation workers were laid off anyway. Meanwhile older sanitation workers feared that wage cuts were in the works, and attrition soared with nearly 200 retiring in July. The sanitation wildcat was both a win and a loss for sanitationmen. Their strike managed to prevent more than 1,000 layoffs, but nearly 2,000 workers were either fired or left the profession early, and the union conceded to new efficiencies that increased workloads and decreased fringe benefits for sanitationmen.[93]

During rush hour on July 1, 500 police officers marched to city hall. Protesting the layoff of some 5,000 officers, they used police barricades to block off traffic at the foot of the Brooklyn Bridge, snarling the commute for thousands.[94] As they blocked the inbound and outbound lanes of traffic, they deflated the tires of several cars, immobilizing them and turning them into impromptu barricades. Fired officers' resentment was expressed in all directions: they attacked motorists who argued with them and threw cans and bottles at police officers trying to control the protest. When Patrolmen's Benevolent Association (PBA) president Ken McFeeley arrived on the scene to confront the 500 laid-off officers, many chanted against his inaction, calling on him to organize an immediate strike of the city's remaining 20,000 police officers. Some even chanted "We want DeLury," in reference to the sanitation workers' total walkout against the crisis budget.[95]

Ironically, McFeeley criticized his own members for being too obedient to his authority and unwilling to organize themselves for their own ends. Of course when disobedience to union authority had reared its head at the end of the 1960s, with police officers forming the Law Enforcement Group of New York, the PBA disavowed its ranks' organizing efforts. While the Law Enforcement Group had faded away, an upsurge in militancy on the part of its leadership perhaps gave some of its members the impression that the PBA would lead them out on strike in the face of budget cuts.[96] In 1971, the union led a five-day wave of sick-outs that saw nearly 20,000 police officers call out each day. Expectations of a repeat of the 1971 strike were misplaced, and the PBA leadership did not move to strike or call a sick-out.[97]

In response to the accusations of inaction and the wildcat mobilization of the sanitation workers, PBA leadership convened on July 2 to determine a course of action. With close to one-quarter of their members fired, the PBA leaders hoped to produce some kind of results to shore up support among the membership. Though the public might disapprove of laying off police officers, it would oppose any strike as well, an action that could be easily cast as an attack on the citizens of New York. PBA leadership adopted a call for all of its working members to follow all operating procedures—a major work slowdown—and the PBA also took over the coordination of pickets outside of the city's seventy-three precincts. That same day, 250 young officers blocked traffic again near the Brooklyn Bridge. On July 3, the laid-off officers gave up their protests, but the PBA kept up picketing, and the city agreed to a temporary rehiring of 2,000 officers; however, Beame wanted escrow payments from the union in case of budgetary gaps and a revision of their previous contract.[98]

Spurred by the sanitationmen's militancy and the protests by police, firemen staged a sick-out against more than 1,500 layoffs. On July 2, 400 firemen called in sick across the city, ten times the normal number. The firefighters union head had hinted at the action in the preceding days, mimicking DeLury: "I cannot control the fire fighters' actions any longer, as a result of the shabby, callous and provocative treatment they are receiving during the layoff."[99]

Meanwhile in neighborhoods like East Harlem and the Lower East Side, young men were barricading entire streets with mountains of trash, which they then set aflame. When police arrived on the scene, local youths attacked them with rocks and bottles. With fewer firefighters on hand to douse the flames, smoldering piles of trash covered several city blocks. McFeeley hoped to leverage the firemen's sick-out and ensuing fires, telling the media, "You know damn well it is 'Fear City.' People will die."[100] Like their counterparts in the uniformed services, firefighters achieved some rehiring, with the city reinstating 750, but with similar demands for union payments and contract revisions.

Perhaps the shortest lived was a wildcat strike by fired DC 37 members at the Transportation Administration. After 570 layoffs, transportation workers picketed at fifteen separate work yards across the city; some even assaulted a supervisor. In shirking their duties, they blocked off the Hudson River Parkway, which runs along half of the city's west side and up to Westchester County, snarling the commutes of thousands of people. DC 37 did not move to organize the protest of its laid-off members, and ultimately none of these workers were reinstated.[101]

The legacy of these short-lived strikes, pickets, and sick-outs was mixed. On the one hand, it showed that rank-and-file workers were able to resist fiscal austerity. Partial rehiring resulted after nearly each case of militant action, and the case with the highest militancy—the sanitation strike—produced the greatest proportion of reappointments. On the other hand, the strikes also showed that union leaders would not lead a concerted resistance to cuts and that they would make major concessions to achieve defensive compromises. Initial rehiring in July involved union funds, which set a precedent for the union investment in city functions threatened by fiscal austerity.[102]

While DC 37 wanted the city's banks and major corporations to shoulder some of the burden of fiscal austerity and economic stagnation, labor and the city's diverse communities would ultimately bear the costs. Additionally, thousands of workers were ultimately laid off, and those who remained were subject to worsening work conditions and pay freezes as well as widespread fear of further layoffs. This new regime went beyond the early July layoffs, however. By the middle of the month, bankers such as David Rockefeller and Walter Wriston were demanding that the city charge tuition in the City University of New York system, raise the subway fare, impose wage freezes, and lay off more workers.[103] At the end of July, Gotbaum agreed either tacitly or directly to all of these demands. Thus if some workers were able to save their own jobs, they were not able to prevent the business elite's broader social aims. In this regard, the July mobilizations were completely unsuccessful and are representative of a failure of the city's labor movement to defend its social values.[104]

The Teachers Strike

New York City's 55,000 teachers mounted the most significant counterattack against austerity. While most unions were negotiating austerity cuts to existing contracts, in 1975 the UFT was fighting austerity in its negotiations for a new contract, with its existing one set to expire at the beginning of the 1975–76 school year. Thus, unlike sanitation, police, or parks service, any agreement would be brought before the UFT membership, giving teachers and paraprofessionals the ability to veto their leaders' decisions in case of poor results. In September 1975, after months of layoffs and what seemed to be only bad news for city workers and the city's working class, rank-and-file anger within the UFT at both budget cuts and their union representatives erupted into a weeklong strike that completely paralyzed the city's education system. But in spite of deep-seated anger, rank-and-file organizing, and even community support, teachers for the most part left their fate in the hands of the union, which ended the strike through the subversion of its own democratic procedures, ultimately bringing its rank and file back to work in defeat.

By the 1970s, the UFT as an organization and teachers as a rank and file had damaged some of their standing with the growing Black and Puerto Rican communities in the city. A series of stances, including crossing the picket lines of the 1964 school boycotts and 1967 contract demands, which included greater punitive power over disruptive students, had caused major friction with communities and sparked rank-and-file opposition on the part of Black teachers through both the African-American Teachers Association and the New Coalition.[105]

The most damaging events were the three strikes during the 1968–69 school year, in which the UFT faced off with community control advocates in a horrible back-and-forth that fueled racial resentment and set organized labor's demands firmly against large parts of the Black community.[106]

The African-American Teachers Association led the charge against the union, but internal opposition was more varied, with the foundation of a Black caucus within the union both supportive of both the strike and community control as well as a primarily white leftist organization willing to cross the picket lines in support of community control. The majority of teachers maintained picket lines even if they thought the strike was hurting their cause.[107] Ultimately the strike reinforced a debilitating white-versus-Black polarization that aligned the political concerns of union teachers with white racism but also aligned the legitimate political demands of Black communities with the likes of the Ford Foundation, a brand of racial nationalism unwilling to think about the question of class.[108]

In the strikes' aftermath, the union rebounded when the thousands of Black and Puerto Rican paraprofessionals voted to join the union over DC 37, which tried unsuccessfully to use the UFT's stance in the 1968 Ocean Hill–Brownsville strike to win support. While paraprofessionals' support for the UFT suggests that the strikes' racial polarization was not all-encompassing, they were more likely an exception to the rule given the desire of many of them to become teachers themselves. While the union's ranks became more integrated, the union's reputation was heavily white and anti-Black.[109]

While the UFT's reputation would certainly be an obstacle, rank-and-file groups within the union had begun to mobilize in early 1975. That spring, the board of education pushed to remove thousands of substitute teachers from its payrolls, the first in a series of major cuts that would see the city's school system left overcrowded and underfunded. Up until those firings, the Teachers Action Caucus (TAC), an opposition faction of Communist Party members and New Left teachers, focused its energy on an unsuccessful bid for power with the union.[110] Founded during the 1968 Ocean

Hill–Brownsville strikes, TAC brought together longtime teachers from the Communist Party with younger teachers who wanted to unite community control advocates and the teachers' rank and file.[111] For these rank-and-filers, the business elite's fiscal crisis demands put into stark relief that teachers' labor conditions were their students' learning conditions, which only a joint effort of the community and union could defend. TAC's chairperson, Anne Filardo, was a guidance counselor in a Queens junior high school and, like many other TAC members, prominently crossed the picket line during the Ocean Hill–Brownsville strike. Many rank-and-filers opposed Albert Shanker and believed the 1968 strike to be a horrible mistake, but they stuck with the strike in solidarity with their fellow union members. TAC's attempt to bridge the teacher-community gap earned the caucus both undying hatred of the UFT leadership and a negative reputation among other teachers.[112]

In fact, teachers associated with TAC or teachers who sympathized with its position and crossed picket lines faced severe ostracization. In the words of one female teacher, "If you went in and the other people were out on strike, you paid the price." She refused to speak to a female teacher associated with Students for a Democratic Society ever again, even though the woman was the sister of her brother's best friend. In other cases, teachers who had crossed the picket lines requested transfers because other teachers refused to speak to them for years afterward.[113] Though such ostracization was largely the case, exceptions were made in strikes throughout the 1960s for single and often younger female teachers who had no other income to rely on during a walkout.[114] Taking a political stand against the UFT and against the 1968 strike may have upheld TAC's principles, but it irreparably harmed their standing among other teachers.

The UFT hoped to mobilize its members and gain public support with a "Day of Mourning" protest against cuts to city education, which it jointly organized with the board of education in June 1975. Rank-and-file groups like TAC hoped the UFT would take a more antagonistic position regarding the cuts, arguing against cuts not simply in education but in the city as a whole.[115] Their leaflets argued that there was in fact no budget shortage, because the city had generated the shortfall by giving millions in tax breaks to the real estate industry and refusing to collect millions in delinquent tax payments from large property owners across the city. TAC also decried the tone of the Day of Mourning. Using an old adage attributed to Joe Hill, "Don't Mourn—Organize!," TAC urged a broad-based community struggle against austerity measures, hoping to influence many UFT members to organize themselves for outreach to parents and students.[116]

Other teachers found Shanker's approach wanting, with a short-lived group of teachers, the Coalition Against Budget Cuts, arguing: "With the demonstration today, Shanker gave out notice to teachers only in the last minute because he could not allow our militancy to hurt his collaborating friendship with the government. Shanker is conducting this show with the Board of Ed. just to trick us."[117] In spite of such criticisms, the union and the board of education mobilized nearly 30,000 people for the rally, bringing together supportive students, parent groups, and rank-and-file UFT members. The image was powerful, but like their counterparts in SSEU Local 371, many New York City teachers believed that much more action was necessary to fight the fiscal crisis.[118]

After the Day of Mourning and the initial layoffs of other municipal workers in July, many New York teachers were dismayed by their union's conciliatory approach. A group of eighty teachers met in late July, founding the Citywide Coordinating Committee to Save New York Schools (CCC). Like the TAC, the CCC criticized the UFT for being too conciliatory and being undemocratic, which in the case of the fiscal crisis negotiations meant that the leadership was unreflective of the base's resistance to firings and class-size increases.[119]

Their initial press release was very clear: the CCC was organizing a militant fight against austerity that could lead directly to a strike in September. The CCC, like the TAC, saw community support as paramount, and on August 9, a month before the school year began, CCC members organized a petition at eleven sites throughout the city to gather support for their antiausterity campaign. At the end of August, the CCC mobilized a picket of the board of education and the UFT negotiations in downtown Brooklyn. Foreshadowing events to come, its press release stated, "Rehire every teacher, or no teacher works in September!"[120]

Importantly, many teachers increasingly resented Shanker, who was insulated from his membership.[121] At the end of the 1974–75 school year, a unanimous vote of the South Shore High School UFT chapter in Brooklyn called upon Shanker to stop his "labor statesman" ways and to begin acting like a "down-to-earth union leader" who communicated directly with his rank and file.[122]

Shanker was increasingly aware of the internal opposition, but he was also in a delicate position wherein a strike could symbolize a strike against the city and could end in defeat. He went so far as to ask the board of education to extend the previous contract, thus allowing him to symbolically maintain his "no contract, no work" position and avoid a strike.

The board refused, and Shanker brought a strike vote before an angry membership.[123]

On the night of September 8, more than 20,000 teachers packed Madison Square Garden. Earlier in the day, the city's teachers had arrived for the first day of school, finding many austerity measures already in place: oversized classes, schools without guidance counselors, and teacher activities extended far beyond the classroom, in addition to the 7,000 layoffs already issued by the board of education. Community solidarity was strongly in effect as well, as many parents across the city kept students out of schools in boycott of deteriorating educational conditions; three schools were closed in Manhattan due to a near-total parent boycott. In many ways, teachers, parents, and students knew that the 1975 school year was not going to go on without interruption.[124]

In Ocean Hill, the focal point of the 1968 strike, TAC members authored and issued a leaflet to community members on the first day of school that apologized for the fact that they would go on strike the following day.[125] The CCC also leafleted at schools where it had active members, reaching out to other teachers as well as parents and students. The teachers emphasized that the strike was for the children and for the maintenance of their children's learning conditions, which was a broadly held sentiment throughout the strike among teachers and not simply an opportunistic use of propaganda.[126]

If many teachers thought teaching as a whole was at stake, so, too, did they think that a strike was the only way to preserve what they had. And though Shanker had done little to rally the troops to the action, in fact repeatedly stating he was against a strike, teachers were ready for confrontation. A massive roar of approval came with the motion to call a strike vote at Madison Square Garden, with the final ballot tallying a landslide 22,870 for and a mere 900 against.[127]

While teachers may have voted down the contract against Shanker's wishes, the UFT's bureaucracy outmatched rank-and-file organizations in both resources and leadership. Its high level of organization and strict hierarchy allowed for an orderly and well-staffed strike, with teachers picketing every school in the city for the entire day and with a reinforced presence during lunch and closing hours. While some teachers designed their own signs and conducted their own conversations with community members, the UFT produced the majority of the propaganda and signage during the strike, leaving it effectively in charge of the strike's representation.[128] Many members expected such organization and leadership. Some older teachers felt an intense bond of loyalty to Shanker, whose shrewd leadership had shepherded them out of precarity and into a stable middle-class position. While they may not have agreed with his every decision or his opposition to this latest strike, they did expect him to lead once the rank and file had spoken.[129]

Doubts about Shanker's commitment to the strike lingered, however. Though the strike may have been well organized, many teachers wanted to ensure its long-term success, such as the more than seventy-five teachers in Washington Heights who issued a letter to Shanker and the UFT executive board members urging them not to end the strike prematurely because of the immensity of the issues at stake. This letter is quite indicative of the rank and file's actual capacity to shape events: it could express and implore the union to action, but like many other rank-and-file-generated strikes, the 1975 teachers strike was in the hands of the union's leadership.[130]

Importantly, the walkout pitted New York City's teachers and many supportive families and community members against the state's newly created Emergency Financial Control Board (EFCB). As William Tabb argues, the MAC was unable to sufficiently impose the will of financial elites on the city and its working class, and in order to more adequately discipline the city into falling in line with their austerity aspirations, business elites, including Rohatyn, Ellinghaus, and Rifkin drafted a law that called for an organization with direct oversight concerning city spending. Though earlier budgets and contracts were sites of power struggles, the EFCB removed any such possibility now by creating a politically insulated organization with the power of life and death over any contract.[131] In spite of this power, the EFCB was careful not to stake its future on the outcome of either the strike or its settlement package, hoping instead to portray it as an instrument of pure economy in which there was no room for negotiation.[132] A prolonged teachers strike had the potential to turn a broad swath of the community and the labor movement against the board.[133]

After months of bargaining and a full week into the strike, the board of education proposed to the UFT that the money saved by not paying tens of thousands of striking teachers be used to rehire some 2,000 laid-off teachers. Shanker scooped up the deal and conceded on teacher productivity, which was an effort by the board of education to compensate for firing teachers with increased teacher workload.[134] The UFT bureaucracy prepared a hasty vote the following day, issuing outlines of an earlier agreement with voting capped at 5:00 p.m. Rank-and-file groups and left-wing groups like the Progressive Labor Party and Coalition for a Labor Party called for a no vote.[135] The TAC called the settlement "a proposal that a *defeated* union accepts."[136]

The union's machinations produced chaos and left thousands locked out, resulting in a much lower turnout and a 10,651–6,695 vote to approve the contract and go back to work. Teachers across the city immediately reacted, collectively petitioning and criticizing Shanker for his undemocratic move and the weakness of the contract.[137] Teachers from PS 90 in Queens collectively penned a letter to Shanker denouncing "the disgraceful way in which this contract offer was accepted and the way in which this most serious and important strike was ended."[138] Teachers at Intermediate School 210, also in Queens, immediately forced their union delegate—a Shanker loyalist—to send a letter on their behalf denouncing the agreement and the undemocratic nature of voting procedures. In spite of the reaction, the teachers were not sufficiently organized to lead their own fight, leaving them to protest and implore the UFT leadership but with little recourse in the face of its decision to orchestrate a return to work.[139]

Unlike SSEU Local 371 members, who maintained a primarily parliamentarian opposition to fiscal austerity, UFT members moved to militancy because of a combination of increased anger at Shanker, a history of militancy, the deleterious effects of austerity on their work environment, and the critical nature of their work. When teachers struck, the city was massively disrupted. Unlike many other rank-and-filers who opposed the fiscal crisis, though, teachers were able to push their leaders forward but were ultimately outflanked. Shanker, like Gotbaum, wanted to preserve collective bargaining and ultimately avoid a strike. By ending the strike, he was able to deliver labor peace and end a conflict that he believed could not be won. Some rank-and-filers linked union subterfuge to the fact that several months after the strike, the UFT obtained an agency shop agreement; in the words of one teacher, Merry Tucker, "The union [was] cutting the throat of the teachers . . . [and] the bureaucracy has set up an interest totally aside from the interest of the teachers."[140]

Though the teachers strike ultimately failed to defend the city's educational services from major cutbacks, it was successful in the very short term at exacting some concessions. Shanker, like other labor leaders, achieved some rehiring of members, who were ironically funded by the money saved by the strike's shutdown of the school system. Shanker, however, conceded to a series of cost-cutting measures that dramatically worsened education in the city. Part of the problem lay in the fact that the business elite's hand had strengthened significantly by the fall of 1975. While the summer strikes had faced off against the business elite's austerity programs implemented through the new fiscal year's budget, teachers were fighting to preserve educational services and their own livelihoods against the EFCB, which would be able to review their contract. When the board ultimately examined the UFT contract, it found the agreement completely inconsistent with austerity priorities and let it hang in limbo for more than a year, a state of exception wherein the rapid rise to power of municipal unions was dramatically curtailed. As Eric Lichten succinctly put it, "The EFCB refused to accept and ratify the contract as punishment for the teacher's militancy."[141] That being said, their refusal to decide on the contract for quite some time also speaks to the effectiveness of teachers' resistance. The EFCB let the process languish rather than making a decision too soon and possibly sparking another strike.

Fiscal Austerity Wins

From the end of 1974 through the end of 1975, rank-and-file municipal workers contested the fiscal crisis, passing militant motions, creating their own propaganda, organizing wildcat strikes, and rejecting leadership-brokered contracts. In many cases union leaders acted directly to halt such independent organizing. At best they leveraged militancy to broker a better settlement for their particular union, which sometimes left them at odds with their fellow labor leaders. Though union leaders disputed the givebacks and layoffs, they ultimately conceded defeat and allowed the financial elite to determine the meaning of the crisis, touting the "common determination" and "common answer" at which they had all arrived.[142]

By the end of 1975, the rank-and-file movement that had spanned more than a decade had come undone. When transit workers again shut down the city in 1980, it was a testament to the ongoing possibility of resisting fiscal austerity and the possibility that internal upheaval could spark militancy. But unlike the 1966 strike, the 1980 shutdown had little wider impact. Failed rebellions in the early 1970s had transformed the attitudes of many of New York's workers, and the punishing effects of stagflation and fiscal austerity left many demoralized. Unemployment remained high throughout the 1980s, wealth moved increasingly up the socioeconomic hierarchy, the national political environment turned against labor with the rise of Ronald Reagan, and in New York City, the working class ceased to be a power to reckon with.[143]

Conclusion

From 1965 to 1975, rank-and-file workers in New York took part in a broad but inchoate rebellion that challenged the power of politicians, business elites, and union leaders. While rank-and-file rebellion in New York City lacked a common political platform, it was characterized by common motivations, similar modes of action, and a collective consciousness. Across many different sectors, powerful strikes shut down essential city services, electoral challenges ousted entrenched bureaucrats, and contract rejections and wildcat strikes defied the authority of New York City's labor hierarchy. Significantly, workers powerfully influenced one another, catalyzing further rebellion across the city, overcoming barriers of race, occupation, skill, and political persuasion. Plumbers inspired sheet metal workers and elevator constructors, sanitation workers encouraged taxi drivers, and transit workers inspired postal workers and even electricians.

New insurgent energies—namely Black militancy and youth revolt—fed the rebellion, as did growing political polarization under Mayor John Lindsay. New York's workers wanted more than just better contracts. They asserted greater control of the work process, contested racism on the job, demanded an end to corruption and more democratic control of representative organizations, and challenged the worker's place in America's socioeconomic hierarchy. In the face of both internal and external limitations, rank-and-file upheaval mostly petered out by the early 1970s, experiencing a brief revival in 1975, when workers led the resistance to the city's business elite and its plans for fiscal austerity. While there were certainly New Yorkers bent on organizing unions in the 1970s, the defeat of the various rank-and-file rebels of this period dramatically undermined the city's social democratic polity and sapped the will to fight of many of the most organized and aggressive working-class New Yorkers.

Important, and thus far untold, stories unfolded in this period. Galvanized by the Harlem riots, a Black motorman and member of the NAACP's Labor and Industry Committee, Joseph Carnegie, established the Rank and File Committee for a Democratic Union, helping push Transport Workers Union leadership into their storied 1966 strike, which in turn sparked rank-and-file upheaval throughout the city in the 1960s and early 1970s. The largely Black committee fought for years against Transport Workers Union leadership and tried to organize rank-and-filers nationwide, salvaging a national meeting of leaders that included the much more famous, but shorter-lived, League of Revolutionary Black Workers.[1] The six-month Local 2 plumbers strike in 1966, which shut down the city's billion-dollar real estate industry, resulted in the ejection of corrupt leaders and only buckled under the international's threat of trusteeship. Their example spread throughout the building trades, and such militant action troubles the predominant image of conservative and satisfied building trades.[2]

In the second half of the 1960s a broader environment of rebellion developed, with wildcat strikes proliferating by telephone workers, Long Island Rail Road engineers, newly unionized taxi drivers, waiters, parking enforcement officers, and even lifeguards. More significant, young workers influenced by the diffuse antiauthoritarianism of the times, as well as the norms and values of working-class New York, contributed to the upheaval. Many sported mustaches, beards, and longer hair, rejecting the straitlaced social conventions of their elders as well as the discipline of the workplace. While scholars have brought some attention to these cultural changes within the working class, they situate this shift in the early 1970s, but it was already prevalent in New York by the second half of the 1960s.[3] Meanwhile, contract rejections also grew among tugboat operators, welfare caseworkers, and firefighters. Finally, a diffuse dissatisfaction proliferated in many workplaces, sometimes manifesting itself as absenteeism or as short-lived strikes. In both 1968 and 1970, the fuel oil drivers of Local 553 rejected their leadership's contract recommendations in boisterous meetings, burning contracts and even attacking the union president. After all, as one former driver described the union leadership, "they ran it with the company, and they ran it against the men."[4] Historians have largely overlooked these strikes and their broad rank-and-file-driven context.[5]

Situating New York's labor struggles in the urban environment also sheds significant light on how they both shaped and were shaped by the city's political fissures. Historians have described how New York City mayor John Lindsay was a focal point for white working-class anger because of his support of Black civil rights aims, but none have sufficiently emphasized the degree to which Lindsay actively opposed the material interests of many rank-and-filers.[6] During the 1966 subway strike, Lindsay gave his mayoralty-defining "power brokers" speech, denouncing organized labor as a force that held a gun to the city's head and which hurt the position of the nonwhite poor.[7] In 1968, during the rank-and-file sanitation strike, Lindsay fought tooth and nail against the Uniformed Sanitationmen's Association, hoping to break the strike with the National Guard and hailing his own recalcitrance as a stand "against illegality, against violence, against extortion."[8] Lindsay also opposed private-sector workers, including taxi drivers who wanted better enforcement of their monopoly on cruising against the predominantly Black livery industry and Communications Workers of America (CWA) members who demanded that he enforce antiscab laws. Such workplace-based political battles helped shape the city's social environment and workers' beliefs and attitudes, demonstrating the workers were not acting against their material interests when they opposed racially liberal politicians. While racial animus did play a role in some strikes, it is hard to ignore that Lindsay publicly championed the plight of Black New Yorkers while publicly battling against predominantly white unions, sometimes intentionally pitting the two against each other.[9]

Yet New York's localized labor militancy resonated with workers of different races and work situations, and importantly even had national reverberations. Spurred by the militancy of public-sector workers and the contract gains of private-sector unions, postal workers in New York led a massive wildcat strike demanding increased wages and a respect befitting the importance of their industry. Black civil rights claims merged with claims to economic citizenship and wider demands to end the era of "collective begging."[10] When New Yorkers walked off the job in 1970, postal workers across the country followed them, leading to real collective bargaining rights and wage gains. When others returned to work, New Yorkers were the last on the picket lines nationwide. Without New York City's localized rank-and-file upheaval, it is likely that the postal wildcat would not have happened when it did.

In other ways, New York's rank-and-file rebellion was both locally generated but equally implicated in nationwide affairs. For years, CWA Local 1101 telephone workers used wildcat strikes to push for better contracts and force workplace rule changes, but they also used union grievance procedures and small-scale sabotage to tie up New York Telephone. In 1971, they would reject both their local and international leaderships during a nationwide walkout against AT&T, continuing to strike for several months in order to gain a better contract more befitting the worsening economic hardships in New York City. In early 1972, though, they would return to work utterly defeated, in what one former shop steward called "the first major industrial strike in recent memory which has ended in undeniable defeat for the labor movement."[11] For a short time, however, CWA Local 1101 was one of the most combative rank and files in the city, if not the nation, because of the way in which diverse insurgent energies combined.

While New York's strikes affected the nation, its political effects were largely local. In 1969, the newly minted Taxi Drivers Union experienced diffuse rank-and-file upheaval, going to war with the city's growing livery cab industry. The city's role in regulating cab service brought Mayor Lindsay into the fray, with the mayor siding with the nascent livery industry. Explosive union meetings resulted in 1971 and 1972, and in the aftermath of the former, the Taxi Rank and File Coalition emerged, putting forth a powerful first-year challenge to Harry Van Arsdale Jr.'s administration. Like other rank-and-filers, they did not obtain immediate victory, and their struggle transformed into a long-term organizing drive that attracted little lasting commitment from their fellow drivers. Drivers remained divided in the early 1970s, with the new battling the old, the full-time against the part-time, the owner-drivers against the fleet drivers, and the yellow cabs against gypsy cabs. Rather than a simple battle between bosses and workers or between insurgents and insulated leaders, the taxi rank-and-file struggle was a maelstrom, a model in miniature of the city's multipolar social breakup.[12]

The rank-and-file attempt to push back against fiscal austerity in 1975 was the last gasp for this era of struggle. Faced with massive debt, declining economic vitality, and elite pressure to gut much of the city's social welfare provision, city employees including social workers, teachers, sanitationmen, police, and others mobilized rank-and-file efforts of varying levels of coordination and strength. In some cases, the resistance was relatively short lived and resulted in some rolling back of firings of city workers; in the case of teachers it was a huge battle eventually put to an end by union leaders who wanted to cut their losses. While financial elites rewrote the rules for New York politics, or perhaps reminded everyone who was really in charge, there had already been a subjective transformation of many of New York's working people.

While the era was charged with powerful working-class challenges to established authority, the legacy of the rebellion is primarily one of defeat. In the early phase of the strike wave, workers were able to extract substantial gains from employers, though as Robert Brenner has shown, many of these were catch-up contracts. Militant action engendered more militancy, but the tide began to turn in the 1970s. Small unions like Local 553 were unable to win their strikes after their contract rejections, leaving militant rank-and-filers isolated from many of their coworkers. Even the largest and most powerful rank-and-file movements—Transport Workers Union Local 100 and CWA Local 1101—could not overcome the combination of union and employer recalcitrance, hamstrung by legal battles and union-run votes or smashed by strikebreakers and automation. Workers continued some of their internal battles but the number of strikes collapsed after 1972, rising again only in 1975 during the fiscal crisis when rank-and-filers confronted the city's business elite in a lopsided battle, which saw the burden of austerity foisted on public-sector workers and working-class communities across the city. The sense of defeat was palpable. As one taxi rank-and-filer put it in the late 1970s, "Elections weren't getting us anywhere, the masses weren't revolting, the industry was falling apart."[13] Workers' struggles had hit a wall and few found a way forward.

When workers' efforts were defeated, either in the aftermath of the years of wildcat strikes and challenges or much more short-lived upheaval, results were similar: rank-and-filers lost confidence, disengaged from challenges, and focused on their own economic survival.

James Haughton captured the challenges of survival in a 1980 interview: "They totally cop out. They just totally withdraw. They accept their alienation, so they live in sort of a cocoon, somewhat isolated from reality, not paying too much attention to anything, as long as number one is getting over."[14] But with earnings eaten away by rising prices and the threat of unemployment growing across the whole of the country, the "getting over" was often self-preservation in the face of seemingly intractable problems. Importantly, a turn inward also meant a rejection of, or at least a declining commitment to, broad social horizons that undergirded both New York's social democratic polity and the labor movement more broadly. Thus, the focus on individual problems was neither the crass individualism of the "Me Decade" nor simply a turn to the right. Instead, it was a strategy of accommodation in the aftermath of failure. Such defeat-engendered norms led to a decline in strikes and rank-and-file challenges, as workers lost confidence in their own ability to shape their future.

If one were to examine the unionization rate of New York City and New York State today, one might think that what remains is a bastion of working-class power and that perhaps Jefferson Cowie's description of the "last days of the working class" or Lane Windham's argument that the "1970s union organizing push never reached its full promise" are overstated.[15] Despite a recent downturn, in 2023 New York City's unionization rate was 17.7 percent, nearly double the national average, and its unions include large numbers of women and people of color. In fact, one-third of all Black and almost one-fifth of all Hispanic workers are unionized, and women are more likely to be union members than men.[16] Yet the city's union members and its working class are in a much less powerful position than in the past. Most union members are in the public sector, and the same juridical mechanisms that managed public-sector rank-and-file rebels in the 1960s and 1970s still hamstring the bulk of New York City's union members. When these workers strike, which they rarely do, they face firings and loss of pay and their unions face the loss of automatic dues collection. While New York's unionization rate is still high, as elsewhere in the country the number of strikes has dropped significantly; to date, the rank-and-file rebellion was the country's last strike wave.

With the renewed interest since the 2016 presidential election in the American working class as a political figure, the political legacy of the rank-and-file rebellion is relevant again. While it's ironic that Donald Trump, the man who best embodied the ethos of the revanchist New York of the 1980s and 1990s, has positioned himself as the champion of working people, it should not be too surprising. As during the 1960s and 1970s, there is a deep well of anger among working-class people, and for the last forty years their social standing has stagnated, with deunionization, deindustrialization, growing personal debt, and the rise of a dual labor market in many areas of the country. Trump criticized some of the very policies that both Democrats and Republicans have championed to the detriment of labor, including the North American Free Trade Agreement, deindustrialization, and increased immigration. His opponent in 2016, Democratic nominee Hillary Clinton, ignored much of the economic reality behind the pro-Trump sentiment, arguing that the bulk of his supporters were simply "deplorables."[17] Though she eventually apologized for the statement, her beliefs are broadly representative of an enduring limousine liberalism that heaps invective on its social inferiors. That those who denounced Trump's supporters as deplorables quickly supported the "racial reckoning" of 2020 also fits the pattern just as well.

While recent years have seen a small increase in strikes and militant negotiations, it seems unlikely that we will witness a return of rank-and-file power in the coming decades. The industries that were once home to the most radical workers have been fundamentally transformed both technologically and geographically, and there are no cities left in the United States where a politically self-aware working class still exists. If American working people are to take their destiny into their own hands, they will have to find other ways to contest the notion of the good life. For now, those solutions remain occluded.

NOTES

ABBREVIATIONS

AF Papers	Anne Filardo Papers on Rank and File Activism in the American Federation of Teachers and in the United Federation of Teachers, Tamiment Library and Robert F. Wagner Labor Archives, New York University
AFSCME Records	American Federation of State, County, and Municipal Employees District Council 37 Records, Tamiment Library and Robert F. Wagner Labor Archives, New York University
BCTC Minutes	Building and Construction Trades Council Meeting Records, Tamiment Library and Robert F. Wagner Labor Archives, New York University
Bellush Papers	Bernard and Jewel Bellush Papers, Tamiment Library and Robert F. Wagner Labor Archives, New York University
CWA Ephemera	Communications Workers of America Printed Ephemera Collection, Tamiment Library and Robert F. Wagner Labor Archives, New York University
CWA Records	Communications Workers of America Records, Tamiment Library and Robert F. Wagner Labor Archives, New York University
HVA Papers	Harry Van Arsdale Jr. Papers, Joint Industry Board of the Electrical Industry, IBEW Local 3 Archives, Queens, NY
JH Papers	James Haughton Papers, Schomburg Center for Research in Black Culture, New York Public Library
JVL Papers	John Vliet Lindsay Papers, Manuscripts and Archives Repository, Sterling Memorial Library, Yale University
Kheel Center	Kheel Center for Labor-Management Documentation and Archives, Cornell University

Municipal Archives	Municipal Archives, New York City Department of Records and Information Services
NAR Records	Nelson A. Rockefeller Gubernatorial Records, Rockefeller Archive Center, Sleepy Hollow, NY
NYCCLC Records	New York City Central Labor Council Records, Tamiment Library and Robert F. Wagner Labor Archives, New York University
NYW	New Yorkers at Work Oral History Collection, Tamiment Library and Robert F. Wagner Labor Archives, New York University
Postal Union Records	New York Metro Area Postal Union Records, Tamiment Library and Robert F. Wagner Labor Archives, New York University
SSEU Records	Social Service Employees Union Records, Tamiment Library and Robert F. Wagner Labor Archives, New York University
Tamiment Library	Tamiment Library and Robert F. Wagner Labor Archives, New York University
TRFC Oral History	Taxi Rank and File Coalition Oral History Collection, Tamiment Library and Robert F. Wagner Labor Archives, New York University
TRFC Records	Taxi Rank and File Coalition Records, Tamiment Library and Robert F. Wagner Labor Archives, New York University
TWUA:RL	Transport Workers Union of America: Records of Locals, Tamiment Library and Robert F. Wagner Labor Archives, New York University
UFT Records	United Federation of Teachers Records, Tamiment Library and Robert F. Wagner Labor Archives, New York University

INTRODUCTION

1. Minutes, special executive board meeting, January 9, 1969, box 117, "NYCCLC Executive Board Meeting Minutes" folder, NYCCLC Records.

2. Minutes, special executive board meeting, January 9, 1969.

3. Freeman, *Working-Class New York*, 55–71. For more on class in postwar New York, see Bellush and Bellush, *Union Power*; Freeman, *In Transit*; Podair, *Strike*; Kahlenberg, *Tough Liberal*; and Philips, *Renegade Union*.

4. The term "rank-and-file rebellion" was not in contemporary use to describe the wave of strikes and workers' challenges, but many commentators referred to upheaval in unions as rebellions or to restive rank-and-filers as rebels. See "Rebellion on Contracts: Rank-and-File Refusal to Take Union Leaders' Advice Is Becoming Chronic," *New York Times*, December 2, 1968; "Rank and File Rebellion Stirs in Mine Union, Posing Threat to Lewis Legacy," *New York Times*, June 13, 1969; and "Teamster Rebellion on Pay Threatens to Tie Up Jersey," *New York Times*, April 21, 1970. The earliest scholarly work to use the term to address the whole of the period is Aaron Brenner, "Rank-and-File Rebellion," but the two most significant recent contributions are Brenner, Brenner, and Winslow, *Rebel Rank and File*; and Cowie, *Stayin' Alive*. Important earlier works on the subject include Friedman, *Teamster Rank and File*; and La Botz, *Rank-and-File Rebellion*.

5. Cowie, *Stayin' Alive*.

6. Windham, *Knocking on Labor's Door*, 3.

7. Freeman, *Working-Class New York*.

8. Strikes peaked in the postwar era in 1958 with some 279 strikes, but by the late 1960s and early 1970s, more than double the number of workers were involved. US Department of Labor, *Analysis of Work Stoppages, 1968*; US Department of Labor, *Analysis of Work Stoppages, 1969*; US Department of Labor, *Analysis of Work Stoppages, 1970*.

9. "Letter Carriers Defy Injunction Ordering Them Back to Work," *New York Times*, March 19, 1970.

10. Podair, *Strike*; Murphy, "Militancy in Many Forms," 229–48; Walkowitz, *Working with Class*.

11. Taylor, "American Petrograd," 311–33.

12. For the best examinations of class in nineteenth-century New York, see Wilentz, *Chants Democratic*; and Beckert, *Monied Metropolis*. See also Stott, *Workers in the Metropolis*. For the best examination of class in postwar New York, see Freeman, *Working-Class New York*. Peiss, *Cheap Amusements*, is also an excellent look at class and gender in the early part of the twentieth century. On the rise of a managerial middle-class professional culture, see Revell, *Building Gotham*. Phillips-Fein, *Fear City*.

13. For exemplary literature on the Right and reaction, see Carter, *Politics of Rage*; Flamm, *Law and Order*; McGirr, *Suburban Warriors*; Rick Perlstein, *Before the Storm*; and Sugrue, *Origins*. On periodization, see Schulman, *Seventies*; and Cowie, *Stayin' Alive*, xxiii. Finally, Cohen, *Consumer's Republic*, stands out as one of the strongest attempts to reorient the story of the 1960s by grounding the northern civil rights movement's language and actions within the discursive field of the emerging consumption-based national politics. For a relatively recent examination of 1970s left politics, see Berger, *Hidden 1970s*. And for a slightly older study that does well to include movements and grassroots politics of the Left and Right in the 1960s, see Isserman and Kazin, *America Divided*.

14. For local AFL-CIO discussion of the "Wallace effect," see minutes, special meeting, October 10, 1968, box 10, "Exec Bd Meetings Minutes 1967–69" folder, NYCCLC Records. For Lindsay on rank-and-file-led strikes' negative effects on the city's poor, see Harry W. Albright Jr. to Nelson Rockefeller, memorandum, n.d., box 90, "New York City Sanitation Strike Key Events" folder, NAR Records. For Lindsay, race, and labor, see Freeman, "Lindsay and Labor." While recent studies have suggested long-standing tendencies toward anti-communism as well as a long-term rise in conservatism, New York City's workers helped build a broad-based social democratic experiment in the two decades prior to the rank-and-file rebellion, and Kenneth D. Durr describes a similar disjunction between liberalism and working-class interest in Baltimore in *Behind the Backlash*. Quote from Moreton, *To Serve God*, 4. See also Cowie, "From Hard Hats," 9–17.

15. For the strike wave locally and nationally, see US Department of Labor, *Analysis of Work Stoppages, 1970*, 41; US Department of Labor, *Analysis of Work Stoppages, 1971*, 51; US Department of Labor, *Analysis of Work Stoppages, 1972*, 55; and US Department of Labor, *Analysis of Work Stoppages, 1973*, 46. For a look at some of the continuing rank-and-file activity at the national level, see Cleaver, "Wildcats"; La Botz, *Rank-and-File Rebellion*; and Murphy, "Militancy in Many Forms." One of the most relevant examinations of New York's rank-and-file rebellion is Aaron Brenner, "Rank-and-File Struggles."

16. Milkman and Luce, *State of the Unions*.

17. For the most substantial examination of the 1966 transit strike, see Marmo, *More Profile Than Courage*. For the complicated political legacy of the building trades, see Freeman, "Hardhats"; Nystrom, *Hard Hats, Rednecks*; and Cowie, *Stayin' Alive*, 136–37.

18. For the sanitation strike and New York City politics, see Cannato, *Ungovernable City*, 196–204. The best work on Wallace's appeal is Carter, *Politics of Rage*. For the postal strike, see Aaron Brenner, "Striking against the State"; and Rubio, *There's Always Work*, 233–74.

19. Jim McMahon, interview with author, New York, January 10, 2017; Rocky Maio, interview with author, New York, January 11, 2017.

20. Aaron Brenner, "Rank-and-File Struggles." For some examination of taxi and rank-and-filers, see Hodges, *Taxi!*; and Biju, *Taxi!* On the 1975 fiscal crisis, see Phillips-Fein, *Fear City*; Moody, *From Welfare State*; Lichten, *Class, Power and Austerity*; and Freeman, *Working-Class New York*, 256–88. For two examinations of the fiscal crisis, one right and one left, see Lachman and Polner, *Man Who Saved*; and Tabb, *Long Default*.

21. Greg Sargent, "Why Did Trump Win? New Research by Democrats Offers a Worrisome Answer," *Washington Post*, May 1, 2017.

CHAPTER 1

1. For "fun city," see Cannato, *Ungovernable City*, 90.

2. For the most substantial examination of the 1966 transit strike, see Marmo, *More Profile Than Courage*. Marmo's work is highly detailed, but he gives little attention to the Rank and File Committee and their efforts in the run-up to the strike.

3. UA Local 2's 1966 strike has received little attention in scholarly literature, overshadowed by the period's many public-sector strikes and lacking readily available archival sources. The small Local 2 collection at the Tamiment Library and Robert F. Wagner Labor Archives mostly contains materials relevant to the 1980s and early 1990s, when the union was shut down, and the earliest documents begin in 1969. The most significant coverage of Local 2 in historical literature pertains to its involvement in a 1964 leadership-organized walkout against the hiring of four nonunion Black and Latino plumbers. For those short mentions, see Purnell, *Fighting Jim Crow*; Waldinger, *Still the Promised Land?*; and Hill, "Bronx Terminal Market Controversy."

4. Freeman, *In Transit*, v–vii.

5. Freeman, *Working-Class New York*, 55–59.

6. Maier, *City Unions*, 38–40.

7. Maier, *City Unions*, 32–33.

8. Maier, *City Unions*, 33–35, quote 33.

9. "Subway Disaster Imminent," August 1965, box 39, "L-100 Rank and File Committee 1964–68" folder, TWUA:RL.

10. For a complete account of the Hogan purge, see Freeman, *In Transit*, 286–317.

11. "15,000 Negro Transit Workers and the Fight for Trade Union Democracy within the TWU," box 10, "Rank and File Committee for a Democratic Union within the New York City Transit Authority" folder, JH Papers.

12. "Strike June 30," box 33, "L-100 Motormen's Benevolent Assn. 1955–1958" folder, TWUA:RL; Marmo, *More Profile Than Courage*, 183–84.

13. "MBA Membership Meeting," box 33, "L-100 Motormen's Benevolent Assn. 1955–1958" folder, TWUA:RL; Maier, *City Unions*, 39–40.

14. "Members Reject Expulsion of TWU Leaders," box 39, "L-100 Rank and File Committee 1954–1955" folder, TWUA:RL; Freeman, *In Transit*, 320–23.

15. Telegram to Matthew J. Guinan, 1955, box 3, "L-100 Correspondence: Members 1957" folder, TWUA:RL.

16. "The Fight Must Go On," box 39, "L-100 Rank and File Committee 1954–1955" folder, TWUA:RL.

17. Marmo, *More Profile Than Courage*, 64–66.

18. "Phoney Union Busting Leaflet Exposed," box 39, "L-100 Rank and File Committee 1954–1955" folder, TWUA:RL.

19. For early discussions of Black hiring in transit, see minutes, executive board meeting, July 25, 1938, box 23, "L-100 Minutes Special Executive Board Meetings 1938" folder, TWUA:RL; and "Bias in the Building Industry: An Updated Report 1963–1967," box 348, "Civil Rights: Union Bias" folder, JVL Papers.

20. Transport Workers Union of America, *Report of the Proceedings*, 158.

21. Freeman, *In Transit*, 150–52.

22. "The Transit Authority and Its 12,000 Negroes," part 1, *Amsterdam News*, June 16, 1962.

23. "The Transit Authority and Its 12,000 Negroes," part 2, *Amsterdam News*, June 23, 1962.

24. "The Transit Authority and Its 12,000 Negroes," part 3, *Amsterdam News*, June 30, 1962.

25. "15,000 Negro Transit Workers and the Fight for Trade Union Democracy within the TWU," 1964, 9, box 10, "Rank and File Committee for a Democratic Union within the New York City Transit Authority" folder, JH Papers.

26. "15,000 Negro Transit Workers," 11.

27. "15,000 Negro Transit Workers," 1.

28. "15,000 Negro Transit Workers," 4.

29. "15,000 Negro Transit Workers," 4–5. Watts became a permanent fixture on the Local 100 executive board; see "Executive Board, 1964–1965," box 1, "L-100 Minutes Executive Board, 1960–1969" folder, TWUA:RL.

30. "15,000 Negro Transit Workers," 6.

31. "15,000 Negro Transit Workers," 4–5. For race and racism in the International Ladies Garment Workers Union, see Hill, "ILGWU Today"; and Lee, *Building*, 61–94.

32. "15,000 Negro Transit Workers," 7–8; James Haughton interview, October 22, 1980, NYW.

33. "15,000 Negro Transit Workers," 12.

34. "15,000 Negro Transit Workers," 14; "Transit Workers Form Rights Unit," *New York Times*, June 9, 1963.

35. "15,000 Negro Transit Workers," 15.

36. Isserman and Kazin, *America Divided*, 90–92.

37. "15,000 Negro Transit Workers," 16–17. For Quill's vocal support of civil rights, see minutes, executive board emergency meeting, June 19–20, 1963, box 1, "L-100 Minutes Executive Board, 1960–1969" folder, TWUA:RL; "N.A.A.C.P. Urges Mass Picketing,"

New York Times, May 8, 1963; and "Rallies Here Decry Suppression of Negro Protests in Alabama," *New York Times*, May 9, 1963.

38. "15,000 Negro Transit Workers," 17–18.

39. Flamm, *In the Heat*, 10–28.

40. Minutes, Labor and Industry Committee meeting, July 20, 1964, box 4, "NY NAACP—Labor and Industry Committee Agenda and Minutes 1963–1965" folder, JH Papers.

41. Minutes, Labor and Industry Committee meeting, July 20, 1964.

42. Minutes, Labor and Industry Committee meeting, August 17, 1964, box 4, "NY NAACP—Labor and Industry Committee Agenda and Minutes 1963–1965" folder, JH Papers.

43. Minutes, Labor and Industry Committee meeting, September 14, 1964, box 4, "NY NAACP—Labor and Industry Committee Agenda and Minutes 1963–1965" folder; and "Transit Workers, Black and White Must Support the Struggles of the People of Harlem," July 1964, box 5, "Rank And File Committee of the Transit Workers Union 1963–1965" folder, both in JH Papers.

44. Haughton résumé, 1969, box 1, "Biographical Information Vital Records, 1929–1977" folder, JH Papers.

45. "15,000 Negro Transit Workers," 9.

46. "17,000 Jobs Sought Here to Avert Summer Violence," *New York Times*, June 5, 1965; Goland, *Constructing Affirmative Action*, 144–45. For Haughton on electricians, see Moccio, *Live Wire*, 115–16.

47. For the Haughton-Carnegie relationship seven years later, see *Rank and File News*, no. 18 (April 1972), box 10, "Rank and File Committee for a Democratic Union within the New York City Transit Authority" folder, JH Papers.

48. Letter to Michael Quill, 1965, box 3, "L-100 Correspondence: Members 1965–1969" folder. For letters and telegrams decrying the June disruption, see J. Connell to Matthew Guinan, June 24, 1965; and John Colleti to Daniel Gilmartin, June 25, 1965, both in box 18, "Enlarged Joint Executive Committee, 1964–1970" folder. For cursory notes from the meeting, see minutes, executive board of Local 100 meeting, June 23, 1965, box 1, "L-100 Minutes Executive Board, 1960–1969" folder. All in TWUA:RL.

49. "Stop the 25cent Care and the Curtailment of Transit Services," June 1965, box 39, "L-100 Rank and File Committee 1964–1968" folder, TWUA:RL.

50. "20,000 Black Transit Workers and the Fight for an Independent Rank and File Union," *Rank and File News*, no. 18 (April 1972), box 10, "Rank and File Committee for a Democratic Union within the New York City Transit Authority" folder, JH Papers.

51. "The TA-TWU Squeeze," 1965, box 39, "L-100 Rank and File Committee 1964–1968" folder, TWUA:RL.

52. "Stop the Curtailment of Transit Services and the Pending Plan for a 25c Fare." The Rank and File Committee was consistent in its opposition to fare hikes; see "Stop Another TWU Contract Sellout," 1969. Both in box 39, "L-100 Rank And File Committee, 1964–1968" folder, TWUA:RL.

53. "T.W.U. to Seek $100 Million; Authority Warns of Rise in Fare," *New York Times*, July 26, 1965.

54. "Transit Workers Picket City Hall," August 1965, box 39, "L-100 Rank and File Committee 1964–1968" folder, TWUA:RL.

55. DeVito to Quill, October 16, 1965, box 3, "L-100 Correspondence: Members 1965–1969" folder, TWUA:RL.

56. "City Transit Union Seeks a Four-Day, 32-Hour Week," *New York Times*, October 11, 1965; Marmo, *More Profile Than Courage*, 28.

57. While some other candidates ran in the TWU election, there was no other full slate. See "Vote the Carnegie-DeVito Slate," 1965, box 39, "L-100 Rank and File Committee 1964–1968" folder, TWUA:RL.

58. For DeVito's membership in the original Rank and File Committee, see "Members Reject Expulsion of TWU Leaders," box 39, "L-100 Rank and File Committee 1954–1955" folder, TWUA:RL.

59. "Vote the Carnegie-DeVito Slate."

60. "Why Do We Picket Our Own Union?," 1965, box 39, "L-100 Rank and File Committee 1964–1968" folder, TWUA:RL.

61. For a summary of their broad appeals period, see "20,000 Black Transit Workers."

62. "Quill's Rank and File: What They Want," *New York Post*, December 14, 1966; "To All T.W.U. Station Division Members," 1963, box 18, "Elections 1962–1963" folder, TWUA:RL.

63. For polling locations, see "To All T.W.U. Station Division Members."

64. Minutes, executive board of Local 100 meeting, October 25, 1965, box 1, "L-100 Minutes Executive Board, 1960–1969" folder, TWUA:RL. For participation in the two previous elections, see press release, December 13, 1963; and tally, 1961, both in box 18, "Elections 1960–1961" folder, TWUA:RL.

65. "Vote the Carnegie-DeVito Slate."

66. Minutes, executive board of Local 100 meeting, October 25, 1965.

67. Hayes to Michael Quill, November 26, 1965, box 3, "L-100 Correspondence: Members 1965–1969" folder, TWUA:RL.

68. Election results, 1965, box 18, "L-100 Elections 1965–1967" folder, TWUA:RL.

69. For the results of the two previous elections, see press release, December 13, 1963; and tally, 1961, both in box 18, "Elections 1960–1961" folder, TWUA:RL.

70. Surface Maintenance Division results, December 1965, box 18, "Elections 1965–1967" folder, TWUA:RL.

71. Conference proceedings, 14–15, box 10, "Rank and File Workers Conferences 1968–1970" folder, JH Papers.

72. For a noncommittee rank-and-file opponent of the TWU, see Ralph Gaspard to Theodore Kheel, 1965, box 55, "NYC Transit II" folder, Theodore W. Kheel Additional Files, Kheel Center; and "Transit Workers Picket City Hall."

73. Alan Lawrence interview, 1986, Transport Workers Union Oral History Collection, Tamiment Library.

74. For skilled worker opposition, see remarks of Richardson, BMT conductor, March 30, 1965, box 1, "L100-Minutes: Joint Executive Committee, 1940–1965" folder, TWUA:RL; "Quill's Rank and File"; and Marmo, *More Profile Than Courage*, 65–67.

75. Cannato, *Ungovernable City*, 82–84.

76. Marmo, *More Profile Than Courage*, 27–28.

77. TA statement, December 14, 1965, box 38, "Bargaining (2) 1965–1966" folder, TWUA:RL.

78. Freeman, "Lindsay and Labor," 120–23. For the committee's understanding of the political nature of the negotiations, see "TA-TWU Squeeze."

79. "Picketing Locations," December 1965, box 55, "Bargaining, 1966" folder, TWUA:RL.

80. "Stoppage of Trains Begin Smoothly," *New York Times*, January 2, 1966; "Pickets on the March Despite the Rain," *New York Times*, January 3, 1966.

81. "Even the Pickets Get There on Foot," *New York Times*, January 2, 1966.

82. Prior to the strike, one transit worker "with little love for Mike Quill and little respect for lying T.A. Managers" wrote to transit negotiator Theodore W. Kheel; see Gaspard to Kheel, 1965. For the best description of the back-and-forth strike negotiations, see Marmo, *More Profile Than Courage*.

83. Henricks to Van Arsdale, January 9, 1966, box 20, "General Files (Includes Transit Strike)" folder, NYCCLC Records.

84. Anonymous Local 2 member, interview with author, New York, January 11, 2017.

85. McMahon interview.

86. Minutes, executive board of Local 100 meeting, January 13, 1966, box 1, "L-100 Minutes Executive Board, 1960–1969" folder, TWUA:RL. For anger at the distribution of the pay increase, see bus maintainers to Matthew Guinan, January 17, 1966, box 38, "Bargaining (2) 1965–1966" folder, TWUA:RL.

87. "We Won!," January 1966, box 55, "Bargaining, 1966" folder, TWUA:RL; bus maintainers to Matthew Guinan, January 17, 1966; Freeman, "Lindsay and Labor," 123; Cannato, *Ungovernable City*, 92.

88. "Working Paper on Employee Relations in the City of New York," n.d., box 59, "Labor Relations 1966–1968" folder, Mayor John Lindsay Collection, Municipal Archives. For Lindsay's public position, see "Statement by Mayor John V. Lindsay," January 13, 1966, box 353, "Labor Relations 1966–1969" folder, JVL Papers.

89. "Letter Carriers Defy Injunction."

90. "Simmering Discontent Sparked Strike," *New York Times*, March 25, 1970.

91. Cannato, *Ungovernable City*, 93.

92. "Transcript of Statement by Mayor Lindsay on Status of Negotiations on the Subway and Bus Walkout," *New York Times*, January 11, 1966.

93. Minutes, special executive board meeting, January 6, 12, 1966, box 117, "NYCCLC Executive Board Meeting Minutes" folder, NYCCLC Records. For Lindsay antilabor supporters, see Mrs. Sawyer to Lindsay, December 5, 1965; and Clara D. Heclet to Lindsay, December 12, 1965, both in box 89, "Mike Quill" folder, JVL Papers. For civil rights calls to end the TWU strike, see Roy Wilkins to Van Arsdale, telegram, January 11, 1966, box 20, "General Files (Includes Transit Strike)" folder, NYCCLC Records.

94. Marmo, *More Profile Than Courage*, 225–39; anonymous Local 2 member interview. For the first Local 100 leadership meeting after Quill's death, see minutes, executive board of Local 100 meeting, March 23, 1966, box 1, "L-100 Minutes Executive Board, 1960–1969" folder, TWUA:RL.

95. The quotation in the subhead above is from Maio interview. For some notable works on the building trades, see Schneirow and Suhrbur, *Union Brotherhood, Union Town*; and Palladino, *Skilled Hands, Strong Spirits*. Sociologists have also produced some notable works, including Riemer, *Hard Hats*; and Silver, *Under Construction*.

96. Segal, *Rise*, 19–34.

97. Montgomery, *Workers' Control in America*, 18–27.
98. Segal, *Rise*, 209–11; Freeman, *Working-Class New York*, 167.
99. Buhle, *Taking Care of Business*, 95–97.
100. "16 Construction Unions Seek New Pacts as Contracts Expire," *New York Times*, June 30, 1966.
101. Minutes, executive board meeting, March 15, 1965, microfilm, BCTC Minutes; Freeman, "Hardhats," 732.
102. Ruffini, *Harry Van Arsdale Jr.*, 159–61.
103. For building trades discussions on unemployment among members, see minutes, executive board meeting, November 16, 1964, February 8, 1965, microfilm, BCTC Minutes.
104. Maio interview; anonymous Local 2 member interview.
105. Maio interview.
106. Anonymous Local 2 member interview.
107. Anonymous Local 2 member interview.
108. Freeman, "Hardhats," 730–33, quote 733. For skill hoarding, see anonymous Local 2 member interview.
109. Freeman, "Hardhats," 730–33.
110. John Feeney, interview with author, New York, January 11, 2017.
111. Maio interview; "Plumbers and Carpenters Agree On How to Install Co-op's Sinks," *New York Times*, October 20, 1962; minutes, executive board meeting, September 20, 1965, BCTC Minutes.
112. Feeney interview.
113. Maio interview. For Cohen indictment, see "Ex-Plumbers' Chief Sentenced on Bribe," *New York Times*, April 8, 1967.
114. Maio interview; anonymous Local 2 member interview.
115. Maio interview; anonymous Local 2 member interview.
116. Maio interview.
117. Feeney interview.
118. Kelly to Lindsay, August 12, 1965, box 89, "Plumbing Industry" folder, JVL Papers.
119. For sentiments similar to Kelly's in different unions, see Charles Henricks to Harry Van Arsdale, January 9, 1966, box 20, "General Files (Includes Transit Strike)" folder, NYCCLC Records; and Old Timers interview, April 15, 1976, TRFC Oral History.
120. Maio interview; Feeney interview.
121. Feeney interview.
122. Maio interview; Feeney interview. For shaping up among carpenters, see Al Filardo interview, October 10, 1986, NYW.
123. Anonymous Local 2 member interview. For fear of intermittent work among electricians, see Moccio, *Live Wire*, 8.
124. Feeney interview.
125. Constitution, 1961, box 4, "Minutes of the Constitution Committee 1971" folder, United Association of Journeymen and Apprentices of the Plumbing and Pipe Fitting Industry, Local 2 Records, Tamiment Library.
126. Zeitz, *White Ethnic New York*, 25–27, 30–32.
127. Maio interview.

128. Waldinger, *Still the Promised Land?*, 178–80; anonymous Local 2 member interview.

129. "Bias in the Building Industry." Forty percent of applicants accepted to Philadelphia plumbers in the late 1960s were sons of plumbers; see Deslippe, *Protesting Affirmative Action*, 30.

130. "Bias in the Building Industry."

131. Gilbert Banks interview, October 22, 1980, NYW; Haughton interview; Purnell, *Fighting Jim Crow*, 28.

132. Waldinger, *Still the Promised Land?*, 183–84.

133. For the story of a Black plumber who was forced to leave the industry, see Freeman, *Working-Class New York*, 179–80.

134. Haughton interview, 43.

135. "Negro Hiring Up in Building Jobs," *New York Times*, April 1, 1965; Sugrue, "Affirmative Action from Below," 156–59.

136. Waldinger, *Still the Promised Land?*, 183.

137. Moccio, *Live Wire*, 112–16.

138. Waldinger, *Still the Promised Land?*, 184.

139. NLRB v. JA of PPI, 360 F.2d 428 (2d Cir. 1966), https://casetext.com/case/nlrb-v-j-a-of-p-pi; Hill, "Bronx Terminal Market Controversy," 363–69.

140. Hill, "Bronx Terminal Market Controversy," 371–72; Purnell, *Fighting Jim Crow*, 280–81.

141. Minutes, executive board meeting, May 18, 1964, microfilm 1966–73, Building Trades Employers Association Meeting Records, Tamiment Library; "Onlookers Crowd Noisy Room for Plumbers' Two-Hour Ordeal," *New York Times*, May 9, 1964.

142. Maio interview.

143. "Bias in the Building Industry."

144. Feeney interview. On hate strikes, see Sugrue, *Origins*, 98–109.

145. Feeney interview; anonymous Local 2 member interview.

146. On the impact of Local 3's victory, see Ruffini, *Harry Van Arsdale Jr.*, 125. Ruffini, however, does not account for the internal dynamics of the unions influenced by Local 3.

147. Due to a dearth of sources on both the management and union side, the 1966 contract negotiations remain opaque. However, both oral history and contemporary press indicate that the demand for a hiring hall was the key issue separating the two sides from the beginning of negotiations in March 1966; see "Contractors Call Plumbers Unfair," *New York Times*, August 6, 1966.

148. Maio interview. Plumbers meeting minutes and correspondence are not held in archives, and there is a dearth of sources to document the plumbers union's internal debates.

149. "Plumbers Union Joins Strike Call," *New York Times*, July 23, 1966.

150. Maio interview.

151. Feeney interview; "Mayor Intervenes in Plumber Strike," *New York Times*, October 28, 1966.

152. Maio interview.

153. "Striking Plumbers Reject New Offer," *New York Times*, October 20, 1966.

154. "Plumbers Strike Brings an Appeal," *New York Times*, October 23, 1966.

155. Shemin to Lindsay, October 13, 27, 1966, box 105, "Strikes & Labor Troubles—Gen. 1966–1967" folder, Subject Files, Mayor John Lindsay Collection, Municipal Archives.

156. Maio interview.

157. "2,200 Plumbers End Strike but 4,000 Remain Off," *New York Times*, September 18, 1966.

158. Maio interview.

159. Shemin to Lindsay, October 27, 1966; minutes, regular meeting, October 17, 1966, microfilm, BCTC Minutes.

160. Minutes, Board of Governors meeting, October 19, 1966, microfilm 1966–73, Building Trades Employers Association Meeting Records, Tamiment Library.

161. Regan, "General Organizers' Report" (January 1967), 12–14.

162. "Parley at City Hall Fails to Halt Plumbers' Strike," *New York Times*, November 3, 1966.

163. Regan, "General Organizers' Report" (January 1967), 12–14.

164. "Plumbers Reject Contract Offer," *New York Times*, November 6, 1966.

165. "Statement by Mayor John V. Lindsay," November 16, 1966, box 353, "Labor Relations 1966–1969" folder, JVL Papers; "What the 131-Day Plumber Strike Is Doing to Us," *Daily News*, December 2, 1966; "Builders Seek Help from Government on Plumber Strike," *New York Times*, November 10, 1966.

166. Press release, November 16, 1966, box 353, "Labor Relations 1966–1959" folder, JVL Papers. A full copy of the proposal was printed in the *New York Times* the day following its rejection: "The Text of Proposals to End the Plumbers' Strike," *New York Times*, December 8, 1966.

167. Regan, "General Organizers' Reports" (February 1967), 15.

168. "Plumbers Still Balk; $500M Tieup Goes On," *Daily News*, December 9, 1966.

169. Regan, "General Organizers' Reports" (February 1967), 15. Machine vote discussed in Maio interview.

170. Maio interview.

171. Feeney interview.

172. Maio interview.

173. Minutes, executive board meeting, January 16, 1967, microfilm, BCTC Minutes.

174. Maio interview.

175. Feeney interview.

176. "Plumbers' Strike Is Ordered Ended: Union President Says There Will Be No Vote on Accord," *New York Times*, December 30, 1966.

177. Segal, *Rise*, 91–92, 206.

178. "Plumbers' Strike Is Ordered Ended."

179. "Plumbers Vote to End Walkout," *New York Times*, January 5, 1967; "Strike by Plumbers Ends after 164 Days," *Daily News*, January 5, 1967.

180. Maio interview.

181. Regan, "General Organizers' Reports" (April 1967), 18.

182. Maio interview.

183. Anonymous Local 2 member interview.

184. Feeney interview.

185. "2 Building Trades Reject Contracts," *New York Times*, July 1, 1969; "Steamfitters Again Reject Proposals to End Strike," *New York Times*, July 8, 1969; "Elevator Constructors Veto Pact, Constructors to Vote on Theirs," *New York Times*, October 12, 1969.

CHAPTER 2

1. For blue-collar blues, see Gooding, "Blue Collar Blues," 70.
2. For racism and Wallace support, see Price, "Right-Wing Politics." For some racist rank-and-file Wallace supporters, see the Law Enforcement Group and its publication *Law Enforcement Group of New York Inc. Bulletin* 1, no. 1 (March 1969), in box 353, "Labor Relations, Police, Fire, Sanitation 1970–1971" folder, JVL Papers.
3. New York State Department of Labor, *Statistics on Work Stoppages* [. . .] *1967*; New York State Department of Labor, *Statistics on Work Stoppages* [. . .] *1968*. A not insignificant portion of days lost in 1968 is attributable to the Ocean Hill–Brownsville teachers strike, but several other majors strikes that year accounted for major losses, including those of electrical workers and sanitationmen.
4. New York State Department of Labor, *Statistics on Work Stoppages* [. . .] *1967*.
5. Brecher, "Decline of Strikes," 74.
6. Glaberman, *Wartime Strikes*; timeline in Brenner, Day, and Ness, *Encyclopedia of Strikes*, xxiv.
7. Mello, *New York Longshoremen*, 45–51, 56–58.
8. "Railway Express Workers Stage a Wildcat Walkout," *New York Times*, January 10, 1967.
9. "3 Restaurants Here Kept from Opening by Wildcat Strike," *New York Times*, May 21, 1967. For restaurant unions and wildcats, see "Strike Called Off at 4 Restaurants," *New York Times*, May 23, 1967; and Brady, "Appetite for Justice," 231–33.
10. "Wildcat Strike Snarls Bus Line," *New York Times*, June 22, 1967.
11. "3-Day Port Strike Settle in Jersey," *New York Times*, October 14, 1967.
12. "Train Service Cut," *New York Times*, September 12, 1967; "L.I.R.R. Expecting 'Full Service,'" *New York Times*, November 29, 1968.
13. Jim McMahon, interview with author, New York, January 10, 2017; "Phone Men Strike Over 'Protection,'" *New York Times*, August 1, 1967.
14. "Phone Men Strike Over 'Protection.'"
15. McMahon interview; Aaron Brenner, "Rank-and-File Struggles," 253–59.
16. McMahon interview. See chapter 4 of this book for Local 1101's rebellion.
17. "Telephone Strike Likely to Spread," *New York Times*, August 7, 1967.
18. Morton Bahr to "All New York Plant Local Presidents," September 12, 1967, box 5, "NY Tel: High Crime Area Dispute (Bargaining)" folder, District 1, CWA Records; McMahon interview.
19. Fortner, *Black Silent Majority*. Flamm, *Law and Order*.
20. "Phone Talks Go On, but Strike Is Expected to Continue Today," *New York Times*, August 4, 1967.
21. Flamm, *Law and Order*.
22. "Walkout Is Staged by 20 Meter Maids," *New York Times*, May 24, 1967.
23. "Plump Ex-Meter Maid Diets to Get Job Back," *New York Times*, August 31, 1965.
24. "City Meter Maids Begin New Duties," *New York Times*, April 20, 1965.

25. "Maid vs. Patrolmen: An Overtime Meter Brings Bronx Clash," *New York Times*, April 15, 1965; "Meter Maids End Two-Day Walkout," *New York Times*, May 26, 1967.

26. Hodges, *Taxi!*, 123–27.

27. Old Timers interview, April 15, 1976, TRFC Oral History.

28. "A Message to All Hackmen [. . .]," 1966, box 1 N5, "Election (Candidates, Circulars, Results 1969)" folder, HVA Papers.

29. "Election Flyer Committee for Taxi Workers Rights," 1966, box 1 N5, "Election (Candidates, Circulars, Results 1969)" folder, HVA Papers.

30. *Taxi News Transport* 4, no. 1 (October 21, 1966), 1, in box 1 N5, "Election (Candidates, Circulars, Results 1969)" folder, HVA Papers.

31. "Strikes Staged by 2,000 Cabbies," *New York Times*, November 12, 1967.

32. Vidich, *New York Cab Driver*, 105–6; "Labor Dispute Tactics," *New York Times*, February 7, 1968.

33. "Wildcat Walkouts Keep 2,500 Cabs off Street," *New York Times*, November 23, 1967.

34. "Taxi Negotiators Reach an Accord Fare Rise Is Seen," *New York Times*, November 25, 1967.

35. "Excerpts from Recommendations on the Taxi Industry by Mayor's Study Panel," *New York Times*, January 5, 1967.

36. "Cab Union Warns of Strikes on January 1," *New York Times*, December 23, 1967.

37. Vidich, *New York Cab Driver*, 106–7.

38. "Tug Strike Begins Here as Crewmen Reject a New Pact," *New York Times*, January 30, 1967.

39. "Firemen to Begin Slowdown Today," *New York Times*, April 6, 1967.

40. Quote from "Statement by Mayor John Lindsay," June 23, 1967. "Statement by Mayor Lindsay on the Threatened Work Stoppage of the Social Service Employees Union against the Welfare Department," June 17, 1967. Both in box 136, "Labor Relations" folder, JVL Papers.

41. Walkowitz, *Working with Class*, 264–74.

42. Gafney, *Teachers United*, 389–91; "Teachers Ratify School Contract; Classes on Today," *New York Times*, September 29, 1967; Ben Occhiogrosso interview, July 6, 1981, NYW.

43. Special Task Force to the Secretary of Health, Education, and Welfare, *Work in America*; "For Many Concerns: An Inadvertent 4-Day Week," *New York Times*, May 14, 1972.

44. Noble, *Progress without People*, 24; Special Task Force to the Secretary of Health, Education, and Welfare, *Work in America*, 38–39.

45. "Sick Leave Abuse in Schools Hinted," *New York Times*, May 31, 1967; "For Many Concerns."

46. "Joseph Maletta, et al.," no. 6021/003, box 1, folder 32, Theodore Woodrow Kheel Arbitration Papers, Kheel Center. This folder documents relatively widespread problems with absenteeism.

47. "Edward McGuire—7/19/1968," folder 20; and for a later suspension for excessive absences, see "William Ford—12/4/1972," folder 24, both in no. 6021/003, box 6, Theodore Woodrow Kheel Arbitration Papers, Kheel Center.

48. "Walworth Drops New York Office," *New York Times*, December 6, 1962.

49. Brockway, "Keep on Truckin'," 42–43.

50. That absenteeism and shirking of work duties were present across many industries confirms these as widespread practices; McMahon interview.

51. "Allied New York Services, Inc. vs. Local 553, IBT," April 6, 1971, no. 5305, box 30, folder 10, Benjamin H. Wolff Papers, Kheel Center.

52. Minutes, board of governors meeting, April 20, May 18, 1966, microfilm 1966–73, Building Trades Employers Association Meeting Records, Tamiment Library.

53. Fenton, "Confessions," 21.

54. Oral history confirms the generational distinction at work sites, with younger workers having fewer long-term financial obligations to deal with in case of strikes or other work interruptions. McMahon interview; Fenton, "Confessions," 24.

55. "Exploratory Study," 1967, box 6, "Exploratory Study of Selected Factors Which May Influence Fatigue and Monotony Associated with the Letter Sorting Task, 1967" folder, Postal Union Records.

56. Judson Gooding, "Blue-Collar Blues on the Assembly Line," *Fortune*, July 1970; Glaberman, "Walter Reuther," 69–70.

57. "470 Strike Pan Am in Wildcat Action," *New York Times*, August 25, 1967; "Employees at Pan Am Vote to End 2-Day Wildcat," *New York Times*, August 26, 1967.

58. "150 Strike Pan Am over a Dismissal," *New York Times*, May 10, 1968; "Pan Am Walkout Ends," *New York Times*, May 11, 1968.

59. Sheppard, *Where Have All*, 3.

60. An oral history of CWA workers confirms the assertion in McMahon interview.

61. "United Parcel Service Will Resume Deliveries after 1-Day Strike," *New York Times*, October 31, 1969.

62. McMahon interview. For more on youth protest and attitudes, see Patterson, *Grand Expectations*, 446–49.

63. "675 Lifeguards Walk Out Here for a Day over Job Conditions," *New York Times*, July 28, 1968.

64. "Conversation: Wilbur Haddock"; "Negro Members Are Challenging Union Leaders," *New York Times*, June 29, 1969.

65. Fogelson, *Violence as Protest*, 43; Darden, *Detroit*, 2–3.

66. Mumford, *Newark*, 136–40; Upton, "Politics of Urban Violence," 243–46.

67. Podair, *Strike*.

68. Denby, *Indignant Heart*, 265–68. Haddock confirms a similar divide in the New York area; "Conversation: Wilbur Haddock," 30–31.

69. Robert Brenner, *Economics of Global Turbulence*, 99–105.

70. "For Many Concerns." For pilferage concerns among building contractors, see minutes, Board of Governors meeting, April 20, 1966, microfilm 1966–73, Building Trades Employers Association Meeting Records, Tamiment Library.

71. Stencel, "America's Changing Work Ethic."

72. Morris, *Cost of Good Intentions*, 104.

73. "Working Paper on Employee Relations in the City of New York," n.d., box 59, "Labor Relations 1966–1968" folder 1099, Mayor John Lindsay Collection, Municipal Archives.

74. "Contracts Expire for City Workers," *New York Times*, July 1, 1966.

75. "De Lury Lashes Back at Kearing on Union Politics," *New York Times*, December 21, 1966.

76. "City Grants Raise to Sanitationmen," *New York Times*, December 17, 1966; "Kearing Seeks Talks with Union to Prevent Sanitation Slowdown," *New York Times*, December 4, 1966.

77. "450 Sanitationmen Shifted to New Jobs 'to Clear the Air,'" *New York Times*, January 24, 1967.

78. "Kearing to Bar Pay for Parading in City," *New York Times*, March 11, 1967.

79. Cannato, *Ungovernable City*, 196.

80. Donovan, *Administering the Taylor Law*, 106–8.

81. For the OCB and settlements of police, social worker, and firefighter contracts, see press release, January 13, 1968, box 136, "Labor Relations" folder, JVL Papers.

82. "Sanitation Union Fails to Strike," *New York Times*, January 31, 1968.

83. Cannato, *Ungovernable City*, 196–97.

84. "Sanitation Strike Begun by 10,000 City Obtains Writ," *New York Times*, February 3, 1968.

85. Joseph J. Chiarelli to Nelson Rockefeller, March 14, 1968, Office Subject Files, reel 70, Sanitation, NAR Records; "Sanitationmen Say Their Pact Has Become Political Football," *New York Times*, February 10, 1968.

86. "Rattle of Garbage Cans in the Streets Marks End of 9-Day Sanitationmen's Strike," *New York Times*, February 12, 1968.

87. Maier, *City Unions*, 86.

88. "Motorists Scramble for Parking Space in Strike," *New York Times*, January 30, 1968; "Bus Strike on L.I. Hits Commuters," *New York Times*, February 2, 1968; "Suspicious Fire Destroys Bus," *New York Times*, February 2, 1968.

89. "Explosive Bargainer," *New York Times*, February 3, 1968.

90. "'A Great Mayor' 'That Bum?,'" *New York Times*, January 1, 1967.

91. Freeman, "Lindsay and Labor," 129.

92. DeLury to Lindsay, November 5, 1970, box 353, "Labor Relations, Police, Fire and Sanitation" folder, JVL Papers.

93. For taxi rank-and-filers and families on Lindsay, see Robert C. Johnson to Harry Van Arsdale, September 27, 1969; and Mrs. Claire B. Dooley to Van Arsdale, October 28, 1969, both in box 3 N4, "Letters to Harry Van Arsdale" folder, HVA Papers; Reeves, "Making of the Mayor," 38; and Hunter-Gault, "Black and White," 47.

94. "'A Great Mayor' 'That Bum?'"; Gonzalez, "Reflections."

95. "The Strike of the New York City Sanitationmen," March 15, 1968, 3, box 75, "Labor" folder, Nelson A. Rockefeller Personal Papers, Rockefeller Archive Center, Sleepy Hollow, New York.

96. Harry W. Albright Jr. to Nelson Rockefeller, confidential memorandum, n.d., 3, box 90, "New York City Sanitation Strike, Key Events" folder, NAR Records.

97. Lindsay to Nelson Rockefeller, February 6, 1968, box 90, "New York City Sanitation Strike, Key Events, 1968 Feb" folder, NAR Records.

98. Albright to Rockefeller, confidential memorandum, n.d., 14.

99. Chronopoulos, "Lindsay Administration"; Purnell, "'Taxation without Sanitation.'"

100. Lindsay to Rockefeller, February 8, 1968, box 90, "New York City Sanitation Strike, Key Events" folder, NAR Records.

101. Ruffini, *Harry Van Arsdale Jr.*, 204.

102. For unification of the labor movement in the face of Lindsay, see "News Conference of Governor Nelson A. Rockefeller Re: Strike of New York City Sanitationmen," February 9, 1968, box 90, "New York City Sanitation Strike, Key Events, 1968 Feb" folder, NAR Records; and "Strike of the New York City Sanitationmen."

103. Albright to Rockefeller, confidential memorandum, n.d., 10.

104. Both quotes in Albright to Rockefeller, confidential memorandum, n.d., 10.

105. Smith, *On His Own Terms*, 506–11.

106. "Governor Warns on Party Future," *New York Times*, October 13, 1966.

107. "Rockefeller Goes on the Offensive," *New York Times*, October 25, 1966.

108. Albright to Rockefeller, confidential memorandum, n.d., 12–15.

109. "Telephone Calls on Strike," February 9, 1968, Diane Von Wie Subject Files, box 23, "Sanitation Strike 1968" folder, NAR Records.

110. "How to Avoid Strikes by Garbagemen, Nurses, Teachers, Subway Men, Welfare Workers, Etc.," *New York Times*, February 25, 1968.

111. For letters in the aftermath of the strike, which are mostly negative but include several commendations of the governor, see Office Subject Files, "Sanitation Strike 1968" folder, NAR Records.

112. "New Conference of Mayor John Lindsay at City Hall, New York," February 11, 1968, box 90, "New York City Sanitation Strike, Key Events, 1968 Feb" folder, NAR Records.

113. "Hearing before New York State Joint Legislative Committee on Industrial and Labor Conditions," 1968, 129, no. 5024, box 2, "Taylor Law 2/23/68" folder, Theodore Woodrow Kheel Arbitration Papers, Kheel Center.

114. Chiarelli to Rockefeller, March 14, 1968, Office Subject Files, reel 70, "Sanitation" folder, NAR Records.

115. For a lively description of his Madison Square Garden appearance, see Carter, *From George Wallace*, 18–21.

116. For a transcription of Wallace's Madison Square Garden speech, see Bush, *Campaign Speeches*, 185–92.

117. Carter, *Politics of Rage*, 204–6.

118. "The Wallace Phenomenon Gets a Big Hand," *New York Times*, September 8, 1968; "Queens Volunteers Mailing Petitions for Wallace," *New York Times*, August 1, 1968.

119. Steinberg, "Social Context."

120. Cowie, *Stayin' Alive*, 98–110.

121. R. W. MacDonald to George Wallace Party, August 21, 1968; Mr. and Mrs. Paul Petaja to Wallace, 1968; Wallace to Hudak, August 28, 1968; and Naporlee to Wallace, August 14, 1968, all in Administrative Files, "Presidential Election 1968 - National Correspondence by State: Alabama-North Carolina" folder, container SG030833, Governors George C. and Lurleen B. Wallace Collection, Alabama Department of Archives and History; Paul R. Petaja obituary, Perry Funeral Home (website), accessed May 8, 2020, https://perryfh.com/tribute/details/881/Paul-Petaja/obituary.html; "Jury Says 21 Faked

Bills for Overtime," *New York Times*, February 17, 1977; National Labor Relations Board, *Decisions and Orders*, 102–5.

122. "Politics: Wallace Is Said to be Hurting Humphrey More Than Nixon in Jersey," *New York Times*, September 13, 1968.

123. "Labor Found Split on the Election," *New York Times*, September 14, 1968.

124. "150 Hunt Ambushers Who Shot Police," *New York Times*, August 3, 1968; "Brooklyn Police Set Up Group to Back 'Vigorous' Enforcement," *New York Times*, August 8, 1968; "Rights Groups Assail Demands of New Police Unity," *New York Times*, August 9, 1968.

125. For LEG's platform, see "A Look Back, a Step Forward," *Law Enforcement Group of New York Inc. Bulletin* 1, no. 1 (March 1969), in box 353, "Labor Relations, Police, Fire, Sanitation 1970–1971" folder, JVL Papers; "5,000 Police Sign Protest Petition," *New York Times*, August 20, 1968; and "Meeting of Policemen Cheers Attack on Complaint Review Board," *New York Times*, August 22, 1968.

126. Darien, *Becoming New York's Finest*, 174–78.

127. Flamm, *Law and Order*, 31–49.

128. For crime statistics, see the chart titled "How New York Changed under Lindsay" in Roberts, *America's Mayor*, 224; and Pileggi, "Crime and Punishment," 80.

129. Flamm, "'Law and Order,'" 655.

130. Johnson, *Street Justice*, 266–69.

131. Quote from "Inquiry Planned on Judge Furey," *New York Times*, August 27, 1968.

132. Alex, *New York Cops*, 198–201.

133. "Wallace Hailed by Police on Tour," *New York Times*, September 8, 1968. There was growing support for Wallace and LEG's position; see "Editorial WCBS News Radio 88," September 18, 1968, box 353, "Labor Relations, Police, Fire, Sanitation 1970–1971" folder, JVL Papers.

134. Herbert L. Haber, memorandum, June 28, 1968, box 59, folder 1095 "Labor Policy—Contract Negotiations and Demand," Mayor John Lindsay Collection, Municipal Archives; "Civil Servants: Wallace Voices Their Frustration," *New York Times*, October 27, 1968; quote from "New Labor Crisis Threatening the City This Month," *New York Times*, September 2, 1968.

135. "All Hands! UFA Bulletin for Delegates," October 21, 1968, Robert Sweet Subject Files, box 7, folder 121 "Labor and Fire"; and Vincent McDonnell to Lindsay, May 1, 1968, box 59, "Labor Relations 1966–1968" folder, both in Mayor John Lindsay Collection, Municipal Archives. For discussions of rank-and-file problems, see "State of New York, Governor's Committee on Public Employee Relations, Interim Report," June 17, 1968, box 4, folder 39, E. Wight Bakke Papers, Kheel Center.

136. For attacks on police officers, see "Attacks on Police Increase," *Law Enforcement Group of New York Inc. Bulletin* 1, no. 1 (March 1969), in box 353, "Labor Relations, Police, Fire, Sanitation 1970–1971" folder, JVL Papers.

137. Flood, *Fires*, 142.

138. For the TWU and crime, see minutes, enlarged joint executive board meeting of Local 100, September 26, 1966, box 1, "L100-Minutes: Joint Executive Committee, 1941–1942 1966–1967" folder, TWUA:RL. For taxis, see chapter 4 of this book.

139. McMahon interview.

140. Isaacs, *Inside Ocean Hill–Brownsville*, 70–71.

141. Quoted in Cannato, *Ungovernable City*, 343. For the most extensive look at the 1968 UFT strikes in relation to Ocean Hill–Brownsville, see Podair, *Strike*. "Red Neck New York: Is This Wallace Country?" *New York*, October 7, 1968, 25–26.

142. Occhiogrosso interview.

143. Jo Yurek, interview with author, New York, April 3, 2018.

144. Quote from Rieder, *Canarsie*, 244–45. Michael Rogin also notes Wallace's weakness among Jews in the 1964 Democratic primaries; Rogin, "Wallace."

145. Podair, *Strike*, 153–58.

146. Occhiogrosso interview.

147. Yurek interview.

148. Podair, *Strike*, 159–82.

149. While Wallace was up in early October nationally, his numbers thereafter began to decline because of Nixon's attacks. See Carter, *Politics of Rage*, 364; and "Wallace Tries to Start That 'Swing,'" *New York Times*, October 6, 1968.

150. "Humphrey Leads Labor Poll, 34–32," *New York Times*, October 9, 1968.

151. Minutes, special meeting, October 10, 1968, box 10, "Exec Bd Meetings Minutes 1967–1969" folder, NYCCLC Records. For news stories, see "Support for Wallace Is Found among Union Members by Poll," *New York Times*, September 11, 1968; "Politics: Wallace Is Said to be Hurting Humphrey"; and "Humphrey Leads Labor Poll."

152. Cowie, *Stayin' Alive*, 82–83.

153. "Wallace Support By Labor Denied," *New York Times*, October 11, 1968.

154. Quote from ". . . And the Pro-Humphrey Labor Chiefs Are Worried," *New York Times*, September 15, 1968.

155. "100,000 Expected in Parade Today," *New York Times*, September 2, 1968; "Parade Security Tight; Crowd Relaxed," *New York Times*, September 3, 1968.

156. "Suggested Guide for Local Unions. Fire House Voters' Registration Drive," box 59, "Voter Registration-Political Campaign" folder, NYCCLC Records.

157. "Report of New York City Central Labor Council AFL-CIO Humphrey-Muskie Campaign," box 59, "Voter Registration-Political Campaign" folder (2 of 2), NYCCLC Records.

158. "Suggested Guide for Local Unions."

159. "Unofficial Registration Totals for Period, Sept. 30th, Oct. 3rd, 4th & 5th," box 59, "Voter Registration-Political Campaign" folder (2 of 2), NYCCLC Records.

160. "Report of New York City Central Labor Council"; Arthur Goldberg to Van Arsdale, telegram, box 59, "Voter Registration-Political Campaign" folder (2 of 2), NYCCLC Records.

161. "Warning: Wallace No Friend of Working People or Their Unions," box 24, "Elections 1968" folder, NYCCLC Records.

162. "Humphrey vs. Nixon 1948–1968"; and "Humphrey and Nixon Speak on Labor," both in box 24, "Elections 1968" folder, NYCCLC Records.

163. "Can We Survive the Assault of '69?," box 24, "Elections 1968" folder, NYCCLC Records.

164. "Labor Press Verdict: GOP Platform Is Bad News," box 24, "Elections 1968" folder, NYCCLC Records; "Humphrey and Nixon Speak on Labor."

165. New York Board of Elections, *Annual Report*, 48–51; "Ethnic Factor Doubted in

Charter Vote," *New York Times*, November 9, 1967; "Gallup Sampling Finds a Catholic Shift to Republicans and Negro-Jewish Democrat Tradition," *New York Times*, November 7, 1968.

166. Kelly, *Neck and Neck*, 208.

167. Zeitz, *White Ethnic New York*, 171–95; Marlin, *Fighting the Good Fight*, 137–43.

168. Sullivan, *New York State*, 90–92.

169. New York Board of Elections, *Annual Report*, 48–51; "Ethnic Factor Doubted"; "Gallup Sampling Finds a Catholic Shift."

170. AFL-CIO meeting notes, n.d., box 5, "NY Tel: High Crime Area Dispute (Arbitration Awards) 1962–1968" folder, District 1, CWA Records.

171. "Wage Rise Brings End to City Incinerator Strike," *New York Times*, November 15, 1968.

172. For the Con Edison strike, see "Con Ed Is Struck but Is Confident of Meeting Needs," *New York Times*, December 1, 1968; "Con Ed Reports Strike Sabotage," *New York Times*, December 4, 1968, 1; and "Sabotage at Con Edison," *New York Times*, December 5, 1968. For union meeting disruption after the strike was concluded, see minutes, regular membership meeting, December 19, 1968, box 1, folder 41, Utility Workers of America, Local 1-2 Records, Tamiment Library. For some rank-and-file *opposition* to the strike, see "Win, Place or Show—Vote Brotherhood," 1968, box 136, "Labor" folder, JVL Papers.

173. Anonymous International Brotherhood of Teamsters Local 553 member, interview with author, New York, January 13, 2017.

174. Minutes, special executive board meeting, January 9, 1969, 1, box 117, folder 1, NYCCLC Records.

CHAPTER 3

1. Minutes, special executive board meeting, January 9, 1969, box 117, folder 1, NYCCLC Records; "Unionist in the Middle: Harry Van Arsdale Jr.," *New York Times*, November 15, 1968.

2. For strike data, see US Department of Labor, *Analysis of Work Stoppages, 1969*, 35; and US Department of Labor, *Analysis of Work Stoppages, 1970*, 41.

3. For complaints and effects of the 1968 strike, see Postmaster Edward J. Quigley to Nelson A. Rockefeller, January 14, 1969; and Stephen A. Hopkins to Miss Ida Krasken, January 20, 1969, both in series 37, Office Subject Files, subseries 3 "Third Administration," Subject "Labor," NAR Records.

4. Blakely, *Mass Mediated Disease*, 132–33.

5. "Fuel Drivers Go on Strike Here," *New York Times*, December 16, 1970.

6. For work on the Teamsters, see Aaron Brenner, "Rank-and-File Teamster Movements"; La Botz, *Rank-and-File Rebellion*; and Friedman, *Teamster Rank and File*.

7. Witwer, *Corruption and Reform*, 64.

8. "New Parleys Fail to End Coal Tie Up: La Guardia Confers with Mediator in Coal Strike," *New York Times*, January 20, 1940.

9. For Local 553 statistics and union gains in the 1950s, see "1955 Negotiation Letter"; "Coal Consumption and Teamsters Wages in New York City Chart"; and Brice P. Disque, statement to the Mayor's Citizens' Committee, 1955, all in Brice P. Disque Papers, coll. 115, Special Collections and University Archives, University of Oregon Libraries.

10. Evidence of Black drivers in photograph of 1955 strike, sent to the author from IBT Local 553. Other than this photograph and generic union publications, the local was not forthcoming with source material.

11. "Tim Costello, Trucker-Author Who Fought Globalization, Dies at 64," *New York Times*, December 26, 2009.

12. Root & Branch was an editorial and organizational group that published a journal from 1970 to 1981, engaging itself in New Left politics and the antinuclear movement. Its ideas were highly critical of the theories and practices of the New Left as a whole, calling instead upon the left communist tradition embodied by Paul Mattick, who, like Rosa Luxembourg, stressed the spontaneity of the working class. A collection of Mattick's essays was published as *Anti-Bolshevik Communism* (White Plains, NY: M. E. Sharpe, 1978).

13. Brockway, "Keep on Truckin'," 42–43.

14. Jeremy Brecher, interview with author, New York, March 15, 2011.

15. Brockway, "Keep on Truckin'," 43.

16. Anonymous IBT Local 553 member, interview with author, New York, January 13, 2017.

17. For documentation of allegations of racketeering and organized crime incursion into the Teamsters in New York City until the 1950s, see Witwer, *Corruption and Reform*, 111–13. For other rank-and-file studies, see Witwer, "Local Rank and File"; and La Botz, "Tumultuous Teamsters."

18. Anonymous IBT Local 553 member interview.

19. Brockway, "Keep on Truckin'," 41–42.

20. Brockway, "Keep on Truckin'," 42.

21. For the contract vote walkout, see "Fuel Oil Men Accept Pact and End Strike," *Daily News*, December 23, 1970; and "Fuel Drivers Vote to Go Back," *New York Times*, December 23, 1970.

22. While Costello mentions a monthly publication produced by Local 553 drivers, I have been unable to locate copies, either in archives or in the possession of former drivers.

23. Brockway, "Keep on Truckin'," 46–48.

24. Anonymous IBT Local 553 member interview.

25. For the 1968 strike, see "Fuel Oil Drivers Strike in the City," *New York Times*, December 16, 1968.

26. Borella to Nelson Rockefeller, memorandum, December 1970, series 37, Office Subject Files, subseries 3 "Third Administration," subject "Labor," "Fuel Oil Drivers" folder, NAR Records.

27. "Fuel Oil Drivers Go on Strike Here," *New York Times*, December 16, 1970.

28. "Fuel Oil Drivers Go on Strike Here."

29. "Fuel Strike On—Supplies Low," *New York Post*, December 16, 1970.

30. Anonymous IBT Local 553 member interview.

31. "Fuel Oil Men Reject Offer and Strike," *Daily News*, December 16, 1970.

32. "Prohiben caseros bajen calefacción," *El Diario La Prensa*, December 18, 1970.

33. "Vote Scheduled Tuesday by 2,200 Teamsters on New Contract," *New York Times*, December 20, 1970.

34. A. G. Marshall to T. N. Hurd, memorandum, December 16, 1970, series 37, Office Subject Files, subseries 3 "Third Administration," subject "Labor," NAR Records.

35. "Fuel Plum: $40 in 2 Jumps," *Daily News*, December 20, 1970.

36. "Fuel Oil Drivers Vote to Go Back," *New York Times*, December 23, 1970; "Vote Scheduled Tuesday." For a broader discussion of the complex intertwining of law-and-order concerns with disdain for social protest, rising street crime, and economic insecurity, see Flamm, *Law and Order*.

37. For landlords filling fuel tanks in anticipation of a strike, see "Fuel Oil Drivers Go on Strike Here."

38. "Possible Strike in Oil Distributing Industry," memorandum, box 53, "Daily Crisis Calendars" folder, JVL Papers; New York Office of Civil Defense, *Spotlight on Disaster Management*, 10. For implementation of the system, see Office of Emergency Control Board—Civil Defense, "Oil Inventory Update," Confidential Subject Files, Mayor John Lindsay Collection, Municipal Archives.

39. "No-Heat Complaints Pour In on the City," *New York Times*, December 21, 1970; "Fuel Drivers Vote to Go Back."

40. "Fuel Oil Men Accept Pact."

41. "Fuel Drivers Vote to Go Back."

42. "Fuel Oil Men Accept Pact"; "Fuel Drivers Vote to Go Back."

43. Anonymous IBT Local 553 member interview.

44. For the last major negotiation, see "Metropolitan Briefs," *New York Times*, December 16, 1974.

45. Anonymous IBT Local 553 member interview. For turning inward and the 1970s, see Schulman, *Seventies*, 78–101.

46. Letter to Mr. Daniel Gilmartin, President, July 17, 1967, box 39, "Rank and File Committee 1964–1968" folder, TWUA:RL; "8 Rank-&-Filers Show at TWU Mass Protest," *Daily News*, December 1, 1967.

47. Freeman, *In Transit*, 338.

48. "The Chairman's Corner," 5–6, box 39, "Rank and File News 1970" folder, TWUA:RL.

49. For workplace complaints, see "Basic Contract Demands of the Rank & File Committee," *Rank and File News*, no. 11, 3–5, in box 39, "Rank & File Committee 1969" folder, TWUA:RL. For the increasing numbers of Black members on the executive council in the late 1960s, see Gilmartin slate election materials "Continue [. . .]," 1966; and "The Team that Won [. . .]," 1969, both in box 18, "Elections 1965–1967" folder, TWUA:RL.

50. "Rank and File Demands Full Investigation: Another Conductor Beaten by Cop While Working," 1968, box 39, "Rank and File Committee 1964–1968" folder, TWUA:RL.

51. "Rank and File Demands Full Investigation"; "Negro Workers Charge Bias in the TA, Union," *New York Post*, December 12, 1968.

52. *Rank and File News*, November–December 1969, in box 39, "The Rank and File News 1967–1968" folder, TWUA:RL.

53. "Negro Members Are Challenging Union Leaders," *New York Times*, June 29, 1969.

54. "Rank and File Transit Workers—Organizational Drive Started for Independent Union," *Fight Back!* 1, no. 2 (November 1968), in box 39, "Rank & File Committee 1969" folder, TWUA:RL.

55. Anonymous Rank and File Committee member, interview with author, New York, August 2, 2017.

56. Letter about the meeting of December 17, 1969, box 39, "Rank & File Committee 1969" folder, TWUA:RL.

57. "Basic Contract Demands," 3–5.

58. For major disruptions of the New York subway system, see chapter 1 of this book.

59. "Transit Authority Guilty of Unfair Labor Practices, Rank and File Wins Access," box 39, "Rank & File Committee 1970–1971" folder, TWUA:RL.

60. Affidavit before the Supreme Court of the State of New York County of Queens, July 15, 1969, box 39, "Rank & File Committee 1969" folder, TWUA:RL; "Transit Authority Guilty."

61. State of New York PERB, "Petition for Certification and Decertification," October 24, 1969, box 39, "Rank & File Committee 1969" folder, TWUA:RL.

62. Thomas R. Brooks, "Subway Roulette: The Game Is Getting Dangerous," *New York*, June 15, 1970, 41, 46.

63. See photograph, *Rank and File News*, no. 18 (April 1972), 14, in box 10, "Rank And File Committee for a Democratic Union within the New York City Transit Authority" folder, JH Papers.

64. Public Employment Relations Board, *Cumulative Digest and Index*, 11023–24.

65. "Rank & File Wins Major Court Decision, P.E.R.B. Plans Appeal," *Rank and File News*, no. 18 (April 1972), in box 10, "Rank and File Committee for a Democratic Union within the New York City Transit Authority" folder, JH Papers.

66. Public Employment Relations Board, *Cumulative Digest and Index*, 11026; "T.W.U Rank and File," *New York Times*, January 11, 1972.

67. Public Employment Relations Board, *Cumulative Digest and Index*, 11026.

68. Matter of Carnegie v. Public Empl. Relations Bd., 40 A.D.2d 519, 334 N.Y.S.2d 416 (1972).

69. Anonymous Rank and File Committee member interview.

70. Freeman, *In Transit*, 339; Hall, "Labor Insurgency." Burton Hall, a prominent New York lawyer who represented several groups of rank-and-file insurgents during the postwar era, argues that working within the web of legal systems that govern and reinforce union representation left a minimal possibility of success because these legal systems tended to entrench labor bureaucracy and produce intimate working relationships among union heads, business owners, and state actors.

71. Minutes, planning meeting for rank-and-file conference in Detroit, October 19, 1968, 1–3, box 10, "Rank and File Workers Conferences 1968–1970" folder, JH Papers.

72. "Random Outline Keynote—Very General, Very Tentative," box 10, "Rank and File Workers Conferences 1968–1970" folder, JH Papers.

73. For some bios of participants, see minutes, planning meeting, October 19, 1968, 1–3.

74. "Random Outline Keynote"; Fred Mueller, "Bankrupt Conference of Rank and File Trade Unionists," *Bulletin: Bi-weekly Organ of the Workers League* 5, no. 18-107 (May 5, 1969), 6–7, in box 10, "Rank and File Workers Conferences 1968–1970" folder, JH Papers.

75. "Random Outline Keynote"; Mueller, "Bankrupt Conference," 6–7. For an insightful account of the battles on the waterfront, see Mello, *New York Longshoremen*.

76. Conference proceedings, 8, box 10, "Rank and File Workers Conferences 1968–1970" folder, JH Papers. For more on the painters, see Hall, "Painters' Union."

77. Conference proceedings, 8–9.

78. Conference proceedings, 1–4.

79. "Organizational Proposals for Assisting Rank and File Groups," 1, box 10, "Rank and File Workers Conferences 1968–1970" folder, JH Papers.

80. "Organizational Proposals," 1–2.

81. "Organizational Proposals," 2–3.

82. "James Haughton on Racism in the House of Labor," History Matters, accessed January 7, 2017, http://historymatters.gmu.edu/d/7038.

83. "Simmering Discontent Sparked Strike," *New York Times*, March 25, 1970.

84. Rachleff, "Postal Strike."

85. Rubio, *There's Always Work*, 31.

86. Quote from Rubio, *There's Always Work*, 155. For a quick summary of key issues in the postal service, see handwritten notes concerning the statement of James Rademacher, June 18, 1968, box 17, folder 5, Nixon Presidential Returned Materials Collection: White House Special Files, Richard Nixon Presidential Library and Museum.

87. "Statement of James H. Rademacher, Vice President National Association of Letter Carriers, before the Subcommittee on Compensation, Committee on Post Office and Civil Service House of Representatives," 5, September 17, 1968, box 17, folder 5, Nixon Presidential Returned Materials Collection: White House Special Files, Richard Nixon Presidential Library and Museum.

88. "$1,000 Pay Rises Offered to Police and Firemen Here," *New York Times*, December 23, 1970.

89. Rubio, *There's Always Work*, 236–37.

90. For New York City and inflation, see "MBPU News Flash," February 4, 1970, box 4, "Officer Files—Presidents—Moe Biller Material Re: Letter Carriers and Strike 1970 (3)" folder, Postal Union Records.

91. US Bureau of Labor Statistics, *New York City*, 50–55.

92. "Statement of James H. Rademacher," 3.

93. "Statement of James H. Rademacher," 11.

94. Rubio, *There's Always Work*, 212–13.

95. "Statement of James H. Rademacher." NALC Branch 36 president Morris Biller concurred with Rademacher's assessment of petty tyrannies; Biller to William Degenhard, August 17, 1971, box 7, "Aborted Strike 1971" folder, Postal Union Records.

96. "Postal Employees Protest 4% Raise," *New York Times*, June 21, 1969; Rubio, *There's Always Work*, 230–32.

97. "Consultative Meeting-Management," June 30, 1969; and US Post Office news release, July 1, 1969, both in box 3, "Officer Files—Presidents—Moe Biller—Kingsbridge Postal Reform, 1969" folder, Postal Union Records.

98. "Carriers' Flash," July 8, 1969, box 3, "Officer Files—Presidents—Moe Biller—Kingsbridge Postal Reform, 1969" folder, Postal Union Records.

99. Walsh and Mangum, *Labor Struggle*, 8–9.

100. For rank-and-file support of the sick-out, see "MBPU News Flash!," July 8, 1969; Joel Schreck et al. to MBPU, July 3, 1969; and Alfred H. Dorsey to Biller, July 9, 1969, all in box 3, "Officer Files—Presidents—Moe Biller—Kingsbridge Postal Reform, 1969" folder, Postal Union Records.

101. "Program of the New York Letter Carriers for all Postal Employees," box 4, "Officer Files—Presidents—Moe Biller Material Re: Letter Carriers and Strike 1970 (1)" folder, Postal Union Records.

102. "US Letter Carrier Demands," box 4, "Officer Files—Presidents—Moe Biller Material Re: Letter Carriers and Strike 1970 (1)" folder, Postal Union Records.

103. "Program of the New York Letter Carriers"; Rubio, *There's Always Work*, 240–41.

104. "NALC Branch 36 Strike Survey," January 20, 1970; and "Our Union," March 17, 1970, both in box 4, "Officer Files—Presidents—Moe Biller Material Re: Letter Carriers and Strike 1970 (1)" folder, Postal Union Records; "Postal Workers' Mood Forced a Strike," *New York Times*, March 21, 1970.

105. "We Won!," January 1966, box 55, "Bargaining, 1966" folder, TWUA:RL; Loyd, "Teachers' Strikes," 255–56.

106. "Letter Carriers Defy Injunction Ordering Them Back to Work," *New York Times*, March 19, 1970.

107. Quoted in Walsh and Mangum, *Labor Struggles*, 7–8.

108. Rubio, *Undelivered*, 56–59.

109. Biller to Nixon, March 3, 1970, box 4, "Officer Files—Presidents—Moe Biller Material Re: Letter Carriers and Strike 1970 (3)" folder, Postal Union Records.

110. "N.Y. Letter Carriers Strike," March 1970, box 4, "Officer Files—Presidents—Moe Biller Material Re: Letter Carriers and Strike 1970 (1)" folder; and "Chronology of Events Leading Up to and through the Postal Strike," 3–6, box 3, "President Biller" folder, both in Postal Union Records.

111. Biller statement, March 18, 1970, box 3, "Officer Files—Presidents—Moe Biller Material Re: Letter Carriers and Strike 1970 (2)" folder, Postal Union Records.

112. "Chronology of Events," 6–7.

113. "Chronology of Events," 8–10.

114. "Letter Carriers Defy Injunction"; Rubio, *There's Always Work*, 241–45; Mikusko and Miller, *Carriers*, 71. Some strike advocacy came a week earlier on Long Island, when NALC Branch 2530 voted for an area wage and called for strike action on March 16; see Howard Speedling to David Silvergleid, March 2, 1970, box 4, "Officer Files—Presidents—Moe Biller Material Re: Letter Carriers and Strike 1970 (3)" folder, Postal Union Records.

115. "Notes by Deputy Chief Inspector Conway in Re: Postal Work Stoppage, March 17–25, 1970," April 29, 1970, box 3, "President Biller" folder, Postal Union Records.

116. Untitled leaflet, box 3, "Officer Files—Presidents—Moe Biller Material Re: Letter Carriers and Strike 1970 (3)" folder, Postal Union Records.

117. "The Pinch Tightens on Businesses Here as Undelivered Letters and Parcels Pile Up," *New York Times*, March 21, 1970.

118. "Postal Blackout Hampers Market," *New York Times*, March 20, 1970.

119. "Notes by Deputy Chief Inspector Conway."

120. Rubio, *There's Always Work*, 254.

121. "Chronology of Events," 12.

122. "Labor Condemns Action, While Business Backs It," *New York Times*, March 24, 1970.

123. This initial deal is mentioned in "Chronology of Events," 22.

124. Agreement, March 29, 1970, box 4, "Officer Files—Presidents—Moe Biller Material Re: Letter Carriers and Strike 1970 (3)" folder, Postal Union Records.

125. "Notes By Deputy Chief Inspector Conway," 13–14.

126. "Offices 3/24 NX," box 4, "Officer Files—Presidents—Moe Biller Material Re: Letter Carriers and Strike 1970 (3)" folder, Postal Union Records.

127. Walsh and Mangum, *Labor Struggle*, 27–30.

128. "Chronology of Events," 18.

129. Rachleff, "Postal Strike," 1116.

130. "NALC President Emeritus, Vincent R. Sombrotto, 1923–2013," January 9, 2013, National Association of Letter Carriers (website), www.nalc.org/news/nalc-updates/nalc-president-emeritus-vincent-r-sombrotto-1923-2013.

131. Rachleff, "American Postal Workers Union," 96.

132. For continued anger at leaders, see Francis F. Soto to Biller, August 6, 1971, box 7, "Aborted Strike 1971" folder. For the continuation of rank-and-file activism in the immediate aftermath of the strike, see "Branch 36 Rank & Filer," box 4, "Officer Files—Presidents—Moe Biller Material Re: Letter Carriers and Strike 1970 (3)" folder. Both in Postal Union Records.

133. Nystrom, *Hard Hats, Rednecks*, 30; "War Foes Here Attacked by Construction Workers: City Hall is Stormed [. . .]," *New York Times*, May 9, 1970; "Police Were Told of Plan," *New York Times*, May 9, 1970.

134. "War Foes Here Attacked"; "Police Were Told of Plan."

135. Bloodworth, *Losing the Center*, 140.

136. Cowie, *Stayin' Alive*, 135–36.

137. For Local 3 and its leadership's presentation of the war effort, see "Habirshaw Picket Line Opens as Strikes Load Copper Reels to Aid U.S. Forces in Vietnam," *Electrical Union World* 29, no. 4 (March 15, 1968); "Letters from Local 3 GI's," *Electrical Union World* 29, no. 6 (April 15, 1968); and "Letters from Local 3 GI's," *Electrical Union World* 29, no. 8 (May 15, 1968), all in HVA Papers.

138. "Why the Construction Worker Holler, 'U.S.A. All the Way,'" *New York Times*, June 28, 1970.

139. Appy, *Working-Class War*, 298–300.

140. "Protests on Cambodia and Kent State Are Joined by Many Local Schools," *New York Times*, May 6, 1970.

141. "Why the Construction Worker Holler."

142. "For Flag and for Country They March," *New York Times*, May 21, 1970.

143. "Why the Construction Worker Holler." Autoworkers in Mahwah, New Jersey, many of them New Yorkers, expressed similar criticisms; "Factory Workers Differ on Protests," *New York Times*, May 8, 1970.

144. "Thousands Assail Lindsay in 2nd Protest," *New York Times*, May 12, 1970.

145. "Thousands in City March to Assail Lindsay on War," *New York Times*, May 16, 1970.

146. Zeitz, *White Ethnic New York*, 177–81; Cannato, *Ungovernable City*, 389–94, 432; "Lindsay vs. Labor," *New York Times*, January 9, 1971.

147. "Workers Debate Students on War," *New York Times*, May 17, 1970.
148. Lizzi, "'My Heart,'" 46.
149. Freeman, "Hardhats," 726–27.
150. Anderson, *Pursuit of Fairness*, 115–27.
151. "Whites in Chicago Continue Protest," *New York Times*, September 27, 1969.
152. Minutes, special meeting of the executive board, May 13, 1970, Executive Board microfilm, BCTC Minutes; quote from "Huge City Hall Rally Backs Nixon's Indochina Policies," *New York Times*, May 21, 1970.
153. On payment and compulsion, see Foner, *U.S. Labor*, 105–8; and "Why the Construction Worker Holler."
154. Rick Perlstein, *Nixonland*, 497–99.
155. Minutes, executive board meeting, March 16, 1964, Executive Board microfilm, BCTC Minutes.
156. Minutes, regular meeting, February 8, 1966, Membership Meetings microfilm, BCTC Minutes.
157. Minutes, regular meeting, April 19, 1966, Membership Meetings microfilm; and minutes, executive board meeting, May 16, 1966, Executive Board microfilm, both in BCTC Minutes.
158. For that summer's negotiations and fall subpoenas, see minutes, executive board meeting, June 20, September 19, 1966, Executive Board microfilm, BCTC Minutes.
159. Minutes, executive board meeting, January 19, 1970, Executive Board microfilm, BCTC Minutes; Banks, "'Last Bastion of Discrimination,'" 270–87.
160. Minutes, regular meeting, January 19, 1970, Membership Meetings microfilm; and minutes, special meeting of the executive board, May 13, 1970, Executive Board microfilm , both in BCTC Minutes.
161. "N.A.A.C.P. Sees 'Hoax' in Plan for Black Workers in Building Trade Here," *New York Times*, April 2, 1970.
162. "City Gets Pledges on Minority Hiring," *New York Times*, March 22, 1970.
163. "Mayor to Order Minority Hiring," *New York Times*, April 12, 1970.
164. Aitken, *Charles W. Colson*, 131–32.
165. For courting of Brennan, see Charles Colson to Nixon, memorandum, July 2, 1971, box 129, "July 1971" folder, Nixon Presidential Returned Materials Collection: White House Special Files, Richard Nixon Presidential Library and Museum.
166. "Hard Hats Finding Fat Raises Do Not Help," *New York Times*, February 6, 1971.
167. "Building Contractors See No Early End to City's 5-Week-Old Construction Strike," *New York Times*, August 6, 1972.
168. "Poll Says Nixon Won Labor Vote," *New York Times*, December 14, 1972. George Meany and most of the AFL-CIO remained neutral in the election, signaling their deep displeasure with George McGovern as the Democratic Party's presidential nominee.

CHAPTER 4

1. For Local 1110 as a vanguard, see "CWA Contract, UTW Contract: Vote No," *Strike Back!* 1, no. 8 (August 1971), 4.

2. Happell v. Genoese, 33 Misc.2d 327 (1962), www.leagle.com/decision/196236033misc2d3271223; "Phone Union Wins Poll," *New York Times*, November 18, 1959; "Union Vote Indecisive," *New York Times*, January 27, 1961.

3. Local 1101 CWA mailout, 1963, box 155, "Local 1101 Mailouts" folder, CWA Records; "Labor News Conference," January 14, 1963, box 4, "Teamsters Raid, 1962–1963" folder, CWA Ephemera; Jim McMahon, interview with author, New York, January 10, 2017.

4. Rust Gilbert, interview with author, New York, April 2, 2018.

5. "2-Hour Telephone Walkout," *New York Times*, October 14, 1961.

6. "Walkout Is Averted at Phone Company," *New York Times*, December 6, 1961.

7. Gilbert interview.

8. Gilbert interview.

9. Gilbert interview.

10. "Rebuttal to the Three Items [. . .]," September 1967, box 63, "Appeal Local 1101 NY Plant Bargaining Unit Election, 1967–1968" folder, CWA Records; Local 1101 CWA mailout, 1963; "Officers of Phone Local Vote to Join Teamsters," *New York Times*, January 3, 1964.

11. "Labor News Conference"; McMahon interview.

12. *United Action*, no. 5 (May 10, 1971), in box 6, "CWA Local 1101 United Action: Serial Publication, Issues 1–21" folder, CWA Ephemera.

13. McMahon interview.

14. Gilbert interview.

15. McMahon interview.

16. Minutes, Big City discussions meeting, August 13, 1970, box 100, "Negotiations (Area Differentials, Big City Problems) 1970–1971" folder, CWA Records.

17. McMahon interview.

18. Aaron Brenner, "Rank-and-File Struggles," 258–59. For a smaller wildcat, see "Wildcat Telephone Strike Settled by Brooklyn Pact," *New York Times*, September 30, 1969.

19. Green, "Race and Technology," S119.

20. Equal Employment Opportunity Commission, *"A Unique Competence": A Study of Equal Employment Opportunity in the Bell System*, part 4, in *Congressional Record* 118:4 (February 15, 1972), E4515–24.

21. Green, "Race and Technology," S128–29.

22. "Protection," *New York Generator*, March/April 1966, box 5, "NY Tel: High Crime Area Dispute (General), 1961–1968" folder, District 1, CWA Records.

23. George M. Miller to "All Local Officers and Stewards, District One," August 3, 1967, box 5, "NY Tel: High Crime Area Dispute (Bargaining)" folder, District 1, CWA Records.

24. Gilbert interview.

25. "Arbitration Award—Discharge of Edward M. Stewart—Local 1101," June 23, 1970, box 16, "Arbitration Awards: Local 1101" folder, Communications Workers of America Local 1150 Records, Tamiment Library.

26. Wooten v. New York Telephone Co., 485 F. Supp. 748 (S.D.N.Y. 1980).

27. *Wooten*, 485 F. Supp.

28. Gilbert interview.

29. McTaggart, *Guerrillas*, 130; "1101 Meeting the Ranks Begin to Move," *United Action*, no. 7 (June 21, 1971), in box 6, "CWA Local 1101 United Action: Serial Publication, Issues 1–21" folder, CWA Ephemera. For more on the International Socialists strategy, see La Botz, "Tumultuous Teamsters," 214–15.

30. "BWAC's Program," *Strike Back!* 1, no. 11 (April 1972). Brenner's work on Local 1101, while providing invaluable insight, overemphasizes the centrality of these left-wing groups to the union's militancy; see Aaron Brenner, "Rank-and-File Struggles," 265–67.

31. Minutes, Big City discussions meeting, July 21, 1970, box 100, "Negotiations (Area Differentials, Big City Problems) 1970–1971" folder, CWA Records.

32. Minutes, Big City discussions meeting, July 21, August 13, 1970, box 100, "Negotiations (Area Differentials, Big City Problems) 1970–1971" folder. On previous contracts as catching up, see Northwestern University School of Management report, box 135, "The Bell System Strikes 1968" folder; and meeting notes, October 29, 1970, box 87, "Bell System Bargaining Council—Meeting Reports and Notes, 1970–1971" folder. All in CWA Records.

33. Beirne to "All Members of the Bell System Bargaining Council," November 16, 1970, box 135, "Effective Strike Bell System—Correspondence, 1970–1971" folder, CWA Records.

34. Meeting notes, October 29, 1970; quote from Charles McDonald to George M. Miller, Subject: "Strike against the Bell System," December 4, 1970, box 135, "Effective Strike Bell System—Correspondence, 1970–1971" folder, CWA Records. For pro-strike letters, see Eugene P. Myers to Beirne, November 30, 1970; Catherine Sugarton to Beirne, December 30, 1970; Betty C. Riley to Beirne, January 2, 1971; Thelma Kreeger to Beirne, January 3, 1971; and Lucile Wooten to Beirne, January 4, 1970. For anti-strike letters, see Bob Nelch to Beirne, December 1970; Michael V. Kennedy to Beirne, December 14, 1970; and G. Robert Stollard to Beirne, December 24, 1970. All letters in box 135, "Effective Strike Bell System—Correspondence, 1970–1971" folder, CWA Records.

35. New York Telephone Company v. Communications Workers of America, AFL-CIO, 445 F.2d 39 (2d Cir. 1971); Gilbert interview; *United Action*, no. 2 (March 8, 1971), in box 6, "CWA Local 1101 United Action: Serial Publication, Issues 1–21" folder, CWA Ephemera.

36. Bahr to Beirne, May 27, 1971, Subject: "Collective Bargaining—1971," box 19, "Executive Board Minutes June 10–11, 1971" folder, CWA Records.

37. "Early Rise Is Seen on Tolls in City to Hold 30C Fare," *New York Times*, January 4, 1970.

38. "6.1 % State Unemployment Most Since December '62," *New York Times*, August 22, 1971.

39. US Bureau of Labor Statistics, *New York City*, 51; "Unemployment Rate Down for First Time in 7 Months," *New York Times*, February 6, 1971.

40. Stein, *Pivotal Decade*, 28–29.

41. US Bureau of the Census, *Historical Statistics*, 210–13; Cullen, *American Dream*; Cohen, *Consumers' Republic*, 199–203.

42. "Bell Negotiations," 1972, box 19, "Executive Board, June 14" folder, CWA Records.

43. "No Turning Back!" and "1101 Meeting the Ranks Begin to Move," *United Action*, no. 7 (June 21, 1971), in box 6, "CWA Local 1101 United Action: Serial Publication, Issues 1–21" folder, CWA Ephemera.

44. "Telephone Strike Is Planned in Much of Nation Tomorrow," *New York Times*, July 13, 1971.

45. For cross-industry comparisons of wages and fringe benefits, see minutes, executive board meeting, August 3–4, 1971, box 19, "Executive Board Minutes, Jul 11–12, Aug 3–4, 1971" folder, CWA Records.

46. "Rebuild the Strike!," *United Action*, no. 8 (July 26, 1971), in box 6, "CWA Local 1101 United Action: Serial Publication, Issues 1–21" folder, CWA Ephemera; Bell Workers Action Committee, "Bell's Nightmare: Plant and Traffic Unite," *Strike Back!* 1, no. 8 (August 1971).

47. Bell Workers Action Committee, "Bell's Nightmare"; "50,000 Workers Continue Strike in State," *New York Times*, July 28, 1971.

48. Minutes, executive board meeting, August 3–4, 1971; "Requests for Special Convention," August 1971, box 19, "Executive Board Meeting Minutes Nov. 15–16, 1971" folder, CWA Records.

49. Glenn E. Watts to Joseph Beirne, George Gill, Gus Cramer, and Louis Knecht, Subject: "Request for Special Convention—1971," August 25, 1971, box 19, "Executive Board Meeting Minutes Nov. 15–16, 1971" folder, CWA Records.

50. "Rank and File from 2nd Ave—TTU, 1101, 1190," *Strike Back!* 1, no. 8 (August 1971).

51. "Rank and File from 2nd Ave."

52. Bell Workers Action Committee, "Bell's Nightmare."

53. McMahon interview; Gilbert interview.

54. "Vietnam———Attica," *Strike Back!* 1, no. 9 (December 1971), 7–8.

55. McMahon interview.

56. For the UA propaganda shift away from cross-union organizing, see programs for CWA Local 1101, in *United Action*, no. 5 (May 10, 1971) and no. 6 (June 7, 1971), in box 6, "CWA Local 1101 United Action: Serial Publication, Issues 1–21" folder, CWA Ephemera; Gilbert interview.

57. O'Farrell and Kornbluh, *Rocking the Boat*, 237–40.

58. Quote from "Forward Looking Union Leader," *New York Times*, July 15, 1971; "Revolution through Democratic Action: New Role for CWA Staff and Locals and the Impact of the Denver Convention," box 19, "Executive Board Meeting Minutes Nov. 15–16, 1971" folder, CWA Records. Despite the growing imbalance of power engendered by automation, Beirne supported automation because he hoped it would lead to a national program for full employment. For more on Beirne and automation, see box 69, "Joseph A. Beirne Materials: Automation" folder, CWA Records.

59. "Bell Breaks Off Contract Talks," *New York Times*, September 3, 1971; "Phone-Strike Talks Here Are Halted by Accusations," *New York Times*, September 14, 1971; "Phone Pact Talks Are Stalemated," *New York Times*, November 6, 1971.

60. "Thomas, Ganser, and Farrar Arbitration," May 7, 1971; "Arbitration Award—Dismissal John C. Byrd Local 1101—N.Y. Plant Bargaining Unit," August 14, 1972; and "Arbitration Award—Discharge—Joseph Nabach New York Tel Co.—Local 1101," December 6, 1972, all in box 16, "Arbitration Awards: Local 1101" folder, Communications Workers of America Local 1150 Records, Tamiment Library.

61. McMahon interview.

62. "Phone Strike Here Is Keeping 100,000 Customers off the Line," *New York Times*, November 11, 1971.

63. For communication between strikers, their families, and the Lindsay administration, see Nicholas Flynn to Lindsay, n.d.; James Kee to Lindsay, November 12, 1971; and "John Conroy," November 15, 1971, all in box 109, "Telephone Strike Correspondence 1971" folder, Subject Files, Mayor John Lindsay Collection, Municipal Archives.

64. Minutes, executive board meeting, November 1971, box 19, "Executive Board Meeting Minutes Nov. 15–16, 1971" folder, CWA Records.

65. McMahon interview.

66. Gilbert interview.

67. "Phone Workers Reaffirm Strike," *New York Times*, November 28, 1971; "Dare to Struggle, Dare to Win," *Strike Back!* 1, no. 9 (December 1971), 3.

68. "Militancy Grows from Local Meeting," *United Action*, no. 10 (December 9, 1971), in box 6, "CWA Local 1101 United Action: Serial Publication, Issues 1–21" folder, CWA Ephemera.

69. "Out of State Picketing," *United Action*, no. 11 (January 3, 1972), in box 6, "CWA Local 1101 United Action: Serial Publication, Issues 1–21" folder, CWA Ephemera.

70. "Militancy Grows from Local Meeting."

71. Gilbert interview.

72. "Telephone Strikes Demonstrate against Management Workers," *New York Times*, January 15, 1972.

73. "Rebuild the Union from the Bottom Up," *United Action*, no. 12 (March 7, 1972), in box 6, "CWA Local 1101 United Action: Serial Publication, Issues 1–21" folder, CWA Ephemera.

74. "Trouble on the Line," *New York Times*, January 16, 1972.

75. "C.W.A Chief Asks Ratifying of Pact," *New York Times*, February 8, 1972; "Phone Workers Ordered to Return to Work Today," *New York Times*, February 18, 1972.

76. McMahon interview; Aaron Brenner, "Rank-and-File Struggles," 275–76.

77. For Brenner's summation of the post-strike period, see Aaron Brenner, "Rank-and-File Struggles," 278.

78. "Don't Mourn Organize!," *Strike Back!* 1, no. 11 (April 1972), 1; "Hundreds Fired!," *Strike Back!* 1, no. 12 (June 1972), 1.

79. For some of the strike-related firings, see "Thomas, Ganser, and Farrar Arbitration"; "Arbitration Award—Dismissal John C. Byrd"; and "Arbitration Award—Discharge—Joseph Nabach."

80. McMahon interview; Famigietti et al. to John Keefe, March 6, 1972, box 19, "Executive Board Meeting Minutes March 20–12, 1972, April 27–28, 1972" folder, CWA Records.

81. John Keefe to Al Ruggiero, March 17, 1972; and Famiegietti et al. to Glenn E. Watts, March 31, 1972, both in box 19, "Executive Board Meeting Minutes March 20–12, 1972, April 27–28, 1972" folder, CWA Records.

82. "Background Information in Support for a Brooklyn Local by Vice President Bahr," April 27, 1972, box 19, "Executive Board Meeting Minutes March 20–12, 1972, April 27–28, 1972" folder, CWA Records.

83. "Background Information in Support."

84. "CWA Executive Board Statement Jurisdiction Local 1101," April 27, 1972, box 19, "Executive Board Meeting Minutes March 20–12, 1972, April 27–28, 1972" folder, CWA Records.

85. Nabach, "Telephone Strike," 46.

86. The agency shop agreement in New York City allowed CWA Local 1101 officials to collect representation fees for nearly 9,000 more employees; see "Back on the Line," *New York Times*, February 18, 1972. Joshua Freeman also cites the 1971–72 telephone strike as a major turning point in the city's postwar labor struggles; see Freeman, *Working-Class New York*, 252–53.

87. For demoralization in the strike's immediate aftermath, see "Rebuild the Union from the Bottom Up." Discussion of longer-term changes in McMahon interview.

88. LaTour, *Sisters in the Brotherhood*, 172.

89. For interviews with New York City workers on 1974 national negotiations and the apprehensiveness, see "A.T.&T. Workers Restless as Wage Talks Near," *New York Times*, April 20, 1974.

90. McMahon interview.

CHAPTER 5

1. Taxi Rank and File Coalition to Van Arsdale, July 9, 1971, box 1, "Bargaining, 1971–1975" folder, TRFC Records.

2. The number of strikes in New York City dropped from 215 in 1970 to 135 in 1971, 148 in 1972, and 128 in 1973. While in 1971 the number of workers involved remained high because of the CWA Local 1101 strike, the numbers dropped afterward from nearly 200,000 workers in 1970 to 74,900 workers in 1973. US Department of Labor, *Analysis of Work Stoppages, 1970*, 41; US Department of Labor, *Analysis of Work Stoppages, 1971*, 51; US Department of Labor, *Analysis of Work Stoppages, 1972*, 55; US Department of Labor, *Analysis of Work Stoppages, 1973*, 46.

3. "Attention Taxi Workers," 1965, box 3 N4, "Taxi Organizations" folder, HVA Papers.

4. For 1966 electoral challenges and differing criticisms of the union, see "Election Flyer Committee for Taxi Workers Rights," 1966, box 1 N5, "Election (Candidates, Circulars, Results 1969)" folder; and Jack Rosen to Harry Van Arsdale, n.d., box 3 N4, "Taxi Organizations" folder, both in HVA Papers.

5. Vidich, *New York Cab Driver*, 104–6.

6. "Sidney Binder for President," 1969, box 3 N5, "Election (Candidates, Circulars, Results)" folder, HVA Papers.

7. Vidich, *New York Cab Driver*, 4–5.

8. Old Timers interview, April 15, 1976, TRFC Oral History.

9. Bret Primack, interview with author, New York, April 2, 2018.

10. John Singer, interview with author, New York, March 22, 2018.

11. Vidich, *New York Cab Driver*, 27–29.

12. Old Timers interview, April 15, 1976.

13. For division and cynicism, see Activists interviews, undated, TRFC Oral History. For distrust and let-down of many union drives, see Old Timers interviews, 1976.

14. Primack interview.

15. "About New York: Belmore Cafeteria Being Sold to Condominium Developers," *New York Times*, August 19, 1981.

16. Biju, *Taxi!*, 51–54; Vidich, *New York Cab Driver*, 120–26.

17. Vidich, *New York Cab Driver*, 106–9.

18. Primack interview.

19. Hodges, *Taxi!*, 128.

20. Singer interview.

21. Primack interview.

22. For deaths and crime, see Walter J. Diaz to Sam Eastman, December 30, 1967, box 2 N5, "Members Correspondence" folder, HVA Papers; and "Taxi Union Drive Quickens Its Pace," *New York Times*, February 12, 1965.

23. For holdup stats, see "Taxi Procession Honors Cabby Slain by Robber," *New York Times*, February 14, 1970; "'Locked Box' May Be Cabbie's Best Friend," *New York Times*, October 4, 1970; and "Special Report on the Stabbing of Jack London," 1969, box 2 N5, "Members Correspondence" folder, HVA Papers; Singer interview.

24. Cohen and Goldstein, "Governing," 175.

25. For demographic shifts in New York City, see Zeitz, *White Ethnic New York*, 13–14, 148–49. For Jewish attempts to stave off white flight, see Pritchett, *Brownsville, Brooklyn*.

26. "The Gypsy Problem: Some Suggestions toward a Workable Solution," fall 1971, box 2, "Gypsies 1969–1978" folder, TRFC Records.

27. Primack interview.

28. Singer interview.

29. The Taxi Rank and File Coalition recorded a frank discussion on driver racism with some older, white, left-wing militants who, in spite of being avowedly antiracist, admitted that because of past robberies by Black people, they were less likely to pick up Blacks or be much more cautious. See "Racism Sum-Up," March 21, 1978, TRFC Oral History.

30. For Black taxi drivers and Black fares, see "Black Drivers on Racism," April 11, 1978; and "Mike Z, Kevin, and John," May 4, 1978, both in TRFC Oral History.

31. "We State Our Case to NYC Council," *Taxi Drivers Voice* 6, no. 1 (January 15, 1971).

32. For incidents of violence between yellow cab drivers and livery cab drivers, see "We Demand Safety [. . .]," *Taxi Drivers Voice* 7, no. 6 (May 18, 1972).

33. For Calvin Williams's estimate, see "Gypsy Cabs Lessen Taxi Strike Impact," *New York Times*, December 9, 1970.

34. "King of the Gypsies," *New York*, June 22, 1970; "Calvin Williams, 61, Car Service Operator and Ex-legislator," *New York Times*, May 7, 1987.

35. West, "Whose Black Power?," 276–78.

36. "Black Drivers on Racism"; Vidich, *New York Cab Driver*, 146.

37. Civil rights groups strongly supported the liveries; see "Gypsy Cabs Lessen Taxi Strike Impact." For one livery cab driver's perspective, see "Interview with a Gypsy," *Hot Seat*, no. 22 (April 1973).

38. For organizing leaflets, see "Gypsy Cab Owners Serve your Community [. . .]," May 1969, box 5 N4, "Gypsy Cabs" folder, HVA Papers. For violence between taxis and liveries, see "We Demand Safety."

39. Proposal, November 1973, box 1, "Conference: Rank and File Program November 3, 1973" folder, TRFC Records; "Gypsy Problem."

40. "City-Wide Committee for the Re-election of Harry Van Arsdale Jr. Officers and Candidates," October 21, 1969, box 3 N5, "Election (Candidates, Circulars, Results)" folder, HVA Papers.

41. "Recommendations to John V. Lindsay by Mayor's Taxi Study Panel," December 1966, box 2 N5, "Mayor's Taxi Panel and Recommendations" folder, HVA Papers.

42. "Procaccino Pledges Safety to Cabbies," *New York Times*, September 29, 1969.

43. "To All Local 3036 Garage Chairmen and Committeemen," October 1969, box 4 N4, "Taxi Cab Industry" folder, HVA Papers; quote in "Cab Driver-Owners Hold Meeting to Protest 'Gypsies,'" *New York Times*, November 10, 1969.

44. Tom Robbins, "Beginnings: The Night the Chairs Flew," *Taxi Rank and File Coalition* (blog), accessed July 25, 2015, https://taxirankandfile.files.wordpress.com/2011/05/beginnings-the-night-the-chairs-flew.pdf.

45. Hodges, *Taxi!*, 134; Robbins, "Beginnings."

46. "Taxi Union Meets on Owners Offer," *New York Times*, November 21, 1970.

47. "Taxi Drivers Call for Citywide Strike," *New York Times*, December 4, 1970; "2 Taxi Strikers Arrested in Brawl over Gypsy Cabs," *New York Times*, December 16, 1970; "Striking Cabbies Here Clash with the Police," *New York Times*, December 18, 1970.

48. "Two Hearings Set on Cab Fare," *New York Times*, December 29, 1970.

49. Old Timers interview, April 15, 1976; Robbins, "Beginnings."

50. Old Timers interview, April 15, 1976.

51. Biju, *Taxi!*, 61–62.

52. Robbins, "Beginnings."

53. Vidich, *New York Cab Driver*, 110–11.

54. "Leaders of Taxi Drivers Union Halt Scattered Work Stoppages," *New York Times*, January 17, 1971.

55. Robbins, "Beginnings."

56. "Meeting of Taxi Union Here Breaks Up Violently," *New York Times*, April 15, 1971.

57. "Administrative Assistants Message," *Taxi Drivers Voice* 6, no. 7 (April 30, 1971).

58. John Garvey, "Taxi Rank and File History: The Early Period," 5–7, *Taxi Rank and File Coalition* (blog), accessed July 25, 2015, https://taxirankandfile.files.wordpress.com/2011/05/rank-and-file-history-the-early-period.pdf.

59. Taxi Rank and File Coalition to Van Arsdale, July 9, 1971, box 1, "Bargaining 1971–1975" folder, TRFC Records; and *Hot Seat*, no. 1, (May 1971).

60. Garvey, "Taxi Rank and File History," 5–7; Hodges, *Taxi!*, 137–39.

61. Garvey, "Taxi Rank and File History"; "Four Years of Fighting Timeline," box 1, "Negotiations 1971–1975" folder, TRFC Records.

62. "Four Years of Fighting Timeline."

63. "Four Years of Fighting Timeline."

64. "Vote Rank and File," 1971, box 2, "Flyers 1970–1978" folder, TRFC Records; "Election Results," *Taxi Drivers Voice* 6, no. 17 (December 1971).

65. "NO Tokenism on Gypsies," *Taxi Drivers Voice* 6, no. 12 (July 31, 1971).

66. "Van Arsdale Argues at City Council Hearings against Licensing of Illegal Cabs" and "All Taxi Workers Organizing against Illegal Cabs," *Taxi Drivers Voice* 7, no 1 (February 1, 1972).

67. "Drivers Jeer and Applaud at Hearing on Gypsy Cabs," *New York Times*, January 25, 1972.

68. "Racism Sum-Up," March 21, 1978.

69. "Van Arsdale Fights Licensing of Gypsy Cabs," *New York Times*, February 1, 1972.

70. "Van Arsdale Argues at City Council."

71. "Strike Spreads—Issues Spread," box 2, "Flyers 1970–1978" folder, TRFC Records.

72. "Fleet Taxi Drivers Strike at 2 Garages over Share of Fares," *New York Times*, February 12, 1972.

73. "Taxi Strike Closes Two More Garages," *New York Times*, February 16, 1972.

74. "Taxi Strike Closes Two More Garages"; "Backpage Photos," *Taxi Drivers Voice* 7, no. 4 (March 28, 1972; "Strike Spreads—Issues Spread."

75. "Don't Buy Harry's Baloney," 1972, box 2, "Flyers 1970–1978" folder, TRFC Records.

76. "Melee of Shouting and Punches Disrupts Taxi-Union Meeting," *New York Times*, April 13, 1972.

77. "The Truth about the Meeting," *Taxi Drivers Voice* 7, no. 5 (April 22, 1972).

78. "Questionable Vote Caused Taxi Melee," *New York Post*, April 13, 1972.

79. "Owner-Driver Unity Meeting," June 6, 1972, TRFC Oral History.

80. "Owner Drivers Unity Meeting," *Taxi Drivers Voice* 7, no. 7 (June 1972); "Owner-Driver Unity Meeting." See also "Stop These Hoods!" and "Goldberg and Gelfand Air Views on Gypsies," *Taxi Drivers Voice* 6, no. 9 (May 30, 1971).

81. "Montano Paroled on Riot Charges," *New York Times*, September 16, 1972.

82. Krohn-Hansen, *Making New York Dominican*, 72–75. For a socialist Puerto Rican perspective, see clipping, *Unidad Latina* 2, no. 12 (1972), 3, in box 2, "Gypsies 1969–1978" folder, TRFC Records.

83. "Gypsy-Cab Owner to Ignore Ruling," *New York Times*, October 4, 1972.

84. Proposal, November 1973, 1–2; "Gypsy Problem"; "Racism in Taxi: Mainly a Comment on the Statement of the Racism Study Group," 1975, box 2, "Gypsies 1969–1978" folder, TRFC Records.

85. Proposal, November 1973, 1–2; "Gypsy Problem"; "Racism in Taxi."

86. "Four Years of Fighting Timeline"; "Dissidents Picket Taxi Drivers Union," *New York Times*, September 16, 1972.

87. For internal debate on group size, composition, and becoming an avowedly socialist organization, see "Some Ideas on Strategy," February 12, 1974, box 1, "Conference: Rank and File Program February 12, 1974" folder, TRFC Records.

88. "Is There Anything Worse Than 22 Months without a Contract," September 1972, box 2, "Flyers 1970–1978" folder, TRFC Records.

89. "Pay Your Dues," *Hot Seat*, no. 16 (August 1972); "Taxi Drivers Here Vote Authorization for Strike," *New York Times*, October 12, 1972.

90. For debate and conflicting views on taking power in the union, see "Some Ideas on Strategy."

91. "Four Years of Fighting Timeline"; "Contract Signed by Cabbies Union," *New York Times*, December 28, 1972; "New Cabbies to Get Higher Commission," *New York Times*, January 20, 1973.

92. "Campaign Notes," *Hot Seat*, no. 31/32 (October 1974).

93. "Elections: Union Runs Out, Drivers Pursue," *Hot Seat*, no. 27 (March 1974).

94. "The Elections Story," *Hot Seat*, no. 33 (January 1975).

95. Paul Wasserman, "Class Struggle in Greenwich Village," *Taxi Rank and File Coalition* (blog), accessed July 31, 2015, https://taxirankandfile.files.wordpress.com/2011/05/class-struggle-in-greenwich-village2.pdf; Gordon, "In the Hot Seat," 36–38; Hodges, *Taxi!*, 140.

96. "Racism Sum-Up," April 11, 1978, CD 1, TRFC Oral History.
97. "Racism Sum-Up," April 11, 1978, CD 1.
98. "Racism Sum-Up," April 11, 1978, CDs 1, 2.
99. "Keeping the Cab Rolling," *Taxi Drivers Voice* 6, no. 2 (January 30, 1971); "Keeping the Cab Rolling," *Taxi Drivers Voice* 6, no. 5 (March 15, 1971). For one driver interview, see "All Taxi Workers Organizing against Illegal Cabs," *Taxi Drivers Voice* 7, no. 1 (February 1, 1972).
100. "Racism Sum-Up," April 11, 1978, CD 2.
101. Singer interview; Primack interview.
102. "Racism Sum-Up," April 11, 1978, CD 1.
103. "Mike Z, Kevin, and John," May 4–5, 1978, TRFC Oral History.
104. For one assessment of growing cynicism in the ranks and a discussion of continued anger but less organizing, see Activists interviews, TRFC Oral History.
105. Freeman, *Working-Class New York*, 254–55.
106. Schulman, *Seventies*, 145. For the original source of this moniker, see Tom Wolfe, "The 'Me' Decade and America's Third Great Awakening," *New York*, August 23, 1976.

CHAPTER 6

1. Freeman, *Working-Class New York*, 256.
2. The literature on the fiscal crisis is roughly divided into left and conservative camps. The former are best exemplified by Phillips-Fein, *Fear City*; Moody, *From Welfare State*; Lichten, *Class, Power and Austerity*; Tabb, *Long Default*; Harvey, *Brief History of Neoliberalism*, 45; and Freeman, *Working-Class New York*, 256–87. For the conservative reading, see Lachman and Polner, *Man Who Saved*; and Morris, *Cost of Good Intentions*.
3. Executive board meeting notes, March 21, 1974, 2, box 117, "1974–1975" folder, NYCCLC Records.
4. For a contemporary account that forefronts worker and community organizations' demands as a driving force in the crisis, see Matter and Demac, *Developing and Underdeveloping*.
5. Fitch, *Assassination of New York*, viii–x; Shefter, *Political Crisis/Fiscal Crisis*, 60–65; Moody, *From Welfare State*, 54–56. For different depictions of the fiscal crisis, see n2, above.
6. Executive board meeting notes, April 18, 1974, 1–3, box 117, "1974–1975" folder, NYCCLC Records.
7. "Tax Rise Opposed by Realty Board," *New York Times*, March 28, 1965.
8. "Publicity Is Said to Bar Better Credit for City," *New York Times*, February 10, 1971.
9. Bailey, *Crisis Regime*, 23–26. On the increased assertiveness of the business elite, see Edsall, *New Politics of Inequality*, 112–15; Moody, *From Welfare State*, 15–17; and Kotz, *Rise and Fall*, 67–69.
10. Greenberg, *Branding New York*, 97–98.
11. Newfield and Dubrul, *Abuse of Power*, 37–41.
12. "Let's Hear It for Wall St. and Some Other Beautiful People," June 1975, box 45, "Fiscal Crisis 1970; 1974–1976" folder, AFSCME Records.
13. "The Big Bank Holdup," box 40, "Fiscal Crisis (1975) General 1975–1976" folder, AFSCME Records.

14. "Testimony by Mayor Abraham D. Beame at Public Hearings Held by the Commerce, Consumer and Monetary Affairs Subcommittee," June 23, 1975, box 070012, folder 9 "June 17–30, 1975," Abraham D. Beame Collection, LaGuardia-Wagner Archives, LaGuardia Community College.

15. For a comprehensive account of community organizing against austerity, see Phillips-Fein, *Fear City*.

16. Phillips-Fein, *Fear City*, 141.

17. "MLC Officers List," 1974, box 1, "MLC General Minutes, 1967–1977" folder, Bellush Papers.

18. Freeman, *Working-Class New York*, 269.

19. For Gotbaum on his supposed influence with financial elites, see "Vic G Notes," n.d., box 4, "Vic Gotbaum, 1970, 1979" folder, Bellush Papers; and Lichten, *Class, Power and Austerity*, 151–53. For a more favorable portrayal of Gotbaum, see Bellush and Bellush, *Union Power*.

20. For Beame's perspective on the source of the fiscal crisis in wider economic issues, see "Remarks by Mayor Abraham D. Beame at Public Hearings Held by the US Senate Budget Committee," March 5, 1975, box 070011, folder 2 "February 25–March 12, 1975," Mayor Abraham Beame Collection, Municipal Archives; and "City Plans to Cut 3,975 off Payroll for '75-'76 Budget," *New York Times*, April 23, 1975.

21. "City's Fiscal Crisis 'Scenario,'" *New York Times*, May 22, 1975; "Mayor Emotional," *New York Times*, May 24, 1975.

22. For layoff pressure from banks, see Lichten, *Class, Power and Austerity*, 171.

23. Mark H. Maier mentions SSEU Local 371's attempts to shift DC 37's course during the fiscal crisis but does not offer any significant examination or discussion; see Maier, *City Unions*, 76.

24. Michael Spear also discusses dissidence in DC 37, but he does not recount how the SSEU Local 371 rank and file led the way; see Spear, "Crisis in Urban Liberalism." Quote from Moody, *From Welfare State*, 31.

25. Maier, *City Unions*, 57–72.

26. Walkowitz, *Working with Class*, 212–13, 264.

27. Walkowitz, *Working with Class*, 242–43.

28. "District Council 37 Calculations Membership, January 1, 1974–December 31, 1974," box 1, "Minutes: Delegates, 1974–1975" folder, AFSCME Records.

29. "Vote the Stan Hill Slate," April 1970; and "The Time is Now . . . Stan Hill is the Man!," 1970, both in box 5, "Local 371, 1967–1972" folder, Bellush Papers; Walkowitz, *Working with Class*, 213, 274, 295.

30. Lonnie Cacchione interview, n.d., NYW. For some rank-and-file protests of contract terms, see Davis et al. to Jerry Wurf, August 8, 1974, box 1, "MLC/OCB Correspondence, 1970–1978" folder, Bellush Papers.

31. Phillips-Fein, *Fear City*, 23–24.

32. Cacchione interview.

33. On welfare costs, see Morris, "Of Budgets, Taxes," 87–89, 95–96; and Walkowitz, *Working with Class*, 257–58.

34. For a short discussion of radical Black social workers, see Walkowitz, *Working with Class*, 313.

35. For the SSEU Local 371 leadership position on the effects of fiscal austerity, see minutes, delegates' assembly meeting, January 22, 1975, box 1, "Delegate Assembly Minutes, 1975" folder, SSEU Records; and Cacchione interview.

36. "Beame Cuts 1,510 Workers and Imposes a Job Freeze to Save City $100 Million," *New York Times*, November 24, 1974.

37. Minutes, executive committee meeting, December 9, 1974; and minutes, delegates' assembly meeting, January 22, 1975, both in box 1, "Delegate Assembly Minutes, 1975" folder, SSEU Records.

38. Minutes, delegates' meeting, November 26, 1974, box 1, "Minutes: Delegates, 1974–1975" folder, AFSCME Records.

39. Minutes, delegates' assembly meeting, January 22, 1975.

40. "Unions to Seek Layoff Sweeteners," *New York Times*, January 20, 1975.

41. Minutes, delegates' assembly meeting, January 22, 1975.

42. Padwee was a member of the New American Movement, an antivanguardist New Left organization; for more on Padwee and the New American Movement, see Padwee Papers, Tamiment Library.

43. Minutes, delegates' assembly meeting, January 22, 1975.

44. Minutes, delegates' assembly meeting, January 22, 1975.

45. Minutes, delegates' meeting, February 25, 1975, box 1, "Minutes: Delegates, 1974–1975" folder, AFSCME Records.

46. Mirengoff and Rindler, *CETA*, 186.

47. "Big Bank Holdup."

48. "News from DC 37: Union Attacks Banks for Overcharging City," February 27, 1975, box 4, "Fiscal Crisis—Readings and Sources" folder, AFSCME Records.

49. Minutes, executive committee meeting, April 14, 1975, box 1, "Executive Committee Minutes, 1975" folder, SSEU Records.

50. Minutes, executive committee meeting, April 14, 1975.

51. Minutes, executive committee meeting, April 14, 1975.

52. Minutes, delegates' assembly meeting, April 23, 1975, box 1, "Delegate Assembly Minutes, 1975" folder, SSEU Records.

53. "March on Washington Extra," April 24, 1975, box 45, "Fiscal Crisis 1970; 1974–1976" folder, AFSCME Records.

54. Minutes, delegates' assembly meeting, April 23, 1975.

55. Minutes, executive committee meeting, June 9, 1975, box 1, "Executive Committee Minutes, 1975" folder, SSEU Records.

56. For Beasley support of Knight, see minutes, special delegates' meeting, June 19, 1975; and for a Gotbaum-backed proposal detailing layoff orders, CETA fund usage, and possibility of "direct action" but not necessarily a strike, see "Resolution to be Presented to the Special Delegates Meeting June 19, 1975," both in box 1, "Minutes: Delegates, 1974–1975" folder, AFSCME Records. For Lillian Roberts's sabotage of the joint rally, see Spear, "Crisis in Urban Liberalism," 157.

57. Minutes, special delegates' meeting, June 19, 1975.

58. Minutes, delegates' meeting, June 25, 1975, box 1, "Minutes: Delegates, 1974–1975" folder, AFSCME Records.

59. Maier, *City Unions*, 172–73.

60. Minutes, delegates' assembly meeting, August 20, 1975, box 1, "Delegate Assembly Minutes, 1975" folder, SSEU Records.

61. Minutes, delegates' assembly meeting, September 17, 1975, box 1, "Delegate Assembly Minutes, 1975" folder, SSEU Records. Unfortunately, the SSEU Local 371 records are incomplete and there are no records of the final vote count.

62. Maier, *City Unions*, 74–75.

63. Spear, "Crisis in Urban Liberalism," 156.

64. For white working-class opposition to welfare, see Reese, *Backlash against Welfare Mothers*, 101–5. One militant rank-and-file social worker, who lamented the increasing divisions generated by self-interest and racial animosity, agreed that former mayor Lindsay had given "too much away to black poverty pimps"; see Cacchione interview.

65. Maier, *City Unions*, 166–67.

66. Spear, "Crisis in Urban Liberalism," 157.

67. "Municipal Labor Committee: Rally and Boycott of First National City Bank," May 20, 1975, box 4, "Fiscal Crisis—Readings and Sources" folder, Bellush Papers; Freeman, *Working-Class New York*, 260–61.

68. Bellush and Bellush, *Union Power*, 393.

69. Freeman, *Working-Class New York*, 269.

70. "Civil Service Rally Assails Bank's Role in City Crisis," *New York Times*, June 5, 1975; "10,000 Protest at Citibank," *Daily News*, June 5, 1975.

71. Minutes, general membership meeting, June 12, 1975, box 1, "MLC General Minutes, 1967–1977" folder, Bellush Papers.

72. "Welcome to Fear City," press release from Police Benevolent Association, June 1975, box 7, "Welcome to Fear City, June 1975" folder, Jack Bigel Collection, Archive on Municipal Finance and Leadership, Baruch College.

73. Greenberg, *Branding New York*, 133–35.

74. "No Budget Cuts! No Layoffs! No Sellouts! Fight to Win!," June 9, 1975, "Fiscal Crisis" folder, United Federation of Teachers Printed Ephemera Collection, Tamiment Library.

75. "New Briefs," *Daily News*, June 17, 1975.

76. Untitled speech transcript, June 28, 1975, box 7, "David Beasley-NYPL-Fiscal Crisis" folder, American Federation of State, County, and Municipal Employees Local 1930 Records, Tamiment Library.

77. Moody, *From Welfare State*, 24–25; Bailey, *Crisis Regime*, 23–26.

78. For MAC minutes, see minutes, meeting of the board of directors, June 19, 1975, MAC Archive, Archive on Municipal Finance and Leadership, Baruch College, accessed online April 11, 2015, https://www.baruch.cuny.edu/mac/Board_of_Directors/06-19-75.pdf; Lichten, *Class, Power and Austerity*, 129–31; and Tabb, *Long Default*, 24–26.

79. The state was also directly consulting not only these members of the MAC but also the heads of major New York–based companies R. H. Macy's and Metropolitan Life Insurance; see Freeman, *Working-Class New York*, 260.

80. "City Yielding on State Plan for Fiscal Rescue Agency," *Daily News*, June 5, 1975.

81. "Chronology of New York City Fiscal Crisis," box 4, "Fiscal Crisis—Readings and Sources" folder, Bellush Papers; "1,200 Provisionals Feel the Ax Today," *Daily News*, June 17, 1975.

82. "Sanitationmen Kicking the City in Garbage Can over Layoff," *Daily News*, June 27, 1975.

83. "Sanitationmen Kicking the City."

84. Press release, June 27, 1975, box 070012, no. 9, "June 17–30 1975" folder, Abraham D. Beame Collection, LaGuardia-Wagner Archives, LaGuardia Community College; "City to Appeal," *Daily News*, June 28, 1975.

85. "Judge Nixes Sanit Layoffs; Sanitmen Back Despite Layoff Threat," *Daily News*, June 29, 1975.

86. "Statement by First Deputy Mayor James A. Cavanagh," July 1, 1975, box 070012, no. 9, "June 17–30 1975" folder, Abraham D. Beame Collection, LaGuardia-Wagner Archives, LaGuardia Community College.

87. Quote from "DeLury Insists Control Is Lost," *New York Times*, July 2, 1975.

88. Joseph DeLury to Abraham Beame, July 9, 1975, roll 4, box 10, folder 295, Sanitation Department, Mayor Abraham D. Beame Collection, Municipal Archives.

89. "DeLury Insists Control Is Lost."

90. For Bigel on the 1975 strike, see Spear, "Crisis in Urban Liberalism," 134.

91. Abraham Beame to James Cavanagh, memorandum, July 1, 1975, roll 16, box 17, folder 280, Sanitation Department, Mayor Abraham D. Beame Collection, Municipal Archives.

92. "McFeeley Scores Accord on Sanitation Rehiring," *New York Times*, July 4, 1975.

93. "City Sanitation Trucks Vandalized in 2 Boroughs," *New York Times*, July 20, 1975. For wages, fringes, and employment numbers in the summer's aftermath, see "Report on the City's Program to Fund COLA for the Uniformed Sanitationmen's Association and the Sanitation Officers' Association from October 1, 1975 to June 30, 1977," box 16 (2), Jack Bigel Collection, Archive on Municipal Finance and Leadership, Baruch College.

94. "Statement by First Deputy Mayor James A. Cavanagh."

95. "Laid-Off Policemen Block Brooklyn Bridge Traffic," *New York Times*, July 2, 1975.

96. Johnson, *Street Justice*, 267–75.

97. "Report of Harry I. Bronstein, Special Assistant to the Mayor on 'Police Job Action' of January 1971," June 1971, box 371, "Job Action" folder, JVL Papers.

98. "PBA Hints at Slowdown; Bars Formal Job Action," *New York Times*, July 3, 1975; "McFeeley Scores Accord on Sanitation Rehiring," *New York Times*, July 4, 1975.

99. "Chronology of New York City Fiscal Crisis"; "Sick Firemen Join in the Protest," *Daily News*, July 3, 1976.

100. "Strike Has Garbage Piling Up," *Daily News*, July 2, 1976.

101. "Chronology of New York City Fiscal Crisis"; "A Strike over Layoffs Causes Hudson Parkway Traffic Jam," *New York Times*, July 3, 1975; Maier, *City Unions*, 166–67.

102. While there are examples of unions paying property taxes in advance, the investment in city functions with union funds was qualitatively different than an advance on taxes owed; see Phillips-Fein, *Fear City*, 127.

103. On the July meeting with Rockefeller and Wriston and the MAC, see Lichten, *Class, Power and Austerity*, 136; and Newfield and Dubrul, *Abuse of Power*, 184–88.

104. This agreement was known as the Americana Agreement because of the hotel where it was brokered; see Phillips-Fein, *Fear City*, 143.

105. Podair, *Strike*, 103–22.

106. For debate within the American Federation of Teachers, see Zeluck, "UFT Strike," 201–12.

107. Ben Occhiogrosso interview, July 6, 1981, NYW.

108. Podair, *Strike*, 190–91.

109. For a more sympathetic take on Albert Shanker and the official UFT position, see Kahlenberg, *Tough Liberal*, 67–112.

110. TAC election flyer, April 1975, box 1, "Teachers Action Caucus November 1974–August 1975" folder, AF Papers.

111. Daniel Hiram Perlstein, *Justice, Justice*, 50–51.

112. Occhiogrosso interview. For background on TAC and Filardo, see "Guide to the Anne Filardo Papers on Rank and File Activism in the American Federation of Teachers and in the United Federation of Teachers TAM.141," NYU Libraries (website), last modified June 2014, http://dlib.nyu.edu/findingaids/html/tamwag/tam_141/bioghist.html; and Spear, "Crisis in Urban Liberalism," 154.

113. Jo Yurek, interview with author, New York, April 3, 2018.

114. Henry Yurek, interview with author, New York, April 3, 2018.

115. "Stop the Bank Interested Rip-Off," box 1, "Teachers Action Caucus November 1974–August 1975" folder, AF Papers.

116. "Don't Mourn—Organize," June 9, 1975, box 1, "Teachers Action Caucus November 1974–August 1975" folder, AF Papers.

117. "No Budget Cuts! No Layoffs!"

118. "School-Fund Cuts Prompt Protest," *New York Times*, June 10, 1975.

119. CCC to Albert Shanker, August 1975, box 135, "Strike 1975" folder, UFT Records.

120. CCC press release, August 25, 1975, box 135, "Strike 1975" folder, UFT Records; "Board and Teachers Seek State Aid in Reaching Pact," *New York Times*, August 30, 1975.

121. Merry Tucker interview, August 25, 1981, NYW.

122. South Shore High School UFT chapter to Shanker, June 24, 1975, box 135, "Strike 1975" folder, UFT Records; Maier, *City Unions*, 175. For a more extensive look at teacher militancy, see Murphy, "Militancy in Many Forms," 229–48.

123. "Shanker Opposed Teachers' Strike," *New York Times*, September 30, 1975.

124. "Frustration and Anger Mark Opening Day," *New York Times*, September 9, 1975; "Talks Broken Off," *New York Times*, September 9, 1975.

125. "We Are Sorry But [. . .]," September 8, 1975, box 1, "Teachers Action Caucus September 1975–Aug 1976" folder, AF Papers.

126. "School Workers, Parents and Community," September 1975, box 43, "Contract Negotiations: Strike '75—Positions Other Than UFT" folder, UFT Records.

127. "On the Picketlines, a Mournful Militance," *New York Times*, September 10, 1975.

128. "Dear Chapter Leader," September 9, 1975; and "Picketing Guidelines," September 1975, both in box 135, "Strike 1975" folder, UFT Records.

129. Jo Yurek interview.

130. Teachers to Shanker and executive board members, September 12, 1975, box 135, "Strike 1975" folder, UFT Records; Maier, *City Unions*, 175.

131. Tabb, *Long Default*, 26.

132. "Strike of Teachers Is First Challenge for New State Unit," *New York Times*, September 10, 1975.

133. Freeman, *Working-Class New York*, 265.

134. "Teachers Vote to Return, but Many Reject Pact," *New York Times*, September 17, 1975; Tucker interview.

135. For left-wing leaflets, see "Vote No!" and "Vote No to Sellout!," September 1975, box 135, "Strike 1975" folder, UFT Records.

136. "Reject the 'Settlement,'" September 15, 1975, box 1, "Teachers Action Caucus September 1975–Aug 1976" folder, AF Papers.

137. Maier, *City Unions*, 175–76; "Teachers Vote to Return."

138. Teachers to Shanker and all members of the executive board, September 17, 1975, box 43, "Contract Negotiations: Strike '75—Positions Other than UFT" folder, UFT Records.

139. John P. Settle to Shanker, September 17, 1975, box 1, "Teachers Action Caucus September 1975–Aug 1976" folder, AF Papers.

140. Tucker interview.

141. Settle to Shanker, September 17, 1975; Lichten, *Class, Power and Austerity*, 141.

142. Quote from Victor Gotbaum statement transcript, October 28, 1975, box 63, "Fiscal Crisis: House Banking Committee and Subcommittee Testimonies 1975" folder, UFT Records.

143. Freeman, *Working-Class New York*, 291–95. For Reagan and labor, see McMartin, *Collision Course*.

CONCLUSION

1. To my knowledge, historians have not written about this gathering, and all source material is held in box 10, "Rank and File Workers Conferences 1968–1970" folder, JH Papers.

2. "Bias in the Building Industry: An Updated Report 1963–1967," box 348, "Civil Rights: Union Bias" folder, JVL Papers; Hill, "Bronx Terminal Market Controversy"; Gilbert Banks interview, October 22, 1980, NYW; James Haughton interview, October 22, 1980, NYW; "Negro Hiring Up in Building Jobs," *New York Times*, April 1, 1965.

3. For Cowie on these changes, see Cowie, *Stayin' Alive*, 21–22, 46–47.

4. Quote from anonymous International Brotherhood of Teamsters Local 553 member, interview with author, New York, January 13, 2017. For documentation of allegations of racketeering and organized crime incursion into the Teamsters in New York City until the 1950s, see Witwer, *Corruption and Reform*, 111–13.

5. Aaron Brenner primarily focuses on Communications Workers of America strikes after 1968 in "Rank-and-File Struggles." For a short mention of taxi wildcats, see Hodges, *Taxi!*, 127. For discussion of the strikes as a strike wave, see Freeman, *Working-Class New York*, 211–12.

6. For exemplary works, see Freeman, "Lindsay and Labor," 118–31; and Cannato, *Ungovernable City*.

7. "Transcript of Statement by Mayor Lindsay on Status of Negotiations in the Subway and Bus Walkout," *New York Times*, January 11, 1966. For several assessments of Lindsay's mayoralty, see Viteritti, *Summer in the City*; and Freeman, "Lindsay and Labor," 129. For a less sympathetic, though exhaustive, account, see Cannato, *Ungovernable City*.

8. "New Conference of Mayor John Lindsay at City Hall, New York," February 11, 1968, box 90, "New York City Sanitation Strike, Key Events, 1968 Feb" folder, NAR Records.

9. Kenneth D. Durr describes a similar disjunction between liberalism and working-class interest in Baltimore in *Behind the Backlash*. See also Cowie, "From Hard Hats," 9–17.

10. Rubio, *There's Always Work*, 155.

11. Nabach, "Telephone Strike," 46. Aaron Brenner devotes significant attention to left organizations in the CWA; see Aaron Brenner, "Rank-and-File Struggles."

12. Freeman, *Working-Class New York*, 254–55.

13. "Carol and Rich," TRFC Oral History.

14. Haughton interview.

15. Windham, *Knocking on Labor's Door*, 178.

16. Milkman and van der Naald, *State of the Unions*.

17. For important changes since the 1970s, including deunionization, debt, and growing inequality, see Massey, "Globalization and Inequality," 9–23. For Clinton's comments, see "Clinton Expresses Regret for Saying 'Half' of Trump Supporters Are 'Deplorables,'" CNN.com, September 12, 2016, www.cnn.com/2016/09/09/politics/hillary-clinton-donald-trump-basket-of-deplorables.

BIBLIOGRAPHY

MANUSCRIPT COLLECTIONS

Alabama Department of Archives and History, Montgomery
  Governors George C. and Lurleen B. Wallace Collection
Archive on Municipal Finance and Leadership, Baruch College, New York, NY
  Jack Bigel Collection
Joint Industry Board of the Electrical Industry, IBEW Local 3 Archives, Queens, NY
  Harry Van Arsdale Jr. Papers
Kheel Center for Labor-Management Documentation and Archives, Cornell University, Ithaca, NY
  Benjamin H. Wolff Papers
  E. Wight Bakke Papers
  Theodore W. Kheel Additional Files
  Theodore Woodrow Kheel Arbitration Papers
LaGuardia-Wagner Archives, LaGuardia Community College, Queens, NY
  Abraham D. Beame Collection
Manuscripts and Archives Repository, Sterling Memorial Library, Yale University, New Haven, CT
  John Vliet Lindsay Papers
Municipal Archives, New York City Department of Records and Information Services
  Mayor Abraham Beame Collection
  Mayor John Lindsay Collection
Richard Nixon Presidential Library and Museum, Yorba Linda, CA
  Nixon Presidential Returned Materials Collection: White House Special Files (Digital)
Rockefeller Archive Center, Sleepy Hollow, NY
  Nelson A. Rockefeller Gubernatorial Records
  Nelson A. Rockefeller Personal Papers

Schomburg Center for Research in Black Culture, New York Public Library
   James Haughton Papers
Special Collections and University Archives, University of Oregon Libraries, Eugene
   Brice P. Disque Papers
Tamiment Library and Robert F. Wagner Labor Archives, New York University
   American Federation of State, County, and Municipal Employees District Council 37 Records
   American Federation of State, County, and Municipal Employees Local 1930 Records
   American Postal Workers Union, Moe Biller Collection
   Anne Filardo Papers on Rank and File Activism in the American Federation of Teachers and in the United Federation of Teachers
   Bernard and Jewel Bellush Papers
   Building and Construction Trades Council Meeting Records
   Building Trades Employers Association Meeting Records
   Communications Workers of America Local 1150 Records
   Communications Workers of America Printed Ephemera Collection
   Communications Workers of America Records
   International Brotherhood of Electrical Workers, Local 3, Meeting Records
   Michael Padwee Papers
   New York City Central Labor Council Collection
   New Yorkers at Work Oral History Collection
   New York Metro Area Postal Union Records
   Social Service Employees Union Records
   Taxi Rank and File Coalition Oral History Collection
   Taxi Rank and File Coalition Records
   Transport Workers Union of America: Local Records
   Transport Workers Union Oral History Collection
   United Action Publication, Printed Ephemera
   United Association of Journeymen and Apprentices of the Plumbing and Pipe Fitting Industry, Local 2 Records
   United Federation of Teachers Printed Ephemera Collection
   United Federation of Teachers Records
   Utility Workers of America, Local 1–2 Records

NEWSPAPERS AND MAGAZINES

Amsterdam News (New York, NY)
Daily News (New York, NY)
El Diario La Prensa (New York, NY)
Fortune
Hot Seat (New York, NY)
New York
New York Post
New York Times
Strike Back! (New York, NY)
Taxi Drivers Voice
Washington (DC) Post

SECONDARY SOURCES

Aitken, Jonathan. *Charles W. Colson: A Life Redeemed.* London: Continuum, 2005.

Alcaly, Roger E., and David Mermelstein, eds. *The Fiscal Crisis of American Cities: Essays on the Political Economy of Urban America with Special Reference to New York.* New York: Vintage Books, 1977.

Alex, Nicholas. *New York Cops Talk Back: A Study of a Beleaguered Minority.* New York: John Wiley and Sons, 1976.

Anderson, Terry H. *The Pursuit of Fairness: A History of Affirmative Action.* New York: Oxford University Press, 2004.

Appy, Christian G. *Working-Class War: American Combat Soldiers and Vietnam.* Chapel Hill: University of North Carolina Press, 1993.

Arnesen, Eric, ed. *Encyclopedia of US Labor and Working Class History.* Vol. 1. New York: Routledge, 2007.

Bailey, Robert W. *The Crisis Regime: The New York City Financial Crisis.* Albany: State University of New York Press, 1984.

Banks, Nancy. "'The Last Bastion of Discrimination': The New York City Building Trades and the Struggle over Affirmative Action, 1961–1976." PhD diss., Columbia University, 2006.

Beckert, Sven. *Monied Metropolis: New York City and the Consolidation of the American Bourgeoisie, 1850–1896.* Cambridge: Cambridge University Press, 2003.

Bellush, Jewel, and Bernard Bellush. *Union Power and New York: Victor Gotbaum and District Council 37.* New York: Praeger, 1992.

Berger, Dan. *The Hidden 1970s: Histories of Radicalism.* New Brunswick, NJ: Rutgers University Press, 2010.

Biju, Matthew. *Taxi! Cabs and Capitalism in New York City.* Ithaca, NY: ILR, 2008.

Biondi, Martha. *To Stand and Fight: The Struggle for Civil Rights in Postwar New York City.* Cambridge, MA: Harvard University Press, 2003.

Blakely, Debra E. *Mass Mediated Disease: A Case Study Analysis of Three Flu Pandemics and Public Health Policy.* Oxford, UK: Lexington Books, 2006.

Bloodworth, Jeffrey. *Losing the Center: The Decline of American Liberalism, 1968–1992.* Lexington: University of Kentucky Press, 2013.

Borstleman, Thomas. *The 1970s: A New Global History from Civil Rights to Economic Inequality.* Princeton, NJ: Princeton University Press, 2012.

Brady, Marnie. "An Appetite for Justice: The Restaurant Opportunities Center of New York." In *New Labor in New York: Precarious Workers and the Future of the Labor Movement,* edited by Ruth Milkman and Ed Ott, 229–245. Ithaca, NY: ILR, 2014.

Brecher, Jeremy. "The Decline of Strikes." In Brenner, Day, and Ness, *Encyclopedia of Strikes,* 72–80.

Brenner, Aaron. "Rank-and-File Rebellion, 1966–1975." PhD diss., Columbia University, 1996.

———. "Rank-and-File Struggles at the Telephone Company." In Brenner, Brenner, and Winslow, *Rebel Rank and File,* 251–80. Atlantic Highlands, NJ: Humanities Press International, 1995.

———. "Striking against the State: The Postal Wildcat of 1970." *Labor's Heritage,* no. 7 (Spring 1996): 4–27.

Brenner, Aaron, Robert Brenner, and Cal Winslow, eds. *Rebel Rank and File: Labor Militancy and Revolt from Below during the Long 1970s*. New York: Verso, 2010.

Brenner, Aaron, Benjamin Day, and Immanuel Ness, eds. *The Encyclopedia of Strikes in American History*. London: Routledge, 2015.

Brenner, Robert. *The Economics of Global Turbulence: The Advanced Capitalist Economies from Long Boom to Long Downturn, 1945–2005*. London: Verso Books, 2006.

Brinkley, Alan. *The End of Reform: New Deal Liberalism in Recession and War*. New York: Vintage Books, 1996.

Brockway, Mac [Tim Costello]. "Keep on Truckin'." In Root & Branch, *Root & Branch*, 39–49.

Buhle, Paul. *Taking Care of Business: Samuel Gompers, George Meany, Lane Kirkland, and the Tragedy of American Labor*. New York: Monthly Review Press, 1999.

Bush, Gregory, ed. *Campaign Speeches of American Presidential Candidates, 1948–1984*. New York: F. Ungar, 1985.

Buttenwieser, Ann L. *Manhattan Water-Bound: Manhattan's Waterfront from the Seventeenth Century to the Present*. Syracuse, NY: Syracuse University Press, 1999.

Cannato, Vincent J. *The Ungovernable City: John Lindsay and His Struggle to Save New York*. New York: Basic Books, 2001.

Carter, Dan T. *From George Wallace to Newt Gingrich: Race in the Conservative Counterrevolution*. Baton Rouge: Louisiana State University Press, 1996.

———. *Politics of Rage: George Wallace, the Origins of the New Conservatism, and the Transformation of American Politics*. Baton Rouge: Louisiana State University Press, 2000.

Chronopoulos, Themis. "The Lindsay Administration and the Sanitation Crisis of New York City, 1966–1973." *Journal of Urban History* 40, no. 6 (November 2014): 1138–54.

Cleaver, William. "Wildcats in the Appalachian Coal Fields." In Midnight Notes Collective, *Midnight Oil*, 169–84.

Cohen, Lizabeth. *A Consumers' Republic: The Politics of Mass Consumption in America*. New York: Vintage Books, 2004.

Cohen, Lizabeth, and Brian Goldstein. "Governing at the Tipping Point: Shaping the City's Role in Economic Development." In Viteritti, *Summer in the City*, 225–39.

"Conversation: Wilbur Haddock on the United Black Brothers." *Souls* 2, no. 2 (Spring 2000): 27–33.

Cowie, Jefferson. "From Hard Hats to NASCAR Dads." *New Labor Forum* 13, no. 3 (Fall 2004): 9–17.

———. *Stayin' Alive: The 1970s and the Last Days of the Working Class*. New York: New Press, 2010.

———. "Vigorously Left, Right, and Center: The Crosscurrents of Working-Class America in the 1970s." In *America in the Seventies*, edited by Beth Bailey and David Farber. Lawrence: University Press of Kansas, 2004.

Cullen, Jim. *The American Dream: A Short History of an Idea that Shaped a Nation*. New York: Oxford University Press, 2004.

Darien, Andrew T. *Becoming New York's Finest: Race, Gender, and Integration of the NYPD, 1935–1980*. New York: Palgrave Macmillan, 2013.

Darden, Joe T. *Detroit: Race Riots, Racial Conflicts, and Efforts to Bridge the Racial Divide*. East Lansing: Michigan State University Press, 2013.

De Angelis, Massimo. *Keynesianism, Social Conflict and Political Economy*. London: Macmillan, 2000.

Denby, Charles. *Indignant Heart: A Black Worker's Journal*. Detroit, MI: Wayne State University Press, 1989.

Deslippe, Dennis. *Protesting Affirmative Action: The Struggle over Equality after the Civil Rights Revolution*. Baltimore: Johns Hopkins University Press, 2014.

Donovan, Ronald. *Administering the Taylor Law: Public Employee Relations in New York*. Ithaca, NY: ILR Press, 1990.

Drenna, Matthew P. "The Decline and Rise of the New York Economy." In *Dual City: Restructuring New York*, edited by John Hull Mollenkopf and Manuel Castells, 25–42. New York: Russell Sage Foundation, 1991.

Durr, Kenneth D. *Behind the Backlash: White Working-Class Politics in Baltimore, 1940–1980*. Chapel Hill: University of North Carolina Press, 2003.

Edsall, Thomas Byrne. *New Politics of Inequality*. New York: W. W. Norton, 1984.

Fainstein, Norman I., and Susan S. Fainstein. "Governing Regimes and the Political Economy of Development in New York City, 1946–1984." In *Power, Culture, and Place: Essays on New York City*, edited by John Hull Mollenkopf, 161–200. New York: Russell Sage Foundation, 1988.

Fenton, Patrick. "Confessions of a Working Stiff." In Zimpel, *Man against Work*, 19–24.

Fitch, Robert. *The Assassination of New York*. London: Verso, 1993.

Flamm, Michael W. *In the Heat of the Summer: The New York Riots of 1964 and the War on Crime*. Philadelphia: University of Pennsylvania Press, 2017.

———. *Law and Order: Street Crime, Civil Unrest, and the Crisis of Liberalism in the 1960s*. New York: Columbia University Press, 2005.

———. "'Law and Order' at Large: The New York Civilian Review Board Referendum of 1966 and the Crisis of Liberalism." *Historian* 64, no. 3–4 (2002): 643–65.

Flood, Joe. *The Fires: How a Computer Formula Burned Down New York City—and Determined the Future of American Cities*. New York: Riverhead Books, 2010.

Fogelson, Robert M. *Violence as Protest: A Study of Riots and Ghettos*. Garden City, NY: Doubleday, 1971.

Foner, Philip S. *U.S. Labor and the Vietnam War*. New York: International, 1989.

Fortner, Michael Javen. *Black Silent Majority: The Rockefeller Drug Laws and the Politics of Punishment*. Cambridge, MA: Harvard University Press, 2015.

Freeman, Joshua. "Hardhats: Construction Workers, Manliness, and the 1970 Pro-War Demonstrations." *Journal of Social History* 26, no. 4 (Summer 1993): 725–44.

———. *In Transit: The Transport Workers Union in New York City, 1933–1966*. New York: Oxford University Press, 1989.

———. "Lindsay and Labor." In Roberts, *America's Mayor*, 118–31.

———. *Working-Class New York: Life and Labor since World War II*. New York: New Press, 2001.

Friedman, Samuel R. *Teamster Rank and File: Power, Bureaucracy, and Rebellion at Work and in a Union*. New York: Columbia University Press, 1982.

Gafney, Dennis. *Teachers United: The Rise of the New York State United Teachers*. Albany: State University of New York Press, 2007.

"General Organizers' Reports." *United Association Journal* 74, no. 4 (April 1967): 18.

Glaberman, Martin. "Walter Reuther and the Decline of the Labor Movement." In

Punching Out and Other Writings, edited by Staughton Lynd, 64–92. Chicago: Charles H. Kerr, 2002.

———. *Wartime Strikes: The Struggle against the No Strike Pledge in the UAW during World War II*. Detroit: Bewick Editions, 1980.

Goland, David Hamilton. *Constructing Affirmative Action: The Struggle for Equal Employment Opportunity*. Lexington: University Press of Kentucky, 2011.

Gonzalez, Juan. "Reflections." In Roberts, *America's Mayor*, 56–57.

Gooding, Judson. "Blue Collar Blues on the Assembly Line." In Zimpel, *Man against Work*, 61–75.

Gordon, John. "In the Hot Seat: The Story of the New York Taxi Rank and File Coalition." *Radical America* 17, no. 5 (July–August 1975): 27–43.

Green, Venus. "Race and Technology: African American Women in the Bell System, 1945–1980." In "Snapshots of a Discipline: Selected Proceedings from the Conference on Critical Problems and Research Frontiers in the History of Technology, Madison, Wisconsin, October 30–November 3, 1991." Supplement, *Technology and Culture* 36, no. 2 (1995): S101–44.

Greenberg, Miriam. *Branding New York: How a City in Crisis Was Sold to the World*. New York: Routledge, 2008.

Hall, Burton, ed. *Autocracy and Insurgency in Organized Labor*. New Brunswick, NJ: Transaction Books, 1972.

———. "Labor Insurgency and the Legal Trap." In Hall, *Autocracy and Insurgency*, 255–64.

———. "The Painters' Union: Autocracy and Insurgency." In Hall, *Autocracy and Insurgency*, 30–40.

Harvey, David. *A Brief History of Neoliberalism*. New York: Oxford University Press, 2005.

Hill, Herbert. "The Bronx Terminal Market Controversy: A Study of Race, Labor, and Power." *Humanities in Society* 6 (Fall 1983): 351–91.

———. "The ILGWU Today: The Decay of a Labor Union." In Hall, *Autocracy and Insurgency*, 147–60.

Hodges, Graham Russell Gao. *Taxi! A Social History of the New York City Cab Driver*. Baltimore: Johns Hopkins University Press, 2007.

Hunter-Gault, Charlayne. "Black and White." In Roberts, *America's Mayor*, 42–54.

Isaacs, Charles S. *Inside Ocean Hill–Brownsville: A Teacher's Education, 1968–1969*. Albany: Excelsior Editions—State University of New York Press, 2014.

Isserman, Maurice, and Michael Kazin. *America Divided: The Civil War of the 1960s*. New York: Oxford University Press, 1999.

Jackson, Ken. *Crabgrass Frontier: The Suburbanization of the United States*. New York: Oxford University Press, 1985.

Jacobson, Matthew Frye. *Roots Too: White Ethnic Revival in Post–Civil Rights America*. Cambridge, MA: Harvard University Press, 2006.

Johnson, Marilyn S. *Street Justice: A History of Police Violence in New York City*. Boston: Beacon, 2003.

Kahlenberg, Richard D. *Tough Liberal: Albert Shanker and the Battle over Schools, Unions, Race, and Democracy*. New York: Columbia University Press, 2007.

Kelly, Robert E. *Neck and Neck to the White House: The Closest Presidential Election, 1796–2000*. Jefferson, NC: McFarland, 2011.

Koscielski, Frank. *Divided Loyalties: American Unions and the Vietnam War*. New York: Garland, 1999.

Kotz, David M. *The Rise and Fall of Neoliberal Capitalism*. Cambridge, MA: Harvard University Press, 2015.

Krohn-Hansen, Christian. *Making New York Dominican: Small Business, Politics, and Everyday Life*. Philadelphia: University of Pennsylvania Press, 2013.

La Botz, Dan. *Rank-and-File Rebellion: Teamsters for a Democratic Union*. New York: Verso, 1990.

———. "The Tumultuous Teamsters of the 1970s." in Brenner, Brenner, and Winslow, *Rebel Rank and File*, 199–226.

Lachman, Seymour P., and Robert Polner. *The Man Who Saved New York: Hugh Carey and the Great Fiscal Crisis of 1975*. Albany: State University of New York Press, 2011.

LaTour, Jane. *Sisters in the Brotherhood: Working Women Organizing for Equality in New York City*. New York: Palgrave Macmillan, 2008.

Lee, Sonia Song-Ha. *Building a Latino Civil Rights Movement: Puerto Ricans, African Americans, and the Pursuit of Racial Justice in New York City*. Chapel Hill: University of North Carolina Press, 2014.

Lichten, Eric. *Class, Power and Austerity: The New York City Fiscal Crisis*. South Hadley, MA: Bergin and Garvey, 1986.

Lichtenstein, Nelson. *State of the Union: A Century of American Labor*. Princeton, NJ: Princeton University Press, 2002.

Lizzi, Maria C. "'My Heart Is as Black as Yours': White Backlash, Racial Identity, and Italian American Stereotypes in New York City's 1969 Mayoral Campaign." *Journal of American Ethnic History* 27, no. 3 (Spring 2008): 43–80.

Loyd, John P. "Teachers' Strikes." In Brenner, Day, and Ness, *Encyclopedia of Strikes*, 252–65.

Maier, Mark. *City Unions: Managing Discontent in New York City*. New Brunswick, NJ: Rutgers University Press, 1987.

Marlin, George J. *Fighting the Good Fight: A History of the New York Conservative Party*. South Bend, IN: St. Augustine's, 2002.

Marmo, Michael. *More Profile Than Courage: The New York City Transit Strike 1966*. Albany: State University of New York Press, 1990.

Massey, Douglas S. "Globalization and Inequality: Explaining American Exceptionalism." *European Sociological Review* 25, no. 1 (February 2009): 9–23.

Matter, Philip, and Donna Demac. *Developing and Underdeveloping New York: The "Fiscal Crisis" and a Strategy for Fighting Austerity*. Brooklyn: New York Struggle against Work, 1976.

McGirr, Lisa. *Suburban Warriors: The Origins of the New American Right*. Princeton, NJ: Princeton University Press, 2001.

McMartin, Joseph A. *Collision Course: Ronald Reagan, the Air Traffic Controllers, and the Strike That Changed America*. New York: Oxford University Press, 2011.

McNickle, Chris. *To Be Mayor of New York: Ethnic Politics in the City*. New York: Columbia University Press, 1993.

McTaggart, Ursula. *Guerrillas in the Industrial Jungle: Radicalism's Primitive and Industrial Rhetoric*. Albany: State University of New York Press, 2012.

Mello, William J. *New York Longshoremen: Class and Power on the Docks*. Gainesville: University Press of Florida, 2010.

Midnight Notes Collective, ed. *Midnight Oil: Work, Energy, War, 1973–1992*. Brooklyn, NY: Autonomedia, 1992.

Mikusko, M. Brady, and John F. Miller. *Carriers in a Common Cause: A History of Letter Carriers and the NALC*. Washington, DC: NALC, 2014.

Milkman, Ruth, and Stephanie Luce. *The State of the Unions 2019: A Profile of Organized Labor in New York City, New York State, and the United States*. New York: CUNY School of Labor and Urban Studies, 2019.

Milkman, Ruth, and Joseph van der Naald. *The State of the Unions 2023: A Profile of Organized Labor in New York City, New York State, and the United States*. New York: CUNY School of Labor and Urban Studies, 2023.

Mirengoff, William, and Lester Rindler. *CETA: Manpower Programs under Local Control*. Washington, DC: National Academy of Sciences, 1978.

Moccio, Fran. *Live Wire: Women and Brotherhood in the Electrical Industry*. Philadelphia: Temple University Press, 2009.

Montgomery, David. *Workers' Control in America: Studies in the History of Work, Technology, and Labor Struggles*. Cambridge: Cambridge University Press, 1979.

Moody, Kim. *From Welfare State to Real Estate: Regime Change in New York City, 1974 to the Present*. New York: New Press, 2007.

———. *An Injury to All: The Decline of American Unionism*. New York: Verso, 1988.

Moreton, Bethany. *To Serve God and Wal-Mart*. Cambridge, MA: Harvard University Press, 2004.

Morris, Charles. *The Cost of Good Intentions: New York City and the Liberal Experiment*. New York: W. W. Norton, 1980.

———. "Of Budgets, Taxes, and the Rise of a New Plutocracy." In Viteritti, *Summer in the City*, 81–105.

Mumford, Kevin J. *Newark: A History of Race, Rights, and Riots in America*. New York: New York University Press, 2008.

Murphy, Marjorie. "Militancy in Many Forms: Teachers Strikes and Urban Insurrection, 1967–1974." In Brenner, Brenner, and Winslow, *Rebel Rank and File*, 229–48.

Nabach, Joseph. "The Telephone Strike: Frozen Militancy." *New Politics* 9, no. 4 (Winter 1972): 40–48.

National Labor Relations Board. *Decisions and Orders of the National Labor Relations Board*. Vol. 135. Washington, DC: Government Printing Office, 1962.

New York Board of Elections. *Annual Report of the Board of Elections in the City of New York*. New York: Board of Elections, 1968.

New York Office of Civil Defense. *Spotlight on Disaster Management: Emergency Control Board Civil Defense Biennial Report 1968–1969; Disaster Management Guide for Agency Heads*. New York: Office of Civil Defense, 1971.

New York State Department of Labor. *Statistics on Work Stoppages New York State, 1967*. New York: Division of Research and Statics, 1968.

———. *Statistics on Work Stoppages New York State, 1968*. New York: Division of Research and Statics, 1969.

Newfield, Jack, and Paul Dubrul. *The Abuse of Power: Permanent Government and the Fall of New York*. New York: Viking, 1977.
Noble, David F. *Progress without People: In Defense of Luddism*. Chicago: Charles H. Kerr, 1993.
Nystrom, Derek. *Hard Hats, Rednecks, and Macho Men: Class in 1970s American Cinema*. New York: Oxford University Press, 2009.
O'Farrell, Brigid, and Joyce L. Kornbluh. *Rocking the Boat: Union Women's Voices, 1915–1975*. New Brunswick, NJ: Rutgers University Press, 1996.
Palladino, Grace. *Skilled Hands, Strong Spirits: A Century of Building Trades History*. Ithaca, NY: Cornell University Press, 2005.
Patterson, James T. *Grand Expectations: The United States, 1945–1974*. New York: Oxford University Press, 1996.
Peiss, Kathy. *Cheap Amusements: Working Women and Leisure in Turn-of-the-Century New York*. Philadelphia: Temple University Press, 1986.
Perlstein, Daniel Hiram. *Justice, Justice: School Politics and the Eclipse of Liberalism*. New York: Peter Lang, 2004.
Perlstein, Rick. *Before the Storm: Barry Goldwater and the Unmaking of the American Consensus*. New York: Nation Books, 2001.
———. *Nixonland: The Rise of a President and the Fracturing of America*. New York: Scribner, 2008.
Philips, Lisa. *A Renegade Union: Interracial Organizing and Labor Radicalism*. Urbana: University of Illinois Press, 2012.
Phillips-Fein, Kim. *Fear City: New York City's Fiscal Crisis and the Rise of Austerity Politics*. New York: Metropolitan Books, 2017.
Pileggi, Nicholas. "Crime and Punishment." In Roberts, *America's Mayor*, 72–83.
Podair, Jerald. *The Strike That Changed New York: Blacks, Whites, and the Ocean Hill–Brownsville Crisis*. New Haven, CT: Yale University Press, 2002.
Polner, Robert. *The Man Who Saved New York: Hugh Carey and the Fiscal Crisis of 1975*. Albany: State University of New York Press, 2010.
Price, Homer Edward. "Right-Wing Politics and Racism in America: The Wallace Movement 1968." PhD diss., University of California, Berkeley, 1973.
Pritchett, Wendell E. *Brownsville, Brooklyn: Blacks, Jews, and the Changing Face of the Ghetto*. Chicago: University of Chicago Press, 2003.
Public Employment Relations Board. *Cumulative Digest and Index: Official Decisions, Opinions and Related Matters*. Vols. 1–20. New York: Public Relations Press, 1981.
Purnell, Brian. *Fighting Jim Crow in the County of Kings: The Congress of Racial Equality in Brooklyn*. Lexington: University Press of Kentucky, 2013.
———. "'Taxation without Sanitation Is Tyranny': Civil Rights Struggles over Garbage Collection in Brooklyn, New York during the Fall of 1962." *Afro-Americans in New York Life and History* 31, no. 2 (July 2007): 61–88.
Rachleff, Peter. "American Postal Workers Union." In Arnesen, *Encyclopedia*, 95–96.
———. "Postal Strike (1970)." In Arnesen, *Encyclopedia*, 1115–16.
Rae, Nicol C. *The Decline and Fall of the Liberal Republicans*. New York: Oxford University Press, 1989.
Reese, Ellen. *Backlash against Welfare Mothers: Past and Present*. Berkeley: University of California Press, 2005.

Reeves, Richard. "The Making of the Mayor." In Roberts, *America's Mayor*, 26–38.

Regan, John. "General Organizers' Report." *United Association Journal* 74, no. 1 (January 1967): 12–14.

———. "General Organizers' Reports." *United Association Journal* 74, no. 2 (February 1967): 15.

Revell, Keith D. *Building Gotham: Civic Culture and Public Policy in New York City, 1898–1938.* Baltimore: Johns Hopkins University Press, 2005.

Rieder, Jonathan. *Canarsie: The Jews and Italians of Brooklyn against Liberalism.* Cambridge, MA: Harvard University Press, 1985.

Riemer, Jeffrey W. *Hard Hats: The Work World of Construction Workers.* New York: SAGE, 1979.

Roberts, Sam, ed. *America's Mayor: John V. Lindsay and the Reinvention of New York.* New York: Museum of the City of New York and Columbia University Press, 2010.

Rodgers, Daniel T. *Age of Fracture.* Cambridge, MA: Belknap Press of Harvard University, 2011.

Rogin, Michael. "Wallace and the Middle Class: White Backlash in Wisconsin." *Public Opinion Quarterly* 30, no. 1 (1966): 98–108.

Root & Branch, ed. *Root & Branch: The Rise of the Workers' Movements.* Greenwich, CT: Fawcett Books, 1975.

Rubio, Philip F. *There's Always Work at the Post Office: African American Postal Workers and the Fight for Jobs, Justice, and Equality.* Chapel Hill: University of North Carolina Press, 2010.

———. *Undelivered: From the Great Postal Strike of 1970 to the Manufactured Crisis of the US Postal Service.* Chapel Hill: University of North Carolina Press, 2020.

Ruffini, Gene. *Harry Van Arsdale Jr.: Labor's Champion.* New York: Routledge, 2002.

Russell, Thaddeus. *Out of the Jungle: Jimmy Hoffa and the Remaking of the American Working Class.* New York: Alfred A. Knopf, 2001.

Schneirow, Richard, and Thomas J. Suhrbur. *Union Brotherhood, Union Town: The History of the Carpenters' Union in Chicago, 1863–1987.* Carbondale: Southern Illinois University Press, 1988.

Schulman, Bruce. *The Seventies: The Great Shift in American Culture, Society, and Politics.* New York: De Capo, 2001.

Segal, Martin. *The Rise of the United Association: National Unionism in the Pipe Trades, 1884–1924.* Cambridge, MA: Wertheim Publications in Industrial Relations, 1969.

Self, Robert O. *American Babylon: Race and the Struggle for Postwar Oakland.* Princeton, NJ: Princeton University Press, 2003.

Shefter, Martin. *Political Crisis/Fiscal Crisis: The Collapse and Revival of New York City.* New York: Columbia University Press, 1992.

Sheppard, Harold L. *Where Have All the Robots Gone? Worker Dissatisfaction in the '70s.* New York: Free Press, 1972.

Silver, Marc. *Under Construction: Work and Alienation in the Buildings Trades.* Albany: State University of New York Press, 1986.

Smith, Richard Norton. *On His Own Terms: A Life of Nelson Rockefeller.* New York: Random House, 2014.

Spear, Michael. "A Crisis in Urban Liberalism: The New York City Municipal Unions and the 1970s Fiscal Crisis." PhD diss., Graduate Center, City University of New York, 2005.

Special Task Force to the Secretary of Health, Education, and Welfare. *Work in America*. Cambridge, MA: MIT Press, 1973.

Stein, Judith. *Pivotal Decade: How the United States Traded Factories for Finance*. New Haven, CT: Yale University Press, 2010.

——. *Running Steel, Running America: Race, Economic Policy, and the Decline of Liberalism*. Chapel Hill: University of North Carolina Press, 1998.

Steinberg, Stephen. "The Social Context of the White Backlash: A Critique of Jonathan Rieder's Canarsie." *Ethnic and Racial Studies* 11, no. 2 (April 1988): 218–24.

Stencel, Sandra. "America's Changing Work Ethic." In *Editorial Research Reports*, edited by Congressional Quarterly, 2:901–20. Washington, DC: CQ Press, 1979.

Stott, Richard B. *Workers in the Metropolis: Class, Ethnicity, and Youth in Antebellum New York City*. Ithaca, NY: Cornell University Press, 1990.

Sugrue, Thomas J. "Affirmative Action from Below: Civil Rights, the Building Trades, and the Politics of Racial Equality in the Urban North, 1945–1969." *Journal of American History* 91, no. 4 (June 2004): 145–73.

——. *The Origins of the Urban Crisis: Race and Inequality in Postwar Detroit*. Princeton, NJ: Princeton University Press, 1996.

Sullivan, Timothy J. *New York State and the Rise of Modern Conservatism: Redrawing Party Lines*. Albany: State University of New York Press, 2009.

Tabb, William. *The Long Default: New York City and the Urban Fiscal Crisis*. New York: Monthly Review Press, 1982.

Taylor, Kieran. "American Petrograd: Detroit and the League of Revolutionary Black Workers." In Brenner, Brenner, and Winslow, *Rebel Rank and File*, 311–33.

Transport Workers Union of America. *Reports of the Proceedings of the 11th Constitutional Convention*. New York: Transport Workers Union of America, 1961.

United States Bureau of the Census. *Historical Statistics of the United States, Colonial Times to 1970*. Bicentennial ed. Pt. 1. Washington, DC: US Bureau of the Census, 1975.

United States Department of Labor. *Analysis of Work Stoppages, 1968*. Washington, DC: Bureau of Labor Statistics, 1970.

——. *Analysis of Work Stoppages, 1969*. Washington, DC: Bureau of Labor Statistics, 1971.

——. *Analysis of Work Stoppages, 1970*. Washington, DC: Bureau of Labor Statistics, 1972.

——. *Analysis of Work Stoppages, 1971*. Washington, DC: Bureau of Labor Statistics, 1973.

——. *Analysis of Work Stoppages, 1972*. Washington, DC: Bureau of Labor Statistics, 1974.

——. *Analysis of Work Stoppages, 1973*. Washington, DC: Bureau of Labor Statistics, 1975.

——. *New York City in Transition: Population, Jobs, Prices, and Pay in a Decade of Change*. Regional report 34. New York: Bureau of Labor Statistics, Regional Office, 1973.

Upton, James N. "The Politics of Urban Violence: Critiques and Proposals." *Journal of Black Studies* 15, no. 3 (March 1985): 243–58.

Vidich, Charles. *The New York Cab Driver and His Fare*. Cambridge, MA: Schenkman, 1976.

Viteritti, Joseph P., ed. *Summer in the City: John Lindsay, New York, and the American Dream*. Baltimore: Johns Hopkins University Press, 2014.

Waldinger, Roger. *Still the Promised Land? African-Americans and the New Immigrants in Postindustrial New York*. Cambridge, MA: Harvard University Press, 1996.

Walkowitz, Daniel J. *Working with Class: Social Workers and the Politics of Middle-Class Identity*. Chapel Hill: University of North Carolina Press, 1999.

Walsh, John, and Garth L. Mangum. *Labor Struggle in the Post Office: From Selective Lobbying to Collective Bargaining*. Armonk, NY: M. E. Sharpe, 1992.

West, Michael O. "Whose Black Power? The Business of Black Power and Black Power's Business." In *The Business of Black Power: Community Development, Capitalism, and Corporate Responsibility in Postwar America*, edited by Laura Warren Hill and Julia Rabig, 274–303. Rochester, NY: University of Rochester Press, 2012.

Wilder, Craig Steven. *A Covenant with Color: Race and Social Power in Brooklyn*. New York: Columbia University Press, 2001.

Wilentz, Sean. *Chants Democratic: New York City and the Rise of the American Working Class, 1788–1850*. New York: Oxford University Press, 1984.

Windham, Lane. *Knocking on Labor's Door: Union Organizing in the 1970s and the Roots of the New Economic Divide*. Chapel Hill: University of North Carolina Press, 2018.

Witwer, David. *Corruption and Reform in the Teamsters Union*. Urbana-Champaign: University of Illinois Press, 2004.

———. "Local Rank and File Militancy: The Battle for Teamster Reform in Philadelphia in the Early 1960s." *Labor History* 41, no. 3 (August 2000): 263–78.

Zeitz, Joshua. *White Ethnic New York: Jews, Catholics, and the Shaping of Postwar Politics*. Chapel Hill: University of North Carolina Press, 2007.

Zeluck, Steve. "The UFT Strike: A Blow against Teacher Unionism." In Hall, *Autocracy and Insurgency*, 201–12.

Zimpel, Lloyd, ed. *Man against Work*. Grand Rapids, MI: William B. Eerdsman, 1974.

Zipp, Samuel. *Manhattan Projects: The Rise and Fall of Urban Renewal in Cold War New York*. New York: Oxford University Press, 2010.

INDEX

absenteeism, 45, 47–48
affirmative action, 94
AFL-CIO (American Federation of Labor–Congress of Industrial Organizations), 26, 32, 60–61, 111, 123
African-American Teachers Association, 58–59
American Postal Workers Union, 91
anti-communism, 13–14, 92–93, 105, 134

baggage handlers, 46
Bahr, Morton, 101, 104, 109
Beame, Abraham, 130–33, 136, 141–42, 145
Beamish, James, 2, 65
Beasley, David, 139, 142
Beirne, Joseph A., 103–4, 106, 109
Bell Workers Action Committee, 102, 105–6, 109
Belmore Cafeteria, 113
Biller, Morris "Moe," 86, 88, 90–91
Black Panther Party, 56–57, 102
Black Pearl Car Service, 116, 123
Black workers, 16, 31, 66, 73–74, 78, 80, 101–2, 126
"blue collar blues," 46
Brennan, Peter J., 94–95

Building and Construction Trades Council, 94–95

Carnegie, Joseph, 12, 16–19, 21–22, 66, 73–79
Carnivale, Ricky, 100, 106–9
Cassesse, John, 51
Central Labor Council, 59–61
Chiarelli, Joseph J., 54
Citywide Coordinating Committee to Save New York Schools, 149–50
Clinton, Hillary, 10, 160
Coalition Against Budget Cuts, 149
Cohen, Jack, 12, 28–29, 33–37
Communication Workers of America: International, 101, 103, 105, 109; Local 1101, 4, 8, 41, 43, 97–11
communists, 58, 83, 105, 115, 134, 147–48
Conservative Party of New York, 62
construction workers, 26–38, 91–96
contract rejections, 33–35, 41, 44, 69–70, 155–56, 159
CORE (Congress of Racial Equality), 31, 47
Costello, Tim, 67–69
craft workers, 14–16, 26, 31, 84, 98, 101–2

crime, 42–43, 54–59, 62, 103, 114–16, 124, 131

deindustrialization, 104, 131, 160
DeLury, John J., 40, 48–53, 143–45
Dempsey, Ed, 107–8
District Council, 37, 130, 132–34, 136–42, 145–47

Emergency Financial Control Board, 151, 153

"Fear City" campaign, 141, 145
Filardo, Anne, 148
fiscal crisis, 129–37, 139–41, 148–53, 159
fuel oil drivers, Local 553, 45, 67–72

"garbagemen," 48, 50, 143
Gilbert, Rust, 102
Gotbaum, Victor, 51–52, 65, 132–33, 136–41, 146
grievances, 41, 46–47, 99–100, 106, 158
gypsy cabs. *See* livery cabs

Habel, Hank, 99–100
Hard Hat Riot, 91–96
Harlem riot of 1964, 18–19
Harlem Unemployment Center, 74, 81–83
Haughton, James, 17, 19, 66, 78–84, 159
Hilderbrand, Richard, 17, 19
Hong Kong flu, 1, 63
Hot Seat (taxi union publication), 120, 124
"hot seat" sensors, 113

inflation, 65, 85, 95, 97–98, 103–4, 132
International Brotherhood of Electrical Workers, Local 3, 1, 12, 24, 29, 31, 33, 92, 98, 118
International Brotherhood of Teamsters, 4, 8, 48, 65–68, 98–100

Katz's Delicatessen, 113
King, Martin Luther, Jr., 15, 48, 75
Knight, Patrick, 133, 136–39

Labor and Industry Committee of NAACP, 17–19
law-and-order politics, 41–43, 47, 56–58, 61, 62, 93
Law Enforcement Group of New York, 56–67
Lazarus, Leo, 120
League of Revolutionary Black Workers, 79–83
"limousine liberals," 93
Lindsay, John, 10–12, 25–26, 34–35, 39–40, 51–57, 89–95, 111–12, 119–26
livery cabs, 44, 111–12, 116–26, 157–58
Lubash, David, 74

Maio, Rocky, 36
Manhattan-Bronx Postal Union, 84, 86, 88, 91
McDonnell, Vincent, 70, 125
McFeeley, Ken, 144–45
McGuire, James, 69–72
Meany, George, 26, 32, 60, 90
Motormen's Benevolent Association, 14, 75
Municipal Assistance Corporation, 141–42, 151
Municipal Labor Committee, 132–33, 136, 140–41
murders, 56, 114–16, 124, 141. *See also* crime

NAACP (National Association for the Advancement of Colored People), 17, 19, 31, 156; Labor and Industry Committee, 17–19
Nabach, Joseph, 109
National Association of Letter Carriers, 84–91
National Welfare Rights Organization, 135
Negro American Labor Council, 16–17, 19, 84
New York City Transit Authority, 14–21, 23, 73, 75–76
New York State Public Employees Relations Board, 74–77
New York Telephone, 97–103, 105–9

New York Times, 7, 25, 55, 57, 60, 70
Nixon, Richard, 59–62, 86–91, 94–96, 137

Ocean Hill–Brownsville Strike, 47, 58, 147–48, 150
Office of Collective Bargaining, 49–51, 53

Padwee, Michael, 136, 138
Pappalardo, Michael, 12, 28–29, 33–37
Patrolmen's Benevolent Association, 144–45
Philadelphia Plan, 94–95
police, 56–57, 85–88, 118–19, 122–23, 141–46
populism, 39–40, 54, 80
postal wildcat strike of 1970, 84–91
Procaccino, Mario, 93
Public Employees Relations Board, 74–77
Puerto Ricans, 31, 51, 73, 76, 102, 123, 147

racial discrimination, 18, 32, 47, 73–74, 83, 101–2, 115–16
Rademacher, Joseph, 85, 90–91
Randolph, A. Philip, 16–17, 19, 84
Rank and File Committee for a Democratic Union, 12, 14–15, 19–24, 38, 72–77
River, José, 123
Rockefeller, Nelson A., 34–35, 42, 52–54, 65, 77, 89, 104

sabotage, 45–48, 106, 108, 143, 158
sanitation workers, 48–54, 57, 62, 142, 145. *See also* "garbagemen"; Uniformed Sanitationmen's Association
scabs, 14, 34, 51, 70, 80, 88, 106, 108, 157
sellout leaders, 37, 44, 45, 70, 103
Serrette, Dennis, 102, 107
Shanker, Albert, 2, 45, 57–58, 65, 130, 148–52
Socialist Workers Party, 105
Social Services Employees Union, Local 371, 130, 133–42

Sombrotto, Vincent, 91
steam fitters, 38, 54
strike violence, 34, 70, 108, 144
Students for a Democratic Society, 57–58, 67, 78, 100, 102, 148
subway fare, 13–14, 19–20, 44, 104, 131, 146

Taxi and Limousine Commission, 119–20, 123
Taxi Drivers Union, Local 3036, 111–13, 117–19, 123, 125–26
taxi fare, 111, 113–14, 118–20, 124–25
teacher rank-and-file organizations. *See* African-American Teachers Association; Citywide Coordinating Committee to Save New York Schools; Teachers Action Caucus
Teachers Action Caucus, 147–50, 152
Teamsters. *See* fuel oil drivers, Local 553; International Brotherhood of Teamsters; Uniformed Sanitationmen's Association
telephone operators, 101–3, 105–6
Telephone Traffic Union, 102, 105–6
Trerotola, Joseph, 52, 65
Trump, Donald J., 9, 60
TWU (Transport Workers Union), 11–25, 40, 45, 47, 49, 66, 72–77, 87

UFT (United Federation of Teachers), 45–47, 58–59, 130, 142–43, 146–53
Uniformed Sanitationmen's Association, 48–54, 141–44
United Action, 102, 105–9
United Association of Journeymen and Apprentices of the Plumbing and Pipefitting Industry, Local 2, 26–38
United Black Brothers, 47
United Telephone Organizations, 98
urban riots, 18–19, 47, 56, 66

Van Arsdale, Harry, Jr., 24–25, 59–60, 65–66, 111–12, 116–22
Vietnam War, 59, 90–93, 105; veterans of, 100

Wagner, Robert, 17, 23, 94, 131
Wallace, George C., 4, 8–9, 39–40, 54–62, 78
Watchdog Committee, 120
welfare, 44, 51, 129–31, 134–35, 139–40
"white-collar woes," 45
white ethnics, 13, 15, 30, 55, 58, 61, 63

wildcat strikes, 39–44, 47–48, 79–80, 84–91, 101–2
Williams, Calvin, 116, 123
women workers, 43–44, 74, 91, 101–2, 105

youth rebellion, 47, 69, 100, 114, 120, 156

www.ingramcontent.com/pod-product-compliance
Lightning Source LLC
Chambersburg PA
CBHW021855230426
43671CB00006B/397